Freedom From Twelve Deadly Sins

Freedom From Twelve Deadly Sins

Secrets To Help You
Press Into Your Destiny

Kelley Varner

Dedication

Years ago I was invited to be part of a major conference for apostles, prophets, and other Christian leaders. After having been introduced, the keynote speaker turned to one of his buddies sitting behind him on the platform. For the next few moments, he shared with us all just how much this man had meant to his life, his family, and his ministry. I will never forget his concluding words of appreciation for this other brother.

He said with tears, "We are not just friends. We are *great friends*."

I now dedicate this volume to one of my "great friends," Destiny Image Publishers of Shippensburg, Pennsylvania.

This personal "life" Scripture describes my assignment. What I see by the Spirit, I am to *"write in a book,"* and send to the whole Church.

For almost 25 years (since 1982), Destiny Image's ministry has encouraged me to write down and distribute 17 messages that the Lord has given me for His ministers and for His people. Their greatest blessing toward my personal race of faith has been to allow me to say these things the way I received them, in words *"which the Holy Spirit teaches"* (1 Cor. 2:13 NKJV).

To visionaries and founders Don and Cathy Nori, along with your national and international team, thank you.

Acknowledgments

To Pastor Wendall Ward, my *"brother, and companion in tribulation"* (Rev. 1:9), for writing the Foreword and for his pastoral and prophetic insight in helping me edit this volume.

To seasoned Pastors Chuck Sexton and Dale Frasier who helped me effectively communicate the burden of Chapters 12 and 13.

To my beloved life companion Joann Dorothy (Armentrout) Varner, who has faithfully run this race beside me for almost 35 years, for helping me write about our personal race of faith.

To the Holy Spirit, who is my Teacher.

Table of Contents

Foreword

For the past four years my wife, Karen, and I have been privileged to labor together at Praise Tabernacle with my friend and pastor, Dr. Kelley Varner. When he asked me to review this manuscript and write the Foreword to *Freedom From Twelve Deadly Sins*, I was deeply honored because I share his passion for the concerns set forth in this volume.

The Church in America is at a critical juncture in its history, and needs to hear and heed the voice of reformation that speaks throughout these pages. This prophetic season requires that the Church recognize and carefully consider the apostolic voices of reformation that can establish us in "present truth" (see 2 Pet. 1:12).

The landscape of American Christianity is littered with the doctrines and traditions of men. For generations, these man-made ideas have nullified the Word of God, thus creating a spiritual vacuum in which a plethora of religious systems has flourished that have no real power to deliver the groaning creation (see Rom. 8:19-23). To make matters worse, in our zeal to propagate the gospel, we have imported these "broken cisterns" (broken systems) to the nations. These broken containers hold the stagnant water of man's religious ideas, not the "living water" of God's eternal purposes (see Jer. 2:13; 29:11).

Freedom From Twelve Deadly Sins is a strong apostolic commission and clear prophetic call. Its timely message urges us to understand and then abandon the doctrines and traditions that have created these impotent religions, delaying our destiny. With the spirit and voice of a reformer, Dr. Varner identifies twelve of these manmade ideas, and shows how each has hindered the individual and corporate advancement of God's Kingdom.

I challenge you to read this book with an open Bible and an open mind. Let the Holy Spirit and the Word of God help you to "rightly divide" these matters, and to remove anything that might hinder your personal race of faith, from pressing into your destiny.

—Wendall S. Ward, Jr.
Pastor, Praise Tabernacle
Richlands, North Carolina

Preface

The Lord called me to write my first book in 1970. Since that *kairos* moment of small beginnings, our own ministry, Tabernacle Press, has printed over 35 titles, including a 15-volume commentary on the books of the Bible, from Genesis to Ezekiel. I will ever be thankful for Don Nori and his team at Destiny Image, with whom I have co-labored and published another 16 titles since 1982.

The volume before you is the 17th and is different from anything that I have ever written.

Jeremiah was graced with his prophetic mantle when he was around 20 years of age; so was I. Jesus washed away my sins with His shed blood when I was 17 and filled me with the Holy Ghost two years later.

In Jeremiah's first 40 years of public ministry to the nation of Judah, this Old Testament seer known to many as "the weeping prophet" witnessed many changes taking place in his nation. So have I. So much has changed in the Body of Christ since the early 1970s. Please don't misunderstand me. Kelley Varner is certainly no

Jeremiah; but I have found an affinity with this man who prophesied over 2,500 years ago.

His heart was broken over the spiritual condition of God's people in his day[1]; so is mine, as I behold the mass confusion and compromise that pervades the American Church.

Jeremiah's nation, the southern kingdom of Judah, had turned from the living God to worship idols. Sometime soon after the consequent fall of Jerusalem and the destruction of its glorious temple by the armies of King Nebuchadnezzar of Babylon (around 586 B.C.), Jeremiah penned these words:

Oh, oh, oh...How empty the city, once teeming with people. A widow, this city, once in the front rank of nations, once queen of the ball, she's now a drudge in the kitchen.

She cries herself to sleep each night, tears soaking her pillow. No one's left among her lovers to sit and hold her hand. Her friends have all dumped her.

After years of pain and hard labor, Judah has gone into exile. She camps out among the nations, never feels at home. Hunted by all, she's stuck between a rock and a hard place.

Zion's roads weep, empty of pilgrims headed to the feasts. All her city gates are deserted, her priests in despair. Her virgins are sad. How bitter her fate.

Her enemies have become her masters. Her foes are living it up because God laid her low, punishing her repeated rebellions. Her children, prisoners of the enemy, trudge into exile.

All beauty has drained from Daughter Zion's face…

Jerusalem remembers the day she lost everything…

Jerusalem, who outshined the whole world, is an outcast…

She played fast and loose with life, she never considered tomorrow, and now she's crashed royally, with no one to hold her hand… (Lamentations 1:1-9 TM).

In all my years of ministry, I have never preached or taught at length from the Book of Lamentations. I've never heard these Scriptures read or spoken publicly from any pulpit. These 154 verses are gut-wrenching, and don't exactly make for one's devotional study.

Yet the prophet has struck a chord in my heart. After hearing his lament over the ancient people of God, and seeing the spiritual condition of the post-modern Church, I can say with Jeremiah,

For all this I weep, weep buckets of tears…(Lamentations 1:16 TM).

A Divine Commission

The Lord Jesus often communicates with me in the middle of the night. Many times I find myself vividly dreaming, and in those dreams I can hear myself preaching the Word of God some place here in America, or even at times in other places throughout the nations.

One minute I am sound asleep, hearing the voice of the Lord through the sound of my own voice, and the next I find myself to be wide awake, listening to the same voice that I heard while dreaming, and often talking out loud.

Several months ago, I woke up from one of those times of "preaching" speaking loudly with great conviction (after 35 years of marriage, my dear wife Joann understands what it means to be married to a man of God who is somewhat "different"). God's words to me were coming through so quickly that I had to get up out of bed and walk next door into my home office to save it all on my computer. I have learned to be instant in season.

I have become [the church's] *servant by the commission God gave me to present to you the word of God in its fullness—*

the mystery that has been kept hidden for ages and generations, but is now disclosed to the saints.

To them God has chosen to make known among the Gentiles the glorious riches of this mystery, which is Christ in you, the hope of glory (Colossians 1:25-27 NIV).

I am a positive person with a positive message. I preach about a great big Jesus and a wee little devil. I focus on Christ, the new creation Man, and not Adam, the old creation. The Lord called me years ago to be one among many who have pioneered the "in Christ" message of truth, a Christ-centered paradigm, across America and around the world. Like the patriarch Noah, I am a preacher of righteousness (see Gen. 7:1).

One of my major concerns as a "grace" preacher is to see God's people delivered from the duality and double-mindedness of sin-consciousness. The thrust of my ministry through the Scriptures is to show God's people who they already are in Christ on the basis of what He has already done. My goal is to help everyone I can on any level to grasp what Jesus' finished work has done with who they used to be. I preach the Good News of the Gospel of the Kingdom.

Now you can begin to see why at the first I fussed with the Lord over His commissioning me to write a book that talks about *sin*. More to the point, His exact words that night to me were, "Tell My people about these twelve *deadly sins* that have aborted the Seed of their destiny."

Above all, I do not want to be misunderstood. Please do not take my words apart from my spirit.

My words are not coming to you with the heated ardor of an Old Testament prophet coming off the back sides of the desert breathing out judgment and denouncing everybody's heathen ways.

Nor am I up on my "soap-box" harping on my favorite subjects or unloading on others all my pet peeves.

I am not trying to straighten everybody out. There are too many weaknesses that remain in my own life, areas that have yet to come under the full jurisdiction of the King of glory.

But I am weeping....

So the Spirit lifted me up, and took me away, and I went in bitter-ness, in the heat of my spirit; but the hand of the LORD was strong upon me.

Then I came to them of the captivity at Telabib, that dwelt by the river of Chebar, and I sat where they sat, and remained there aston-ished among them seven days (Ezekiel 3:14-15).

I am weeping for all of us. Jesus was called "the son of man" throughout the four Gospels (34 times in Matthew alone) because He totally identified with the human situation. The prophet Ezekiel was known as well by that name (over 90 times). In that spirit, I am not pointing my finger at anyone, for I have "sat" where you sit. Like Nehemiah and Daniel, I am not ashamed to identify myself with the people or our problem. Admittedly, "*We* have sinned...."[2]

Following His triumphal entry into Jerusalem, King Jesus "wept over it" because the people of God did not recognize or discern the time of their "visitation" (Luke 19:41-44).

For these things I weep...(Lamentations 1:16).

This Book's Title

It was not until I began to write this manuscript that the Lord answered my prayer with the title of this book, *Freedom From Twelve Deadly Sins*. To my, and my ministry team's relief, Jesus gave me a positive way to communicate the negative.

Know ye not that they which run in a race run all, but one receiveth the prize? So run, that ye may obtain (1 Corinthians 9:24).

Brethren, I count not myself to have apprehended: but this one thing I do, forgetting those things which are behind, and reaching forth unto those things which are before,

I press toward the mark for the prize of the high calling of God in Christ Jesus (Philippians 3:13-14).

Wherefore seeing we also are compassed about [amphitheatered] *about with so great a cloud of witnesses, let us lay aside every weight, and the sin which doth so easily beset us, and let us run with patience the race that is set before us,*

Looking unto Jesus the author and finisher of our faith; who for the joy that was set before Him endured the cross, despising the shame, and is set down at the right hand of the throne of God (Hebrews 12:1-2).

These three Scriptures were given to me as the basis for this writing. The apostle Paul uses the metaphor of the runner in the games who reaches the goal and wins the prize.

Moreover, the Lord emphasized that the goal or destination of this race—our *destiny* (see the next chapter)—is contained in the Seed of the Word of the Kingdom.

Sin has distorted and aborted that Seed. Obstacles and impediments are strewn along our path. We must watch out for them and hurdle them in Jesus' name!

Although there is much to be said about running this race of faith, it remains that we must beware the sin which "does so easily beset" us.

The Greek word, used only here in Hebrews 12:1, is *euperistatos*, meaning, "well standing around, a competitor thwarting a racer in every direction; skillfully surrounding." It is a compound of *eu* (good or well) and *peri* (around or all about) and *histemi* (to stand); it thus describes sin as having advantage in favor of its prevailing.

The danger to us who run the race is that sin is a *mistaken identity*.

Sin Is a Mistaken Identity

Hamartiology is the theological term for the Doctrine of Sin. The simplest meaning of the Greek word *hamartia* is, "to miss the mark."

Another Greek word for "mark" is *charagma*, which can be transliterated to the English word, "character."

To sin is to fall short of the character of Christ!

Sin is a mistaken identity. We do not know who we are in Christ as the Seed of Abraham and the Seed of David (see Matt. 1:1 with 1 John 4:17).

The Bible declares that Christ "is the image of God" (2 Cor. 4:4). Therefore, the spirit of antichrist is any other image!

As I have shared in many of my previous writings, there are only two kinds of men on the planet: Christ and Adam, the "new man" and the "old man"[3]—beauty and the beast!

My little children, of whom I travail in birth again until Christ be formed in you, (Galatians 4:19).

...Do you know how I feel right now, and will feel until Christ's life becomes visible in your lives? Like a mother in the pain of childbirth... (Galatians 4:19 TM).

The apostolic anticipation of Paul was for Christ to be fully formed in a people—Christ in you (a plural pronoun) reveals a corporate Man with a corporate anointing. The cry of the groaning creation is for the nature of the Pattern Son to be unveiled in a vast company of sons, male and female (see Rom. 8:19).

For the gifts and [the] *calling of God are without repentance* (Romans 11:29).

There is one body, and one Spirit, even as ye are called in one hope of your calling; (Ephesians 4:4).

There is but one calling—*the* calling (the definite article is here in the Greek language). The "high (upward) calling" of Philippians 3:14 and the "heavenly calling" of Hebrews 3:1 is that each of us has been summoned forward and upward to *be like Jesus*, to be conformed to His image and likeness! There is no nobler aspiration in this life or the life to come. This alone is His will and purpose, and our destiny.

The *individual* goal and destination, the finish line of this race of faith is to be like Christ!

Each of us has been called into His presence to be transformed by His grace, and from thence to be sent to our particular assignments. But our singular calling and our "blessed hope" is to become like Him (see Titus 2:13 with 1 John 3:1-3).

Neither pray I for these alone, but for them also which shall believe on Me through their word;

That they all may be one; as Thou, Father, art in Me, and I in Thee, that they also may be one in Us: that the world may believe that Thou hast sent Me.

And the glory which thou gavest Me I have given them; that they may be one, even as We are one:

I in them, and Thou in Me, that they may be made perfect in one; and that the world may know that Thou hast sent Me, and hast loved them, as Thou hast loved Me (John 17:20-23).

Till we all come in the unity of the faith, and of the knowledge of the Son of God, unto a perfect man, unto the measure of the stature of the fulness of Christ: (Ephesians 4:13).

Our *corporate* goal and destination, the finish line of this race of faith is "the unity of the faith" for which Jesus prayed—one corporate Man! We are to become one in Him.

The third dimension is marked by maturity: love and unity.

Our Hope Is in the Seed

The theme of the next chapter, the introduction to this writing, will more fully develop the underlying truth that our aforementioned destiny comes wrapped up in the Seed, the living Word of God.

"Christ *in* you" (Col. 1:27) is the divine Seed, incorruptible[4] and indestructible, by which we were born again. The Message Bible calls this, "a life conceived by God Himself." We have been "born again" (John 3:7), regenerated or re-GENE-rated with the very DNA of our Father God![5] We are partakers of His "divine nature" (2 Pet. 1:4). His hope of glory, which is now our hope of glory, is in the Seed. The Bride of Christ, His "glorious church" (Eph. 5:27), is marked by the indwelling Seed, and that seed is Christ (Gal. 3:16).

According to the Scriptures, our adversary the devil is a liar and was a murderer from the beginning (see John 8:44). He is an assassin. His purpose is simple and singular: abortion—he wants to destroy the divine Seed!

And I will put enmity between you [the serpent] *and the woman, and between your seed and her Seed; He shall bruise your head, and you shall bruise His heel* (Genesis 3:15 NKJV).

This first promise of the coming Messiah is called the Protevangel. Throughout the Old Testament and into the New, the devil attempted and failed to snuff out the Messianic Seed, the royal lineage of Jesus through Abraham and David.[6] Satan is terrified by the thought of that Seed coming to fruition and maturation in and through a people who will, as did their Elder Brother, "bruise" (crush completely, shatter) his head (see Rom. 16:20). When the Church becomes this second Witness, his demise and defeat will be established in the earth. David slew Goliath; David's mighty men slew Goliath's kinfolk (see 1 Sam. 17; 1 Chron. 20). Jesus defeated the devil; the Church is arising to rid the earth of his influence!

"ITES" and "ISMS"

When the LORD thy God shall bring thee into the land whither thou goest to possess it, and hath cast out many nations before thee, the Hittites, and the Girgashites, and the Amorites, and the Canaanites, and the Perizzites, and the Hivites, and the Jebusites, seven nations greater and mightier than thou; (Deuteronomy 7:1).

Moses' church in the wilderness was told about these "seven nations"[7] (Acts 13:19). Each of these "ites" had to be overcome for them to possess the land of their inheritance.

And these are the kings of the country which Joshua and the children of Israel smote on this side Jordan on the west...all the kings thirty and one (Joshua 12:7,24).

Moreover, Joshua and his army had to drive out another 31 kings in order for the tribes to inherit the Promised Land. We must disinherit these enemies or they will disinherit us. As with King Saul, that which we do not kill will come back and kill us (1 Sam. 15:1-23 with 2 Sam. 1:1-13).

The night that God woke me up to write, He whispered in my ear, "Go and tell My people that divine destiny is being aborted."

"Aborted by what, Lord?" I asked.

"By religious confusion and manmade teachings that have nothing to do with My Word or My Spirit," He replied.

Do you remember that the prophet Ezekiel was weeping over the fact that his nation Judah had been carried away by Babylon? *Babylon* means, "confusion;" it also means, "the gate of God." Babylon is *religious confusion*, and God is not the Author of confusion (instability, disorder), but of peace (see 1 Cor. 14:33). Our destiny has been aborted by religious confusion and man-made ideas.

> *See to it that no one takes you captive through hollow and deceptive philosophy, which depends on human tradition and the basic principles of this world rather than on Christ* (Colossians 2:8 NIV).

The Lord continued to share with me His burden, "Help My people to understand that the god of this world, the fabricator of all religion, has blinded their minds lest the light and understanding of the gospel of My glory should shine unto them" (see 2 Cor. 4:4).

> *Furthermore He said to me, "Son of man, do you see what they are doing, the great abominations that the house of Israel commits here, to make Me go far away from My sanctuary? Now turn again, you will see greater abominations"* (Ezekiel 8:6 NKJV).

Then, as I lay there in the dark that night, He begin with the Outer Court and walked me through the Holy Place and then into the Most Holy Place, showing me, like Ezekiel of old, the *sin* and idolatry in all three dimensions.[8] There is sin in every camp (see Josh. 7:11).

The Lord didn't call these enemies of our maturity and unity "ites;" He called them "isms." Each of these twelve deadly sins that cause us to forfeit our destiny is an "ism." They are listed and named in the next section of this Preface.

Once in my office, I wrote these things down as fast as I had heard them in my bed. With each one of these problems, the Lord reminded me of His keeping power during my own journey since 1969, when He first called me. A parade of people and experiences passed through my mind, helping me understand how, over the last four decades, I had faced and, like the praiser David (see 2 Sam. 22:30; Ps. 18:29), leaped over many of these "isms" by His grace. My race, my course, is not finished, but I pray that my testimony will be like that of Paul.

But none of these things move me, neither count I my life dear unto myself, so that I might finish my course with joy, and the ministry, which I have received of the Lord Jesus, to testify the gospel of the grace of God (Acts 20:24).

I have fought a good fight, I have finished my course, I have kept the faith: (2 Timothy 4:7).

The word used for "course" in these two verses (and only elsewhere in Acts 13:25) is *dromos*, and it means, "a race; career; the course of life or of office." Compare *trecho*, which means, "to run or walk hastily; to exert oneself, to strive hard." *Trecho* was used of persons in haste or of doctrine that is being rapidly propagated, and occurs in Greek writings denoting to incur extreme peril, which requires the exertion of all of one's effort to overcome.

What is more, King David divided the Levitical priesthood into 24 "courses" or divisions (see 1 Chron. 24:7-18). The priest Zacharias, the father of John the Baptist, ministered in the eighth "course" (daily service) of Abia or Abijah (see 1 Chron. 24:10 with Luke 1:5-8).

This is the "set time" to favor Zion, the season for our "course" (see Ps. 102:13). But this is also a serious time, for this racecourse of faith is strewn with impediments that compromise the Seed and impede our progress. Watch your step!

The Twelve Obstacles to our Faith

After the Preface and introductory first chapter showing the importance of the Seed, subsequent chapters will follow this same format:

- Define and identify each of these particular sins, or "isms." Each is an obstacle to maturity and unity.

- Show its workings in the post-modern Church, and give examples. What does this stuff look like?

- Explain how each particular sin or "ism" has aborted the Seed of the Kingdom and our destiny. How does it operate?

- Share a litany of my own personal relationships with key people and a variety of personal experiences over the last 40 years that have helped me face and overcome (come over) these enemies.

Therefore we also, since we are surrounded by so great a cloud of witnesses, let us lay aside every weight, and the sin which so easily ensnares us, and let us run with endurance the race that is set before us, (Hebrews 12:1 NKJV).

Listed below are the *obstacles* to our race of faith, *twelve deadly sins* that the Holy Spirit showed me that eventful night. A closer look at each of them forms the bulk of this manuscript.

Each of these hindrances we must overcome and hurdle is called a "weight." This Greek word, used only in Hebrews 12:1, is *ogkos*, and it means, "a mass (as bending or bulging by its load), burden (hindrance); whatever is prominent, a protuberance, a bulk, a mass; hence, a burden, a weight, an encumbrance."

But the Lord said to Joshua, "Get up off your face! Israel has sinned and disobeyed my commandment..." (Joshua 7:10 TLB).

The beginning stage of our race is marked by truths that we hear and believe and preach, and by which we become spiritual *children* (see 1 John 2:12). The Outer Court (of the Mosaic Tabernacle), paralleled by the Feast of Passover—where we are born again by His blood (at the Brazen Altar) and baptized in water (at the Brazen Laver)—is beset with *cessasionism, Stoicism,* and *easy believism.* There is sin in the evangelical camp.

The middle and most critical part of our journey is marked by truths that we hear and believe and preach, and by which we become spiritual *adolescents* (see 1 John 2:13). The Holy Place or the Feast of Pentecost, after we have been Spirit-filled, is complicated with *legalism, ascetism, dualism, elitism, tribalism, traditionalism,* and *futurism.* There is sin among classical Pentecostals, Charismatics, and the Faith Movement.

The final section of our course is marked by truths that we hear and preach and believe, and by which we become spiritually *mature* (see 1 John 2;14). The Most Holy Place, corresponding to the Feast of Tabernacles is not without its difficulties. We must also overcome and hurdle *mysticism* and *Gnosticism* if we are to finish strong in this way of righteousness, and finally reach the goal of individual

Christ-likeness and corporate unity, our being one in Him. There is sin in the Kingdom camp among Third Day people.

And I will put enmity between thee and the woman, and between thy seed and her seed; it shall bruise thy head, and thou shalt bruise his heel (Genesis 3:15).

And I will put enmity between you [the serpent] *and the woman, and between your offspring and hers; He* [Messiah] *will crush your head, and you will strike His heel* (Genesis 3:15 NIV).

These twelve deadly "isms"—the obstacles we must overcome in the race of faith—constitute the "enmity" (hostility, hatred) between the serpent and the Seed of the woman. Each has matured to express itself as a major religious idea to usurp the anointing of the Holy Spirit and to abort the Seed. These "antichrists" (1 John 2:18), something "instead of Christ," are weights that encumber us.

Each of these twelve obstacles can stand by itself as a particular hindrance that operates in one of the three aforementioned realms. But it is also true that all twelve are at work in all three arenas of Christian experience. All along the Christian journey—during childhood, adolescence, and maturity—these seducing mind-sets and evil spirits can be at work. At times, they overlap each other or join hands to conspire against the runner.

God hates religion (and so do I) because it is the invention of the devil, the "god of this world" (2 Cor. 4:4).

And a certain woman…had an issue of blood… (Mark 5:25).

These twelve weights or encumbrances have weakened the people of God. Like the woman who was hemorrhaging with the "issue" of blood, the Church is bleeding to death because of man-made issues (see Mark 5:25-34).

God hates this mixture (and so do I) because it always contaminates the Seed and slows us down in our race.

For there shall arise false Christs [anointings], *and false prophets, and shall shew great signs and wonders; insomuch that, if it were possible, they shall deceive the very elect* (Matthew 24:24).

That we henceforth be no more children, tossed to and fro, and carried about with every wind of doctrine, by the sleight of men, and cunning craftiness, whereby they lie in wait to deceive; (Ephesians 4:14).

Furthermore, each of these twelve hindrances are deceptive in their workings to seductively entice the runner off the divine course onto some man-made side road that ultimately comes to a "dead end"—the Bible calls each of these side paths "the way to hell, going down to the chambers of death" (Prov. 7:27).

The primary word for "deceive" (used over 50 times in the New Testament)[9] is *planao*, meaning, "to cause to roam from safety, truth, or virtue); to cause to stray, to lead astray, to lead aside from the right way; to wander, to roam about; to lead away from the truth, to lead into error, to deceive." This key word is derived from *plane* (fraudulence; a mental straying from orthodoxy or piety; delusion, error), and from *planos* (roving as a tramp or vagabond; an impostor, misleader, corrupter, or deceiver).

The kinds of people and teachings that have tried to attach themselves to our heavenly assignment are like "wandering stars" and planets that have broken loose from the orbit of faith (see Jude 1:13).

...My people are destroyed [dumb, silent, cut off] *for lack of knowledge...* (Hosea 4:6).

...My people are dying for lack of knowledge... (Hosea 4:6 Phillips).

...My people are ruined because they don't know what's right or true... (Hosea 4:6 TM).

Again, sin is a mistaken identity. Religion has confused us. We don't know who we are in Christ.

May the Lord help us to understand that our destiny is in the Seed!

It is time to *press into destiny and gain freedom from these twelve deadly sins!*

The Scriptures clearly outline the rules that govern the race run with His faith. All the warning signs have now been read and understood.

It is time to begin. Come run with me. The track has been made ready. Our course is clear.

Come look with me unto our Goal—He is Jesus, the Author and the Finisher of our race of faith.

Endnotes

1. Jeremiah's heart was broken over the spiritual condition of his people (see Jer. 4:19).

2. See Nehemiah 1:6 and Daniel 9:5,8,11,15.

3. Paul describes the "new man" (2 Cor. 5:17; Eph. 2:15; 4:24; Col. 3:10) and the "old man" (Rom. 6:6; Eph. 4:22; Col. 3:9).

4. First Peter 1:23 declares that we were "born again" by (through) the Word of God, which is an "incorruptible" seed. This is the Greek word *aphthartos* meaning, "undecaying, not liable to corruption, imperishable."

5. Our heavenly Father is called "the father of spirits" (Heb. 12:9) and "the Father of lights" (James 1:17).

6. We see this hellish scheme of the evil one in the killing of the Hebrew males in the days of the Egyptian Pharaoh Seti (see Exod. 1:22), in the horrible slaughter of the royal seed by the wicked Queen Athaliah (see 2 Kings 11:1), and by the senseless butchering of the babies of Bethlehem in Herod's mad attempt to kill this newborn King of the Jews (see Matt. 2:16-18).

7. In my book, *Principles of Present Truth From Exodus-Deuteronomy*, I give the Hebrew meanings of each of these "seven nations," and, accordingly show that Moses' church had to overcome the "ites" of violence, ignorance, pride, the love of money, the lack of vision, human effort, and fear.

8. My previous writings, especially *Prevail* (pages 84-85), teach about the "excellent" or "three-fold" things of God (Prov. 22:20-21). Using the Tabernacle of Moses as a pattern (see Exod. 25:8,40), as well as the Feasts of Jehovah—Passover, Pentecost, and Tabernacles (see Deut. 16:16)—we understand Jesus Christ to be our Savior, our Baptizer (in the Holy Ghost), and our King and Lord (see Luke 2:9-11; Acts 2:36). Our growth in God is in three realms: we are born again (see John 3:7), Spirit-filled (see Acts 2:4), and then mature (see Eph. 4:13). God showed the prophet (see Ezek. 8) that there was sin and idolatry in the Outer Court, the Holy Place, and the Most Holy Place.

9. Don't be led off the path. The primary Greek word for "deceive" is *planao*, and is used over 50 times in the New Testament (read and study Matt. 18:12-13; 22:29; 24:4-5,11; Mark 12:27; 13:5-6; Luke 21:8; 1 Cor. 6:9; 15:33; Gal. 6:7; 2 Tim. 3:13; Tit. 3:3,10; Heb. 3:10; 5:2; James 1:16; 1 Pet. 2:25; 2 Pet. 2:15; 1 John 1:8; 2:26; 3:7; and Rev. 2:20; 12:9; 13:14; 18:23; 19:20; 20:3).

Our Destiny
Is in the Seed

It is time to press into destiny!

This Christian journey is a race of faith, and there are many obstacles along the way that can hinder the runner.

Before we begin, it is good to know that the "faith" of which we speak is not ours, but His! As with all other things that we believe and practice, our faith must be Christo-centric. The centrality and supremacy of pure Christology—the Person and Work of Jesus Christ—must ever be our focus and emphasis.

The Race of Faith—From Faith to Faith

The subject of faith from a Christ-centered view includes two major Kingdom paradigms:

First, real faith is not our faith, but rather "the faith of God" (Rom. 3:3). Second, as with salvation that is progressive as well as once for all, real faith gradually moves us around the Christian racecourse "from faith to faith" (Rom. 1:17).

The Hebrew word for *faith* means, "established, trusty, trustworthiness." Its root *aw-man'* (confirmed, established, sure, reliable, certain) is transliterated to the English word, "amen." The Greek word is *pistis*, meaning, "persuasion, credence; moral conviction." *Pistis* is also translated in the King James Version as, "assurance, belief, believe, faith, fidelity."

Moreover, the Bible itself defines faith.

Now faith is the substance of things hoped for, the evidence of things not seen (Hebrews 11:1).

Now faith is the assurance (the confirmation, the title-deed) of the things [we] hope for, being the proof of things [we] do not see and conviction of their reality—[faith perceiving as real fact what is not revealed to the senses] (Hebrews 11:1 AMP).

The "race of faith" that we have been called to run is all about His faith, not ours. To underscore and illustrate this truth, there are essential differences between *foundational faith* and *finishing faith*.

For therein is the righteousness of God revealed from faith to faith… (Romans 1:17).

It takes a lifetime to press into destiny. This contest is not a quick sprint of 100 meters—it is a long-distance marathon. To run it well and win, we must move "from (foundational) faith to (finishing) faith."

Foundational faith jumps us off the starting line. It is crucial that we do well in our beginnings. The rest of the race depends upon that.

Therefore leaving the principles of the doctrine of Christ, let us go on unto perfection; not laying again the foundation of repentance from dead works, and of faith toward God, (Hebrews 6:1).

The phrase "faith toward God" is literally, faith "upon" God. We cast all our cares upon Him because He cares for us (1 Pet. 5:7).

Foundational faith is mankind's faith in God to get his or her needs met. It is wholly man-centered, and brings to us the following blessings:

- We are justified by faith (Rom. 5:1).

- Our hearts are circumcised in water baptism by faith (Col. 2:11-12).

- We receive the Pentecostal experience of the Holy Ghost Baptism by faith (Gal. 3:1-5).

- We receive divine healing for our physical bodies by faith (1 Pet. 2:24).

- We receive financial blessings by faith (Phil. 4:19).

This constitutes the "faith message" as we have known it. These five principles are not profound. They are to be taught and learned in first principles (catechism) class, in spiritual elementary school.

These five new creation realities are vital, not optional. Each must be experienced in the beginning part of God's course for us.

For by it [faith] *the elders obtained a good report* (Hebrews 11:2).

These all died in faith, not having received the promises... (Hebrews 11:13).

And these all, having obtained a good report through faith, received not the promise:

God having provided some better thing for us, that they without us should not be made perfect (Hebrews 11:39-40).

Our faith begins in Hebrews 11, but it does not end there. There we learn two more things about elementary or first principles faith:

- We can die in foundational faith.

- With foundational faith we can die without the promise.

Men and women have testified, "Pray my strength in the Lord. Pray that I will make it to Heaven. All I want is to hear the Master say, 'Well done!'" Some, like the elders of the Old Testament, are content with a good report card.

That is right and noble, but this race involves much more than just dying and going to Heaven. We began this pursuit to finish, and finish strong. God brought us out of Egypt to bring us into the land (see Deut. 6:23)—we have been *purchased* and *purposed*! There is a purpose, a predestined goal that lies before us.

That eternal purpose is realized in *finishing faith!*

A word of balance is needed here. The most important part of any building is its foundation. Many have experienced foundational faith who may never hear the whole truth about finishing faith. But no one can taste the sweetness of finishing faith without experiencing the basics of foundational faith.

Which of these two principles is the more important? Foundational faith! Nonetheless, we are to keep running as we move forward "from faith to faith."

...Nevertheless when the Son of man cometh, shall He find faith on the earth? (Luke 18:8)

I am [have been] *crucified with Christ: nevertheless I live; yet not I, but Christ liveth in me: and the life which I now live in the flesh I live by the faith of the Son of God, who loved me, and gave Himself for me* (Galatians 2:20).

Wherefore seeing we also are compassed about with so great a cloud of witnesses, let us lay aside every weight, and the sin which doth so easily beset us, and let us run with patience the race that is set before us,

Looking unto Jesus the author and finisher of our faith... (Hebrews 12:1-2).

Though it began in Hebrews 11, "our faith" is found in Hebrews 12, where Jesus Christ is the "Author" (chief leader, prince) and the "Finisher" (completer, consummator, perfecter) of it!

It is Jesus Himself who develops and matures His own faith in our hearts. The rules to this race are governed by the "law of [His] faith" (Rom. 3:27).

Finishing faith is the faith of God Himself, operating and manifesting itself in and through a Corporate Man.

Finishing faith is Jesus' faith, the "faith of the son of God." Again, in this race of faith, it is all about *His* faith, not ours.

Unlike the limitedness of foundational faith, Jesus' faith conquered death and obtained the promise! When the Son of God came into our hearts, He brought with Him this "measure of faith" (Rom. 12:3).

Simply stated, foundational faith is about *us*. Finishing faith is all about *others*. The faith of God is for the nations and will ultimately deliver His creation.

Now that we know whose faith is at work here, it is time to begin the race. This course has been marked off beforehand. It is His will, and plan, and purpose for each of our lives.

In Him we were also chosen, having been predestined according to the plan of Him who works out everything in conformity with the purpose of His will, (Ephesians 1:11 NIV).

Our Destiny Is Our Destination

Declaring the end from the beginning, and from ancient times the things that are not yet done, saying, My counsel shall stand, and I will do all My pleasure: (Isaiah 46:10).

Known unto God are all His works from the beginning of the world (Acts 15:18).

Our Creator not only knows and sees all things, but He declares the end from the beginning! He has predestined us. He knows our destination.

My two previous books, *Sound the Alarm* and *The Secrets of the Ascended Life*, had as their underlying theme the "high (upward) calling" as mentioned in Philippians 3:13-14. As noted in the Preface, this Scripture also helps to form the basis of this writing.

To press into our destiny is to press into our high calling, to press toward the mark for the prize.

Webster's Dictionary defines *destiny* as the "state or condition appointed or predestined; ultimate fate; lot, fortune, destination; invincible necessity or fixed order of things established as by a divine decree, or by an indissoluble connection of causes and effects."

He adds that one's *destination* is "the purpose for which something or someone is intended or appointed; the end of ultimate design; the place to which a person or thing is going or sent; the predetermined end of a journey or voyage."

For whom He did foreknow, He also did predestinate to be conformed to the image of His Son, that He [Jesus] might be the firstborn among many brethren.

Moreover whom He did predestinate, them He also called: and whom He called, them He also justified: and whom He justified, them He also glorified (Romans 8:29-30).

The Bible has much to say about our destiny and destination. The word for "predestinate" in these verses is *proorizo*, and means, "to limit in advance, predetermine; to decide beforehand (used of God decreeing from eternity); to foreordain, to appoint beforehand." It is a compound of *pro* (fore, in front of, prior, before) and *horizo*, which means, "to mark out or bound ('horizon'); to appoint, decree, specify; to define; to mark out the boundaries or limits; to determine, to appoint, ordain." *Proorizo*, or "predestinate," is used in the following:

For to do whatsoever Thy hand and Thy counsel determined before to be done (Acts 4:28).

But we speak the wisdom of God in a mystery, even the hidden wisdom, which God ordained before the world unto our glory: (1 Corinthians 2:7).

Having predestinated us unto the adoption of children by Jesus Christ to Himself, according to the good pleasure of His will…

In whom also we have obtained an inheritance, being predestinated according to the purpose of Him who worketh all things after the counsel of His own will: (Ephesians 1:5,11).

My book *Chosen for Greatness* establishes that each of each is a Word from God, chosen out of the *Logos* from the foundation of the world (see Eph. 1:4). You and I were actually "pre-seeded" (pre-worded) before we were born, predestined for His eternal purposes. Our destiny is in the Seed! Our path, our race, was predetermined and premeasured by His Word. We have been hemmed in by His love and goodness.

The Bible further declares our destiny or destination to be the *end* of this race, "the end of our faith, even the salvation of your souls" (1 Pet. 1:9). This word for "end" is *telos*, taken from a primary *tello* (to set out for a definite point or goal), and means, "the point aimed at as a limit; the conclusion of an act or state; result of ultimate or prophetic purpose; that by which a thing is finished, its close, an issue; the aim, purpose." Our whole soul—intellect, emotions, and will—and, consequently, our body, will be delivered when we finish our course.

As we prepare to run the race throughout this writing, it is good to understand how *telos* is used to describe the "end" of the race.[1] Of particular interest is its usage by John in the Book of Revelation.

And He [Jesus] *said unto me, It is done. I am Alpha and Omega, the beginning and the end. I will give unto him that is athirst of the fountain of the water of life freely* (Revelation 21:6).

I am Alpha and Omega, the beginning and the end, the first and the last (Revelation 22:13).

In these verses *Telos* is a Person—the "end" is a *Person!* The End is the same One who is the *Alpha* (the beginning of our race) and the *Omega* (the ending of our race). *The End is Jesus!* He is the Goal.

Therefore leaving the principles of the doctrine of Christ, let us go on unto perfection... (Hebrews 6:1).

Looking unto Jesus the author and finisher of our faith... (Hebrews 12:2).

This awesome truth is corroborated by the word for "perfection" in Hebrews 6:1, and the same word "finisher" in Hebrews 12:2.

Related to *telos*, this key word is not *telioo* the verb (to complete, accomplish, or consummate), nor *telios* the adjective (complete, finished). Used only in these two verses, it is the noun *teliotes* (Strong's Bible Concordance #5051), "a completer, consummater; a perfector."

The End, the Goal of our race of faith is not some spiritual state of perfection or maturity—again, the End, the Goal of our race is a *Person!* Jesus is the One who has in His own Person raised faith to its perfection and so set before us the highest example of faith.

Now that we know where we are headed in this race—to be like Jesus—and now that we have clarified and identified our destiny, our destination, we must next realize that all of our destiny is wrapped up in the Seed.

Jesus Is the Seed

Every born-again Christian knows that the Bible is the Word of God.

These 66 books, written by 40 authors over a period of hundreds of years, tell a story—the story of the Seed.

Jesus Christ is the eternal *Logos*, the Word of God (see John 1:1).

The Bible is a narrative of history—it is *His* story!

And I will put enmity between you [the serpent] *and the woman, and between your seed and her Seed; He shall bruise your head, and you shall bruise His heel* (Genesis 3:15 NKJV).

The book of the generation of Jesus Christ, the son of David, the son of Abraham (Matthew 1:1).

Jesus Christ is the Seed of the woman, the Seed of Abraham, and the Seed of David. In that we see, respectively, His pain, His promise, and His power as He relates to the human family racially, redemptively, and royally.

Jesus, the Seed, is the sum total, the *Alpha* and the *Omega*[2] of everything that the Father ever wanted to say to us. He is the *Logos*, the Word, the complete discourse of God to man.

For those God foreknew He also predestined to be conformed to the likeness of His Son, that He [Jesus] *might be the firstborn among many brothers* (Romans 8:29 NIV).

The dream of the Father came to earth as a Seed. God, through the Person of His Son, wrapped Himself in flesh and time, and then the Virgin Mary wrapped Him in swaddling clothes and laid Him a manger. He came to be the federal Head of a new creation, the Head of a family of sons.

The apostle Paul called His incarnation a great mystery (see 1 Tim. 3:16). God came down to us bundled in eight pounds of love, with all the fullness of the Godhead encased in that tiny body (see Col. 2:9).

I tell you the truth, unless a kernel of wheat falls to the ground and dies, it remains only a single seed. But if it dies, it produces many seeds (John 12:24 NIV).

Jesus was that "corn of wheat" (KJV) who fell into the ground and died. His death, burial, and resurrection constitute the essence of the Gospel (see 1 Cor. 15:3-4). His glorious resurrection has produced a mighty harvest, His glorious Church.

The Story of the Seed

Chapter Six of my book, *The Priesthood is Changing* (1991), teaches in depth about the Bible being His story, the story of the Seed. In 1996 I wrote another book titled, *The Time of the Messiah: A Prophetic Picture of the End-time Church*. Chapter One of that writing is titled, *Christ, the Anointed Seed*. Both are recommended reading to underscore this present chapter before you.

There (in the latter) I explained: "When Paul wrote to the Church at Corinth, he defined 'Christ' as 'the image of God' (2 Cor. 4:4). The image of God, our future and destiny, is held within the Messianic Seed! The pragmatic application and manifestation of Jesus' present reign is the Father's ultimate intention and expectation: a vast family of sons conformed to the image of the Firstborn, a corporate expression of Jesus' life and nature (compare Gen. 1:26-28)."[3]

Using the time of Jesus' first Advent (the Christmas story) as recorded in Matthew 1-2 and Luke 1-2 as the historical backdrop for that book, I showed how the Seed that was planted in the womb of the Virgin Mary when she was overshadowed and impregnated by the Holy Spirit, the power of the highest, is the *same Seed* that was planted in each of us when we were born from above!

Paul calls this experience, "Christ in you" (Col. 1:27), and adds that God has sent forth "the Spirit of His Son" into our hearts (Gal. 4:6).

Thus, individually and corporately, we Christians have become the ongoing incarnation of God in the earth!

Quoting again from *The Time of the Messiah*:

"The generation of Jesus Christ (Matt. 1:1) is a people who have been birthed out of Him! We are the offspring[4] of God (Acts 17:29), His family. Adam was the federal head of a natural race; Jesus is the federal Head of a spiritual people[5] who have been regenerated or born from above (John 3:7).

"In that Seed is God's name or nature—all that God is, all that God has, and all that God does! The story of Bible history is 'His story,' the story of the Seed. In the volume of the Book, it is written of Him.

From Genesis to Malachi, the Seed comes (Gen. 3:15).

In the four Gospels, the Seed dies (John 2:24).

In the Book of Acts, the Seed lives (Acts 2:24).

From Romans to Jude, the Seed speaks (Heb. 1:1).

In the Book of Revelation, the Seed reigns (Rev. 11:15).

"Isaiah prophesied that Messiah would 'see His seed' and that they would 'prolong His days' (Isa. 53:10). The story of the New Testament Church in the Book of Acts is the continuation of "all that Jesus began both to do and teach' (Acts 1:1)."[6]

This Seed Is the Word of the Kingdom

When any one heareth the word of the kingdom, and understandeth it not, then cometh the wicked one, and catcheth away that which was sown in his heart. This is he which received seed by the way side (Matthew 13:19).

Another parable put He forth unto them, saying, The kingdom of heaven is likened unto a man which sowed good seed in his field: (Matthew 13:24).

And He said, So is the kingdom of God, as if a man should cast seed into the ground; (Mark 4:26).

It is important for every Christian to understand that this Seed is not just any word—it is the Word of the *Kingdom*!

Both John the Baptist and Jesus came preaching the Gospel of the Kingdom (see Matt. 3:2; 4:17). Stephen, Paul, and the other ministers of the Church in the Book of Acts preached the Gospel of the Kingdom (see Acts 8:12; 14:22; 19:8; 20:35; 28:31).

And when they had appointed him [Paul] a day, there came many to him into his lodging; to whom he expounded and testified the kingdom of God, persuading them concerning Jesus, both out of the law of Moses, and out of the prophets, from morning till evening (Acts 28:23).

This is the best definition I have discovered in the Scriptures that clearly defines the Gospel of the Kingdom. The message and Person we herald has but one purpose: to persuade men "concerning Jesus"—He is the King!

Don't Contaminate the Seed

Everything is in the Seed. Our *destiny* is in the Seed!

Again, the devil's sole intent is to kill the Seed. But that is impossible, for we have shown already that this Seed is "incorruptible" (1 Pet. 1:23), indestructible.

We are not ignorant of satan's devices, his evil purposes, schemes, and strategies (see 2 Cor. 2:11). Having learned that he cannot destroy this Seed, he has but one remaining resolve: through the centuries, he has attempted to *contaminate* it!

There has always been a "mixed" multitude (Ex. 12:38; Neh. 13:3), a mongrel race, hanging around God's chosen people. When King Sennacherib carried away captive the northern kingdom of Israel into the land of Assyria, he left such a mixture of peoples in the land (2 Kings 17:23-41). These heathen families with all their heathen gods (religious ideas) came to be known as Samaritans.

Howbeit every nation made gods of their own, and put them in the houses of the high places which the Samaritans had made, every nation in their cities wherein they dwelt (2 Kings 17:29).

But these foreigners also worshiped their own gods. They placed them in the shrines on the hills near their cities (2 Kings 17:29 TLB).

This mixed multitude of religious traditions and ideas want to run this race alongside us. Their assignment is to hinder or even thwart our progress toward Him who is our Goal. We must not allow these sins which so easily beset us in the race (Heb. 12:1) to mill around us or run beside us, and thus rob or waste our time, energy, and finance by distracting us with lesser issues.

All this false religion was orchestrated by "the god of this world" (2 Cor. 4:4) in his relentless purpose and pursuit to contaminate the coming Messianic Seed.

There is an interesting Old English word used in the King James Version that clearly illustrates this type of mixture.

Thou shalt not sow thy vineyard with divers seeds: lest the fruit of thy seed which thou hast sown, and the fruit of thy vineyard, be defiled [unclean, unholy, taboo] (Deuteronomy 22:9).

The Hebrew word for "divers" here means, "dual, separated; two heterogeneities; two kinds." The same word is translated in Leviticus (KJV) as "a diverse kind" and "mingled seed."

Thou shalt not plow with an ox and an ass together (Deuteronomy 22:10).

This next verse in Deuteronomy shows the same truth. The ox (domesticated) nature reveals the Christ nature. The ass (untamed) nature points to the Adam nature. Paul spoke about this "unequal yoke" in his second letter to the Corinthians (2 Cor. 6:14-7:1).

Thou shalt not wear a garment of divers sorts, as of woollen and linen together (Deuteronomy 22:11).

The Hebrew word for "divers" in the above verse is a different word from that given in verse 9. Here it means, "linsey-woolsey, cloth of linen and wool carded and spun together; mixed stuff, fabric of mixed weave." This is most significant, for linen is a symbol for righteousness (see Rev. 19:8), and wool speaks of the sweat of sin and the curse of the law.[7] Again, we see exemplified the two natures, two diverse mind-sets: Christ the new man, and Adam the old man.

The New Testament usage of the word "divers" (KJV) explains more clearly its meaning.

For we ourselves also were sometimes foolish, disobedient, deceived, serving divers lusts and pleasures, living in malice and envy, hateful, and hating one another (Titus 3:3).

Be not carried about with divers and strange doctrines. For it is a good thing that the heart be established with grace... (Hebrews 13:9).

Both these verses use the Greek word *poikilos*, which means, "motley, various in character; various colors, variegated; of various sorts." Vine's Expository Dictionary adds that the verb *poikillo* means, "to make gay."

It is sad but true that "divers lusts" flow out of "divers and strange doctrines (teachings)." Men and women play with the Word and calling of God, but their party is about to end (see Dan. 5).

God hates the mixture of compromise.

Having established my motive for this writing, and having verified the preeminence of the Seed, we are ready to examine the first of twelve of these teachings that are "strange (foreign, alien)" to the Person and Work of Jesus Christ, "strange" to the clear teaching of the Word of God, and "strange" to the Holy Spirit, the One who authored the Scriptures. We must learn to run past these strangers.

Our destiny is in the Seed. Don't contaminate it.

Hurry! Get to the starting blocks. I trust that you are prepared. This contest is about to begin.

Are you ready to run with me? Are you ready to press?

Endnotes

1. The Greek word *telos* describes the "end" of our race of faith (Matt. 10:22; Rom. 6:22; Heb. 3:14; 6:11).

2. The *alpha* is the first letter of the Greek alphabet, and *omega* is the last letter. Jesus is called the "Alpha and Omega," the beginning and the end (Rev. 1:8,11; 21:6; 22:13).

3. See pages 4-5 of *The Time of the Messiah*. Order online at www.kelleyvarner.org or by calling 910-324-5026.

4. The Greek word for "offspring" in Acts 17:29 is *genos*, and it means, "kin; race, family, stock, nation." Peter used the same word in First Peter 2:9 to describe the Church as God's chosen "generation."

5. As such, Jesus is called by John "the beginning of the (new) creation of God" (Rev. 3:14). The word for "beginning" is *arche*, and it means, "a commencement, or chief; beginning, origin; the first person or thing in a series; the leader."

6. See pages 8-9 of *The Time of the Messiah*.

7. Consequently, the priesthood of Zadok in Ezekiel 44 is dressed from head to foot in linen, in righteousness. Zadok (the faithful priest under David's administration), which means, "righteous," is a nickname for Melchisdec, which means, "King of righteousness" (Heb. 7:2). Ezekiel says of this king-priest ministry, "they shall be clothed with linen garments; and no wool shall come upon them, whiles they minister" (Ezek. 44:17). No wool, no sweat. No sweat, no curse. No curse, no death, just the power of an endless life (see Heb. 7:16)!

Cessasionism

My heart is broken because of all the confusion and mixture that I see operating among the people of God.

I am especially concerned for our children and young people, who have trusted us to tell them the truth about God and His Word.

The previous chapter set forth the supremacy and centrality of Jesus Christ as the Seed, the Word of God. God's will, plan, purpose, and our destiny, is wrapped up in the Seed, the Word and Gospel of the Kingdom!

We are now ready to press into destiny, to begin running the good race of faith. At the starting line, we immediately notice that some things want to run with us. These odd-looking and odd-sounding creatures are religious traditions, the besetting sins of Hebrew 12:1. Beware! These ideas concocted by the god of this world will compete for Jesus' love and attention. Our adversary has attempted to skillfully surround us with compromise that he might thwart us in our progress and possibly get us kicked out of the race, disqualified as a "castaway," unapproved and rejected (1 Cor. 9:27).[1]

Beginning with this section and the next 11 chapters, I am going to fearlessly expose the false teachings that have mixed with the Seed and even aborted the destiny of many sincere contenders.

I am not afraid of the devil. He is afraid of me and every apostle or prophet who dares to lift his or her voice in protest of his schemes.

Interestingly, the name "Goliath," the champion of the Philistines (see 1 Sam. 17:4), and a type of satan, comes from a primitive root which means, "to denude (especially in a disgraceful sense); by implication, to exile (captives being usually stripped); figuratively, to reveal; to uncover, to disclose, to discover, to lay bare." Through God's Word and Spirit, I am about to unmask and strip the enemy until he has no place to hide! The plain teaching of the Bible will lay him bare!

I will define each of these problems ("isms") and then show how each is at work in the Church today. I will clearly show how each of these dangerous teachings have compromised the Word of God and even aborted the Seed of destiny, and will then share from my own personal journey how I have faced and, by His grace, overcome these enemies in my own life—in my mind, my family, my church, and my ministry.

From the moment of our new birth in Christ, we discover that this good race of faith is the "good fight" of faith (1 Tim. 6:12; 2 Tim. 4:12). From the starting gun, it is so important that each of us learns and memorizes the Word of God.

Do you have your Bible in hand? In your heart (Ps. 119:11)? Don't even think about starting this race without it!

Our first obstacle that we must hurdle is just up ahead. It is the man-made tradition called *cessasionism.*

What Is Cessasionism?

Cessasionism is the first of many adversaries who wants to tag along with us and plagues the evangelical church world.

Cessasionism, according to Webster's Dictionary, means, "to cease; a ceasing, a stop; the act of discontinuing motion of action of any kind, whether temporary or final." Also, "a cessasion of arms" is "an armistice or truce agreed to by the commanders of armies."

Cessasionism is the teaching that the supernatural demonstration of signs, wonders, and miracles "ceased" with the early Church and the Book of Acts once the Canon of Scripture was completed. In so doing, cessasionists have signed a truce with the enemy.

This hand-me-down religion purports that the *charismata*, the gifts and manifestations of the Spirit (see 1 Cor. 12:8-10), especially *glossalalia*, or speaking with other tongues, are not for us today. Some go as far as to preach that any contemporary manifestations of the Spirit are of the devil. Moreover, one who is a cessasionist does not believe in the present-day ministry of the apostles and the prophets.

Like the Sadducees who opposed Jesus in the days of His earthly ministry, these folks refuse to acknowledge the power of the Holy Ghost through the Name of Jesus Christ to perform the supernatural; they are marked by a disbelief in the spiritual world. Known for their denial of the bodily resurrection, the Sadducees came from the leading families of the nation—the priests, merchants, and aristocrats.

Even the Jewish historian Josephus repeatedly designates these proud aristocrats as those who court only the rich and have not the people on their side (Ant. 13.10.6). He adds, "This doctrine is received but by a few, yet by those still of the greatest dignity" (Ant. 18.1.4); in other words, the Sadducees were persons of rank.

The high priests and the most powerful members of the priest-hood (the old order) were mainly Sadducees. Many modern-day Sadducees have relished "Higher Criticism," appealing to their rea-son rather than the plain teachings of the Bible.

At this point, one is tempted to launch this writing into a trea-tise of apologetics, and absolutely dismantle each of these "isms" by speaking the truth in love (see Eph. 4:15). However, we must stay true to the Lord's assignment in presenting this volume, and therefore briefly state what the Bible says about each of these man-made ideas that want to block our path to destiny.

Cessasionism Is at Work

I weep to think of the millions of young men and women with a genuine call of God upon their lives who have been robbed and spoiled by cessasionism. Full of God and a genuine passion for the things of the Spirit, they find themselves in some Bible school or seminary, listening to ungodly professors making light of the Scriptures. Gradually but inevitably, the light in these young, impressionable minds and hearts goes out, until the time of their graduation, when empty hands will be laid upon their empty heads.

It is too difficult to bear the thought of these young warriors spending the rest of their lives defending their tribe and particular brand of faith. I don't even want to think about the day when they grow old, die and go to Heaven, only to discover the end result: a saved soul and a lost life (see 1 Cor. 3:9-15).

The experience of the Holy Ghost Baptism with the evidence of speaking with other tongues was restored to the Church (Joel 2:25) at the turn of the 20th century. Then, in the early 1960s and throughout the 1970s, this birthright of every believer was embraced by almost every traditional denomination, including Roman Catholicism.

Cessasionism is one of the hallmarks among evangelicals. The issue of *glossalalia*, or speaking with other tongues, has often sparked many a feud among staunch fundamentalists. The primary proof text for their traditional stance to fight against the present reality of the supernatural power of the Holy Ghost is found in Paul's first letter to the Church at Corinth, and in of all places, the "love" chapter.

Charity never faileth: but whether there be prophecies, they shall fail; whether there be tongues, they shall cease; whether there be knowledge, it shall vanish away.

For we know in part, and we prophesy in part.

But when that which is perfect is come, then that which is in part shall be done away.

When I was a child, I spake as a child, I understood as a child, I thought as a child: but when I became a man, I put away childish things (1 Corinthians 13:8-11).

Love never fails. But where there are prophecies, they will cease; where there are tongues, they will be stilled; where there is knowledge, it will pass away.

For we know in part and we prophesy in part,

but when perfection comes, the imperfect disappears.

When I was a child, I talked like a child, I thought like a child, I reasoned like a child. When I became a man, I put childish ways behind me (1 Corinthians 13:8-11 NIV).

Across the Christian spectrum, one usually finds three interpretations to this important passage.

First, cessasionists see verse 10—"when that which is perfect is come"—to mean the completion of the Bible, the Canon of Scripture. But if this be so, then knowledge has also ceased (Hos. 4:6). This view is but a convenient rationalization of the obvious lack of real New Testament power in ministry, much as the higher critics' silly idea that Mark 16:9-20 was not in the original manuscripts!

Second, some classical Pentecostals say that "that which is perfect" is Jesus Christ at His Second Coming. Accordingly, at that time, we shall have been transformed into a greater dimension of life and ministry. While there is a measure of truth in that thought, we must understand that the Bible itself explains this passage—"in Thy light we see light" (Ps. 36:9).

And He gave some, apostles; and some, prophets; and some, evangelists; and some, pastors and teachers;

For the perfecting of the saints, for the work of the ministry, for the edifying of the body of Christ:

Till we all come in the unity of the faith, and of the knowledge of the Son of God, unto a perfect man, unto the measure of the stature of the fulness of Christ: (Ephesians 4:11-13).

In both these passages, Paul refers to the Church as becoming (developing, maturing into) a "perfect (mature) man." The in-part realm of Pentecost will end only when the many-membered Body of Christ is brought to the stature of a complete, fully developed, Corporate Man. The Holy Ghost Baptism, the gifts of the Spirit, and the fivefold ministry are the means (tools) that Jesus and the Holy Spirit have ordained and given to the Church to equip His people to this end.

These gifts and graces will not cease until God has fulfilled His purpose. These blessings have not ceased; rather, they are necessary, vital to our Christian heritage and apostolic orthodoxy!

Cessasionism Aborts the Seed

How has the man-made idea of cessasionism impacted our destiny and impeded our progress?

The devil has contaminated our theology and our race with the notion that there are no more apostles and prophets.

This presents an immediate problem, for God has stewarded to these ministries the revelation of the mystery (see Eph. 3:1-5). Besides the twelve "apostles of the lamb," more commonly known as Jesus' original twelve disciples (see Rev. 21:14 with Matt. 10:1-8), there are many other apostles of the Spirit mentioned in the Bible, including a woman.[2]

There are diversities of gifts, but the same Spirit.

There are differences of ministries, but the same Lord.

And there are diversities of activities, but it is the same God who works all in all.

But the manifestation of the Spirit is given to each one for the profit of all: (1 Corinthians 12:4-7 NKJV).

Moreover, the *charismata*, the gifts or manifestations of the Spirit are given for the edification and the building of up the Body of Christ. We need to see them operating in and among the saints more than ever before.

For to one is given by the Spirit the word of wisdom; to another the word of knowledge by the same Spirit;

To another faith by the same Spirit; to another the gifts of healing by the same Spirit;

To another the working of miracles; to another prophecy; to another discerning of spirits; to another divers kinds of tongues; to another the interpretation of tongues (1 Corinthians 12:8-10).

There is the *speaking* ministry—we can talk like God, and say things that natural men cannot say. These three include the simple gift of prophecy (to edify, exhort, and comfort, as in First Corinthians 14:3), divers kinds of tongues (the message in tongues for the public assembly), and the interpretation of tongues.

There is the *knowing* ministry—we can think like God, and know things that natural men cannot know. These three include the word of knowledge, the word of wisdom, and the discerning of spirits.

There is the *doing* ministry—we can act like God, or do the works of God, and do things that natural men cannot do. These three include faith (the God-given ability to believe for the impossible), the working of miracles (the God-given ability to perform the impossible), and the gifts of healing.

But one and the same Spirit works all these things, distributing to each one individually just as He wills (1 Corinthians 12:11 NASB).

These gifts or manifestations of the Spirit should be actively operating in every local church and the lives of every Spirit-filled believer!

Therefore let us leave the elementary teachings about Christ and go on to maturity, not laying again the foundation of repentance from acts that lead to death, and of faith in God,

instruction about baptisms, the laying on of hands, the resurrection of the dead, and eternal judgment (Hebrews 6:1-2 NIV).

Finally, the elementary and foundational things that Jesus taught, His first principles included "the doctrine of baptisms (including the Holy Ghost Baptism)" and the "laying on of hands" (KJV). The basics of our faith include the workings of the Holy Spirit in the realm of the supernatural.

The quickening power of the Holy Ghost is our strength for the race (see Acts 1:8; Rom. 8:11). The primary word for "power"— used 120 times in the New Testament (see Acts 1:15)—is *dunamis,* and primarily means, "ability."

The Pentecostal experience of the Holy Ghost Baptism—with the historical, experiential, and biblical initial evidence of speaking with other tongues (see Acts 2:4; 10:46; 19:6)—is the indwelling dynamo through whom we have the ability to run!

And these signs shall follow them that believe; In My [Jesus'] *name shall they cast out devils; they shall speak with new tongues* (Mark 16:17).

Yet cessasionists refuse to acknowledge even the first principles and the plain doctrine of what Jesus taught and practiced. These religious traditions have drained us before we can ever get up a head of steam. In exasperation and much sadness, I exclaim with the psalmist,

> *If the foundations be destroyed, what can the righteous do?* (Psalms 11:3).

My Personal Race of Faith

Many times I am asked this question, "Dr. Varner, what is your background?"

My reply is quick and to the point, "Heathen. What's yours?"

I grew up heathen, a church-going sinner. My parents were good moral people, and my father was a great provider for me (an only child) and my mother; but I was not reared in the nurture and admonition of the Lord (see Eph. 6:4). I knew very little about God, about His race, or His faith to run it.

My mom, Lucy, along with my dad, Kelley, Sr., and I went to church as far back as I can remember. We regularly attended the Church of the Brethren (an Anabaptist denomination) in Keyser, West Virginia. I cannot ever remember hearing what I would now call a "salvation" message preached from that pulpit, yet I know that there were and are many fine churches in that movement. Some at that time were evangelical because their pastor was genuinely born again. But the message that I heard as a child and youth concerned itself more with a "social" gospel and especially with an emphasis upon pacifism (because of the Vietnam War). As young men of draft age, we were asked to be conscientious objectors.

Yet some of the people in that little church on South Mineral Street were really saved. Cletus Blackburn, Oma Smith, and Prema

Lipscomb all taught me in Sunday School, and undoubtedly planted good seeds into my unregenerate heart.

One man who especially touched my life was Delmar Cook, our Sunday School Superintendent. I learned early on that the Lord had given me a good singing voice, and had joined the church choir. But Delmar would take me on Sunday afternoons all over those West Virginia hills into little Methodist churches to be part of their church fall homecomings and all-day "singings" on the grounds.

Little by little, the Lord was awakening my heart to spiritual things. My experiences as a camper and counselor at my church youth camp, Camp Galilee, in Terra Alta, West Virginia, also watered my early Christian stirrings. The late Reverend Laurean "Bud" Smith, pastor of the Moorefield, West Virginia church, especially loved on me and impacted my life (I would later meet Bud again when courting Joann, for that was her home town). Looking back, I honestly believe that Pastor Smith sensed the calling of God on my life for the ministry.

Besides all this, several of my relatives belonged to fundamental Baptist churches, which, of course, preached a strong message that we all must be "born again" (John 3:7). I know that they were praying for my salvation, but later would not fully understand my associating myself with tongue-talking Pentecostals.

My conversion happened May 12, 1966, during my junior year of high school. My dad died during open-heart surgery at the age of 49, and this shocked me into realizing that I was fooling myself and everybody else, but not God. No long after Dad's death, I was saved in McCoole, Maryland, under the preaching of Richard Richardson. When I walked the aisle that night, Jesus met me at my first step. I finally knew that I was saved!

Over 100 pounds ago, with my 6'3" frame poured into a junior choir robe that was far too small, and wearing tennis shoes, I stood in front of that little Brethren congregation and sang, "Amazing Grace." Puzzled looks asked, "What got into Him?"

The Lamb!

That wonderful night, my mother and her mother (my grandma, Elizabeth Summers who went to Heaven at the age of 96), and I were all baptized in water. I had been baptized before at the tender age of nine, but that one didn't "take."

My journey had begun, and the Lord was going to see to it that I would not be detoured by cessasionism or anything else.

So the same year, 1966, He led me to Larry Shrout, who sang tenor in our second period choral class. Through his witness and invitation to sing bass in their gospel quartet, I was introduced to Tim Miller (the baritone) and Dave Dawson (the lead). The name of this group was "The Ambassadors," taken from the name of the youth group in the Keyser Assemblies of God Church where Larry and Tim attended.

Those were the days of the great Charismatic Renewal of the 1960s and 1970s, and our locale was already being impacted by the move of God in the Pittsburgh area (through the ministry of Kathryn Kuhlman and others). Timing is such a key to our race of faith!

I remember one Sunday night at the Assemblies church, a little "praying grandma" came up to me after the service. She stood about 4 1/2' high, but was over 5' tall with the neat little bun of grey hair on the top of her head. I will never forget her words.

"Young man, I certainly enjoyed your singing tonight, but I can't wait until you get filled with the Holy Ghost!"

Like the Ephesian disciples said to Paul when asked, "Have you received the Holy Ghost since you believed?" (Acts 19:2), I had not heard whether there be any Holy Ghost! Thank God that His sovereign hand had kept my ears from hearing the evil teaching of cessasionism.

Not long after, in the fall of 1968, that same sovereign hand touched my life once and for all. Some men and women are simply called of God, but others, like Saul of Tarsus and me that life-changing evening, have to be "suddenly" cornered (Acts 9:3)!

Christians were gathered in the old Shaw Mansion in Barton, Maryland (a meeting place for worship and then a Bible School, but now a lovely bed and breakfast). Our gospel quartet stood around the piano, singing an old song, "The Ark is Coming Up the Road." In my ignorance, I didn't know what the Ark was, or even what road it was on! I was just singing the bass part to an old song, when...

Suddenly, I could not stand. As with Paul on the Damascus Road, I found myself glued to the floor, unable to rise. What a rush of emotions—fear, amazement, and unknown anticipation—all hitting me at once. I gathered my faculties enough to say in my best religious voice, "Lord, what meaneth this?" (see Acts 2:12).

Then I heard a voice....

Not just any voice, but His voice. The One who called me from my mother's womb and who had guarded my life and mind from religious traditions the first 19 years of my life, was now speaking to me.

"Be still and know that I am God," the Lord said (Ps. 49:10).

Then, for five solid hours, from 8 P.M. until 1 A.M., Jesus did for me what the Holy Spirit did for King Saul of old—He turned me into "another man" (1 Sam. 10:6). For five hours I preached, I prophesied, and I talked in tongues. That was over 38 years ago. Somebody asked, "Pastor Varner, what have you been doing all these years?"

"Preaching, prophesying, and talking in tongues...."

God was good to me at the starting line, and kept me from being swept aside by the teaching of cessasionism. Divine destiny is still my portion. Some will never press into destiny because they have gotten knocked out of the race at the start.

In those days, while armchair theologians debated the present reality of being filled with the Holy Spirit just like they were in the Book of Acts, hungry people were being baptized with the Holy Ghost. A man with an experience is never at the mercy of a man with an argument.

I am tempted to tell more of the story, but this book would get too long to print. But the next time the quartet went to sing, something else happened. In one of those little churches on the other side of the tracks, I asked to testify. After 20 minutes, the other guys just smiled and sat down while I finished my first sermon!

Others soon followed my steps, and the little Church of the Brethren in Keyser, West Virginia, was never quite the same.

Oma, Delmar, and others were soon filled with His love. I especially remember the night under a tent with a sawdust floor when Cletus Blackburn received her personal Pentecost. You must understand that this classy lady was always in control; every hair was always in place. My fondest memory of Cletus was when she went over the altar rail backward that night. About an hour later, with disheveled grey hair and sawdust everywhere, she came up smiling, and talking in a heavenly language!

Unashamedly, I find myself weeping tears of joy as I remember those glorious days and pen these words. How good God has been to me!

And yet I also weep tears of intercession because so many have been taught that the Book of Acts is a separate age, and that these blessings are not for us to today because they have ceased.

How many are in Heaven today with only a partial inheritance, robbed of their spiritual birthright by some ignorant Sadducee?

We must understand that one day with the Lord is but a thousand years (see 2 Pet. 3:8), and that the Book of Acts happened just the day before yesterday! We are now living in the last days of the same age begun by Peter and Paul.

Thank God that Jesus is the *same* today as then (see Heb. 13:8)!

Do you need salvation? Come to Him today.

Do you need healing in your body or mind? Come to Him today.

Have you received the Holy Ghost Baptism since you believed?

Do you need a miracle? He is the mighty, right-now God who stands ready to lavish His love upon you.

Just humble yourself and come. The God of the Bible has never changed.

Don't ever let any person or any teaching talk you out of your destiny and your break-through. And then get happy about it!

We've only begun this exciting race. Let's run a little farther.

Endnotes

1. The word for "castaway" in First Corinthians 9:27 is *adokimos*, and it means, "unapproved, rejected, worthless; not standing the test, not approved, properly used of metals and coins; unfit for, unproved, spurious, reprobate" (see Rom. 1:28; 2 Cor. 13:5-7; Tit. 1:16; and Heb. 6:8).

2. Note the many apostles of the Spirit. Nowhere is it taught that the apostolic ministry would cease; rather, it is needed until the Church is perfected (matured) and presented to Jesus her Husband. We need every *doma* gift given by Jesus to the Church (see Eph. 4:11-13). Note the following list of those named as apostles in the New Testament: Barnabas and Paul (Acts 14:4,14; Rom. 1:1; 1 Cor. 9:5-6); Andronicus and Junia, a woman (Rom. 16:7); Titus (2 Cor. 8:23—"messengers" is *apostolos*); Epaphroditus (Phil. 2:25—"messenger" is *apostolos*); Silvanus (Silas) and Timothy (1 Thess. 1:1; 2:6); James and the Lord's brothers (1 Cor. 9:5; 15:5-8; Gal. 1:19); Apollos and Sosthenes (1 Cor. 1:1; 4:6-9); and "all the apostles" (1 Cor. 9:5; 15:5-7; Rev. 18:20).

CHAPTER THREE

Stoicism

God has packaged our destiny in the Seed of His Word. That Seed is "incorruptible" (1 Pet. 1:23), indestructible. Nothing can stop it.

Yet our adversary is determined to spoil and ruin our lives and ministries. He has contaminated the Word of the Kingdom with incredible mixture.

The Lord showed me twelve deadly sins, twelve obstacles in the race of faith. Each has the potential to abort the Seed and distort our reaching the Goal.

These religious traditions operate all the way around the course, from our beginnings in the Outer Court to our maturation in the Most Holy Place, from spiritual conception to spiritual perfection (maturity).

The previous chapter explained how the evangelical camp has been hampered by the blight of cessasionism, the idea that anything supernatural—the gifts of the Spirit, including signs, wonders, and miracles, along with the ministry of apostles and prophets—ceased with the Book of Acts and the finalization of the Canon of Scripture.

The next barrier to hurdle is the subtle sin of *Stoicism*.

What Is Stoicism?

Webster's defines "Stoicism" to be "the philosophical system of the Stoics; a real or pretended indifference to pleasure or pain; the bearing of pain without betraying feeling; impassivity."

The Stoics were disciples of the philosopher Zeno, who founded a sect about 308 B.C. He taught that men should be free from passion, unmoved by joy or grief, and submit without complaint to the divine will and unavoidable necessity by which all things are governed. Thus a Stoic is a person who is not easily excited, an apathetic or stoical person, indifferent to pleasure or pain.

Simply, Stoicism does not believe in any show or manifestation of emotion or passion. Paul met some of these folks in Athens.

Then certain philosophers of the Epicureans, and of the Stoicks, encountered him. And some said, What will this babbler say? other some, He seemeth to be a setter forth of strange gods: because he preached unto them Jesus, and the resurrection (Acts 17:18).

Stoicism among Christians again relegates itself to the Outer Court, and is most evidenced among the traditional denominations, with regard to their style of worship, especially in public meetings. A stoic church service is very, very quiet. These folks take the following verse very literally.

But the LORD is in His holy temple: let all the earth keep silence before Him (Habakkuk 2:20).

From this traditional view, there is to be no show of emotion in public gatherings. Stoics also like to use this verse by Paul to stifle any spiritual rowdiness.

Let all things be done decently and in order (1 Corinthians 14:40).

But all things must be done properly and in an orderly manner (1 Corinthians 14:40 NASB).

Stoicism Is at Work

The Bible and Church history is filled with examples of men and women who have responded with great emotion when touched and changed by the power of God.

Again, my heart aches for the millions of young people in this nation and the nations who have yet to experience the overflowing joy of their salvation in the House of the Lord. They may go all through their lives without experiencing the true liberty of the Holy Ghost in worship, for "where the Spirit of the Lord is, there is liberty (freedom)" (2 Cor. 3:17).

In that day will I raise up the tabernacle of David that is fallen, and close up the breaches thereof; and I will raise up his ruins, and I will build it as in the days of old:

That they may possess the remnant of Edom, and of all the heathen, which are called by My name, saith the LORD that doeth this (Amos 9:11-12).

In that day I will restore David's fallen tent. I will repair its broken places, restore its ruins, and build it as it used to be, (Amos 9:11 NIV).

I will restore...and return it to its former glory... (Amos 9:11 TLB).

God has promised to restore the Tabernacle of David—revealing the restoration of the Church in the areas of worship and ministry.

Just as there were two priesthoods in operation for the 40 years following the crucifixion of Jesus (from A.D. 30-70)—the old Jewish order along with His new king-priest order of Melchisedec—so in the days of David. The Tabernacle of Moses (the old order) was still going through the motions on Mount Gibeon while the Tabernacle of David (God's new thing) was operating on Mount Zion.

The legal order on Gibeon (established from Mount Sinai) was void of the Ark of the Covenant, the very presence and glory of God—it was Ichabod (see 1 Sam. 4:21), for the glory (the Ark) had departed! The Brazen Altar, the Laver, the Golden Candlestick, the Table of Shewbread, and the Golden Altar of Incense remained on Mount Gibeon in the structure that God had ordained and blessed in a previous day (see Exod. 25:40)—the only thing missing was the Ark of His glorious Presence!

The Tabernacle of David—a simple, single tent prepared by King David—was the transplanting of the Ark of the Covenant and the Most Holy Place to the "holy hill of Zion" (Ps. 2:6; 15:1; 99:9).

What simplicity! How different from many of the churches in America. Stain-glassed windows, high arching ceilings, lavish altars covered with vessels of silver and gold, some even surrounded by images and icons—all geared to overwhelm the worshipers and stupefy their senses. Everything is in its place, except the presence of the Lord. God is not impressed, and His manifested Presence is no where to be found. No emotion, no joy, no laughter—just deafening silence. Little wonder that the Bible calls such places "the congregation of the dead" (Prov. 21:16). The joyful sound of Spirit-anointed praise is not heard in Babylon because there is no sound of a millstone there (see Rev. 18:22). No corn of the Word is ever rightly divided in the house of the "strange woman," for "her house is the way to hell" (Prov. 7:5-27).

By contrast, the Tabernacle of David was a place where men and women worshiped God "in spirit and in truth" (John 4:23-24)!

There were no Stoics in David's tent! Two tabernacles and two priesthoods were operating at the same time. It was really quiet on Mount Gibeon, the old order. The ritual and liturgy of worship was monotonously the same as usual. None had access to His Presence.

Stoicism is without feeling, without emotion, without passion. The worship in old order churches (on any level) is much like that on Mount Gibeon. There was no singing, no musical instruments, no recording (testimony), no thanksgiving, no praise, no clapping of the hands, no lifting of the hands, no shouting, no corporate bowing or kneeling, and certainly no dancing!

The tendency among some Spirit-filled groups in recent years to move back to the formalism of traditional liturgical forms and dress—what some have dubbed "bells and smells"—has accentuated the "high church" ambiance of Stoicism.

But the mood, environment, and order of the church services in David's Tabernacle were full of feeling, strong emotion, and passionate praise! All the aforementioned ways of thanksgiving, praise, and worship were a way of life under David's tent in *Zion*,[1] the place and environment that the Lord has "desired" (craved, longed for) and chosen for "His habitation (seat, abode)" (Ps. 132:13).

> *...when they that bare the ark of the LORD had gone six paces, he* [David] *sacrificed oxen and fatlings.*

> *And David danced before the LORD with all his might* [physical strength];

> *and David was girded with a linen ephod. So David and all the house of Israel brought up the ark of the LORD with shouting, and with the sound of the trumpet* (2 Samuel 6:13-15).

> *Glory ye in His holy name: let the heart of them rejoice that seek the LORD* (1 Chronicles 16:10).

In the Tabernacle of Moses (the old order), joy had to be commanded, legislated. In the Tabernacle of David, there was heartfelt joy! In Gibeon's order, only the High Priest (the pastor, the leader, or the speaker) went beyond the veil (to the high altar or to the pulpit). In Zion, all the priests could go before the Ark—there was "access" (admission, permission) with boldness (Rom. 5:2; Eph. 3:12). Whosoever will may come (Acts 2:21; Rev. 22:17).

As with legalism and license in Chapter Five, there is also a flip side to Stoicism.

> *And Isaac said unto Jacob, Come near, I pray thee, that I may feel* [touch] *thee, my son, whether thou be my very son Esau or not. And Jacob went near unto Isaac his father; and he felt him, and said, The voice is Jacob's voice, but the hands are the hands of Esau* (Genesis 27:21).

Some of God's children show no emotion or passion. Others govern their lives completely by how they "feel." Isaac, deceived by his son Jacob, had a "goat-hair" feeling! Those who always go by "how they feel" often make mistakes. We are to be "led" by the Spirit and Word of God, not our feelings (see Rom. 8:14).

An added thought is that *Judas*, like "Judah," means, "praise." There is a praise that betrays Jesus (as did Judas), when we just go through the motions and feelings of the outward praise of our lips, but our hearts are far from Him (see Mark 7:6).

But as we dart around the track with our heart in our praise, we are a noisy lot. Without taking time to explain why or apologize, we sing, and shout, and clap our hands, and even dance while we run! Real worshipers don't love Him because they have to; we want to, and get to. We do it because we are running with God, in God, and toward God!

We run toward freedom through praise.

Stoicism Aborts the Seed

God knew what He was doing when He created us in His image and likeness (see Gen. 1:26-28).

We are just like God. Essentially, we are "spirit" (John 3:6 with John 4:23-24), we have a soul—intellect, emotions, and will (Ps. 34:1-2; 103:1 with Heb. 10:38), and we live in a body (1 Cor. 6:19 with 1 Cor. 12:27; Eph. 4:12).

Our emotions are in the soul. Stoicism, the philosophical idea that we are not to show our emotions in public or private, kills our passion and our love for God and others.

The religious tradition of Stoicism destroys the joy of the Lord, which is our strength (see Neh. 8:10). The enemy knows that if he can rob us of our joy, he's got us. Without strength, one cannot walk, let alone run. But true worshipers have learned to experience joy in every circumstance. We have refused to let anything on the track get in our way.

There is not enough time and space in this volume to go through the Scriptures and note all the emotions that are expressed by God Himself. One of my favorites is in the following verse.

He who sits in the heavens laughs...(Psalms 2:4 NASB).

Laughter is a symbol of conquest. God laughs because He has no enemies. They are all under His glorious feet (see Eph. 1:20-23)!

God is the God of passion. I don't have the vocabulary to adequately describe His range of emotions revealed in one of the most familiar verses in all of Scripture:

God **so** *loved...*(John 3:16, emphasis added).

When He first made man, God "breathed into his nostrils the breath of life; and man became a living soul" (Gen. 2:7).

Can you begin to imagine the roar of God's passion as He breathed into Adam's nostrils all of His life and love at once?

Who in his right mind would want to stifle that? To keep God's people from experiencing that? Not only in our churches, but in our homes, and schools, and workplaces, let us ever be a people of passion, unashamedly and fearlessly expressing our great love for our great God!

We press and pursue after Him with all that is in us.

One word that is universally understood among the nations is, "Hallelujah!" If we really know that the blood of Jesus Christ has washed away our sins, and that we have been truly forgiven, we cannot speak that word without emotion!

And he leaping up stood, and walked, and entered with them into the temple, walking, and leaping, and praising God (Acts 3:8).

When the man by the Gate Beautiful received a double miracle—he was healed *and* learned to walk immediately—he ran into Solomon's Porch, shouting and praising God. If some Stoic had stopped him and said, "Now, brother, calm down, you're in church." He would have kept right on shouting, "There ain't no quiet in me!"

Every great revival from Martin Luther to the present has been marked by the outpouring of the Holy Spirit, and God's people have always responded to His love with great passion and emotion, especially joy and laughter. Little wonder that the god of this world wants us to keep quiet.

These are spots in your feasts of charity, when they feast with you, feeding themselves without fear: clouds they are without water, carried about of winds; trees whose fruit withereth, without fruit, twice dead, plucked up by the roots; (Jude 1:12).

...They are like fruit trees without any fruit at picking time. They are not only dead, but doubly dead, for they have been pulled out, roots and all, to be burned (Jude 1:12 TLB).

The apostle Jude was pretty rough on church-going sinners, but it's quite simple. People who are alive have feelings and passion. People who are still dead in their sins are just that, graveyard dead, graveyard quiet!

Not as though I had already attained, either were already perfect: but I follow after, if that I may apprehend that for which also I am apprehended of Christ Jesus (Philippians 3:12).

The apostle Paul tells us that we have been "apprehended" for the high calling. This Greek word is *katalambano*, and is taken from two other words: *kata* means, "down," and *lambano* means, "to lay hold of, to seize upon, to embrace."

This wonderful word *katalambano* reveals the very incarnation of the Lord Jesus Christ, the Word made flesh. He came "down" here and "embraced" us! Now He waits patiently for a people to humble themselves (*kata*) and to embrace Him with the *same passion* wherewith we have been embraced! We call that, "worship."

> *His disciples remembered that it was written, "Zeal* [heat, ardor, fervor] *for Your house will consume Me* [Messiah]*"* (John 2:17 NASB).

Stoics are afraid to show emotion or heart. But in this race of faith, the baton of purpose has been passed to a people who will be known as the "anchor leg." When the anchor leg wins, the whole team wins. That final runner is not just the fastest person on the squad. He or she is the one with the greatest zeal and passion to win! Jesus, our Coach and Leader, will never put a Stoic on the anchor leg.

As with cessasionism, Stoicism is one of the twelve obstacles in our pursuit of Him Who is the Goal. Both will cause us to stumble on this path of righteousness toward freedom.

My Personal Race of Faith

As I shared previously, I grew up in a traditional Mount Gibeon kind of church. The services were quiet and always predictable. We were always out of there by 12 noon, sharp.

I have always loved to sing, but I never heard real singing until I started hanging around my newfound Pentecostal friends. For the first time, I witnessed people praising the Lord with heartfelt joy and unabandoned, unabashed love for their Savior.

I will never forget the night that the Lord healed Sister Ruth Moomau of cancer. She was an ample woman; notwithstanding, it was humanly impossible for her to twirl in a dancing circle before the Lord as long as she did, as fast as she did.

When our quartet would sing the songs of Zion, I saw grown men weep and shout. This was a whole new world for me.

I won't kid you. When I was a sinner, I did it all the way. Now that I am a Christian, I sing with passion and I preach with passion. May God help us all to run with passion as we love Him and live for others!

I began to study voice as a sophomore in high school. By the time I started as a freshman music major at Potomac State College in Keyser (a branch school of West Virginia University), I had the basic mechanics down. I sang Italian opera and German Lieder along with the English folk songs. I never would have ended up on the operatic stage—that was too stiff, too stoic, for me.

I backslid that first year of college (because of dating the wrong kind of girls), and ended up spending my weekends playing my sax in the clubs around the Keyser and Cumberland (Maryland) areas. When I came back to the Lord in my sophomore year, our quartet rented the newly built Church-McKee Arts Center on our campus and performed a Gospel concert the Wednesday before Easter in 1969. "Music for Him" attracted the saints of God down out of those mountain "hollers" where we had sung in dozens of little churches. Students came, and even some of the faculty members attended that night. The four of us hit the stage hard and fast, singing at the tops of our voices, "I'm saved, and I know that I am." Like the cripple who had been healed in Acts 3, there was just no "quiet" in me.

The years have passed. We moved from the mountains of West Virginia and Maryland at the end of 1977 and the beginning of 1978. Since that time, my wife Joann has given me four awesome children: April, Jonathan, Joy Beth, and David. All of them are real worshipers. I have seen each of them bowing before the Lord in tears of humility, and dancing before the Lord with the exuberance of Judah's ancient king, who, was, by the way, a "man after His own heart" (1 Sam. 13:14; Acts 13:22).

Our kids were not born in Egypt. Nor were they conceived in the wilderness. Their generation was "born" in Zion (Ps. 87:5), in the House of the Lord. They have grown up in "present truth" (2 Pet. 1:12), and will never be robbed of their passion for God!

I would be remiss I if did not mention Nathaniel W. Rand, affectionately known to all as "Brother Nat." Now 75 years young, he has been an elder in Praise Tabernacle since its beginnings in 1978. Like the rock that he was prophesied to be, this faithful man has stood by me and the Lord through all these years. But let me warn you. Don't sit beside or in front of Nat during a church service. His shout is infectious to the weary and intimidating to the stoic. Demons flee at the sound of Nat's voice. When he prays or prophesies over the people of God, he does so with great passion.

People always ask me, "How is Nat?" My answer is always, "He is just like Jesus—the same, yesterday, and today, and forever!"

Whether in the Piggly Wiggly (the local food store) or a hospital corridor, this apostle of great joy has impacted hundreds of lives. I don't know if Nat knows what a Stoic is (most folks do not), but he sure does know what one is not. Thank you, Nathaniel, for showing us all how to be ourselves in God, and how to run the race of faith with great joy.

I remember the words of a great man who was taken from us far too soon. As we traveled together among the churches, he personally taught and showed me the true meaning of great grace. I will never forget the Word of the Lord that he brought to our church in a critical moment.

As Scotty Todd would say, "Children, enjoy the journey!"

Endnote

1. In David's Tabernacle, men and women worshiped with their voices (speaking, singing, and shouting), with their hands (lifting, clapping, and the playing of instruments), and with their whole body (corporate standing, bowing, kneeling, and dancing). Study these verses (see 1 Chron. 15:1,16,28; 16:1,4,8,36,41 with Ps. 28:2; 47:1; 63:4; 80:1; 134:1-3; 149:3; and 150:4).

CHAPTER FOUR

Easy Believism

All the way through our race of faith, we must ever keep before us the mind and motive of the Lord. What is this all about? What is important to His heart? What is His concern? What really matters to Him? It is not enough to see His acts as we move along the path of righteousness. We must know His "ways" (Ps. 103:7).

Thus, from a posture of brokenness, the Lord has commissioned me to write, for this generation and the generations to come, His present burden for His people.

Throughout the Old Testament, the prophets received what they called the "burden of the Lord" (Jer. 23:33-38) or the "burden of the Word of the Lord" (Zech. 9:1; 12:1; Mal. 1:1). Isaiah, in particular, received a word or "burden" for certain nations.[1] This Hebrew word for *burden* means, "porterage, a load; an utterance." In the King James Version, it is also translated as, "prophecy" (Prov. 30:1; 31:1).

How can a young man keep his way pure? By living according to Your word (Psalms 119:9 NIV).

Seasoned ministries in the Body of Christ carry a prophetic burden, a load. We have been sent by Jesus to the Church with His Word. Having faced many obstacles along the way, our concern is His concern, that the foundation of the House of the Lord be kept plumb and true to the Scriptures. We are showing a new generation that we overcome adversity and keep ourselves pure by giving heed to God's Word.

Religious tradition has weakened our base. Men and women have turned away their ears from the truth, and have been carried off the path into what Paul in his Pastoral Epistles called "fables" (see 1 Tim. 1:4; 4:7; 2 Tim. 4:4; Titus 1:14). This is the Greek word *muthos*, and it means, "a tale, fiction ('myth'); an invention, a falsehood." Vine's adds that *muthos* is to be contrasted with *aletheia*, the word for "truth," and with *logos* (the "Word" of John 1:1). We have walked away from the Word.

We have already examined two of these "fables" that have infected the Outer Court realm of the Church world, our evangelical friends. The popular teachings of cessasionism and the common practice of Stoicism have obstructed the Word and Seed of the Kingdom, turning many from the pursuit of destiny.

Now we come to a third obstacle that has weakened and compromised the Gospel in that first dimension—*easy believism*.

What Is Easy Believism?

Easy believism is a term that I have coined to describe the third hurdle of our race. Easy believism has soddened (and saddened) the Passover Lamb. The old English word for "sodden" in Exodus 12:9 means, "to boil." Men and women have "watered down" true evangelism and compromised the Gospel with *easy believism*.

In evangelistic meetings and crusades, in door-to-door witnessing and in open-air gatherings, in one-on-one conversations, sinners are encouraged to accept the Lord. That is right and good. What is not so right and good are the traditional methods we are using to reach the lost.

We have taken them down the Roman road[2] and had them repeat a "sinner's prayer." Then we have announced to them, "You are saved!" Don't get me wrong. That technique can and has worked with certain people, but it has also led others into confusion. A simple mental assent to the Scriptures is no substitute for the quickening, regenerative power of the Holy Ghost!

Moreover, evangelists have preached what I call "graveyard" stories, and threatened people in the pews with their going to hell or missing the "Rapture." The problem is that many have been stirred in their emotions and shed a lot of tears, but have never been impacted in their will. Learn this: whatever means one uses to get sinners to the altar is the means that he or she will have to continue to use to keep them there!

For God hath not given us the spirit of fear; but of power, and of love, and of a sound mind (2 Timothy 1:7).

If you "sing" folks there, you will have to keep singing to them. If you scare folks there, you will have to keep them scared. Admittedly, popular eschatology (with all its trappings of a coming Tribulation Period with its antichrist) will do that. But any system of theology or eschatology that is based upon the "spirit of fear" cannot be of God!

*Therefore leaving the principles of the doctrine of Christ, let us go on unto perfection; not laying again the foundation of **repentance*** *from dead works, and of **faith** toward God,* (Hebrews 6:1, emphasis added).

As seen below, there are two basic elements to real conversion—*repentance and faith*. Both are a gift from God ministered to us by the Holy Spirit. We have encouraged sinners to have faith in God without telling them of the necessity of real repentance and the consequent fruit of that repentance, which is an immediate change of heart and life that is openly evident to family and old friends.

Easy believism results in weak, wimpy preaching without the power to really save. Only the energizing presence, power, and anointing of the Holy Spirit can convict and then draw the lost to Christ; otherwise, sinners end up just going through a bunch of religious motions.

No one is able to come to Me unless the Father Who sent Me attracts and draws him and gives him the desire to come to Me... (John 6:44 AMP).

Finally, a person cannot get "saved" any time he or she chooses—each must be "drawn" by the Spirit. This "space of grace" is a season when the Lord draws near to the sinner, and it is imperative that one responds to His love and seek Him while He may be found (see Isa. 55:6). Unless the Holy Spirit of God has brooded over the sinner's heart (a theologian calls this "prevenient grace"), there can be no real conversion. If God by His Spirit has not spoken to one's heart about his or her sinful condition and the consequent need of the Savior, it is useless for anyone to try to talk to that person about accepting His finished work. Disciples must be led by the discerning voice of the same Holy Spirit as we witness our faith to others (see Rom. 8:14).

Now is not the time to take it easy, to saunter along at our own pace and leisure. Now is the time to run!

Easy Believism Is at Work

Churches across America are filled with folks who assume that they have been born again. These good people have heard the Gospel in their minds, but the Good News has yet to drop 18 inches into their hearts. As noted, too many have but given mental assent to the truth. As I testified about my own life in Chapter Two, so it is that local assemblies everywhere are packed on Sunday mornings with "church-going sinners."

I have been crucified with Christ and I no longer live, but Christ lives in me. The life I live in the body, I live by faith in the Son of God, who loved me and gave Himself for me (Galatians 2:20 NIV).

The bad fruit of easy believism intensifies when exasperated pastors admonish their members to live for God. This is impossible, for a sinner is still governed by the beast nature, and must act accordingly. The old Puritans used to say, "Living the Christian life is not difficult, just impossible!" The Christian life is the exchanged life as the life of Another lives through us.

Every person is a saint or an "ain't"! Try as we may, one cannot live the Christian life until the Person of Christ Himself indwells and empowers the believer. It is in and through *Him* that we live, and move, and have our being (see Acts 17:28).

For he cometh in with vanity, and departeth in darkness, and his name shall be covered with darkness.

Moreover he hath not seen the sun, nor known any thing... (Ecclesiastes 6:4-5).

Church-going sinners are still lost "without God" (Eph. 2:12). Easy believism has caused them to be spiritually stillborn. The above passage vividly describes one who has never produced the fruit of truly being "born of God."[3] This person has repeated the sinner's prayer, has walked to the front of the church, has shaken the pastor's hand, and perhaps been baptized in water. Yet these sinners remain in spiritual darkness. They have never seen the "Sun of righteousness," the Son of God (Mal. 4:2), or known the reality of His forgiveness. Such methods of "easy" evangelism are but "vanity," leaving folks empty and void of spiritual reality.

And you He made alive, who were dead in trespasses and sins, (Ephesians 2:1).

A sinner without Christ is spiritually dead—his spirit is dead unto God. He is asleep and needs to be awakened! He must be "quickened" (KJV) and energized by the Holy Spirit, the same Spirit that raised Jesus from the dead (see Rom. 8:11).

Beyond this, easy believism has taken on new meaning and form in the last several years—the current trend of "seeker-sensitive" churches.

Again, I am grateful for anyone who wants to reach others with the Gospel by any means, but not when our notion of success (our love for nickels, noses, and names)[4] takes the place of effectiveness. A canned, pre-packaged, 45-minute church service, with a 15-minute homily, a sermonette for "Christianettes," has become very popular in certain "church growth" circles.

But in so doing, we worship and serve the creature more than the Creator (see Rom. 1:25). We have allowed our fast-food, get-rich-quick, I-want-it-now American culture to dictate *how* we have "church." The disgusting "politically correct" climate of our governmental leaders in Washington, D.C., has flowed over and filtered down into the Christian sphere. Sadly, these heathen mind-sets have impacted us more than we have impacted them!

"Don't offend anybody!" is the banner over American politics. That has translated into the easy believism of American Christianity to sound like this: "We need to keep it simple. Folks need to feel good about themselves. Let's make it easy and convenient for them." An ancient king felt the same way:

Jeroboam thought to himself, "The kingdom will now likely revert to the house of David.

If these people go up to offer sacrifices at the temple of the LORD in Jerusalem, they will again give their allegiance to their lord, Rehoboam king of Judah. They will kill me and return to King Rehoboam."

After seeking advice, the king made two golden calves. He said to the people, "It is too much for you to go up to Jerusalem. Here are your gods, O Israel, who brought you up out of Egypt."

One he set up in Bethel, and the other in Dan.

And this thing became a sin; the people went even as far as Dan to worship the one there.

Jeroboam built shrines on high places and appointed priests from all sorts of people, even though they were not Levites.

He instituted a festival on the fifteenth day of the eighth month, like the festival held in Judah, and offered sacrifices on the altar. This he did in Bethel, sacrificing to the calves he had made. And at Bethel he also installed priests at the high places he had made.

On the fifteenth day of the eighth month, a month of his own choosing, he offered sacrifices on the altar he had built at Bethel. So he instituted the festival for the Israelites and went up to the altar to make offerings (1 Kings 12:26-33 NIV).

Jeroboam also announced that the annual Tabernacle Festival would be held at Bethel on the first of November (a date he decided upon himself), similar to the annual festival at Jerusalem... (1 Kings 12:32 TLB).

So he offered upon the altar which he had made in Bethel the fifteenth day of the eighth month, even in the month which he had devised of his own heart... (1 Kings 12:33).

...Jeroboam built forbidden shrines all over the place and recruited priests from wherever he could find them, regardless of whether they were fit for the job or not.

To top it off, he created a...festival....

This was strictly his own idea to compete with the feast in Judah; and he carried if off with flair... (1 Kings 12:31-33 TM).

Did you know that the first "seeker-sensitive church" in the Bible was invented and "devised" (contrived, feigned) by King Jeroboam I, the son of Nebat? He led the ten northern tribes in secession and rebellion from Judah and Jerusalem, the true priesthood, and the Messianic line through David. Reminiscent of Israel's rebellion under Moses (Exod. 32), this evil king set up two golden calves, false gods, for the people to worship.

Jeroboam reasoned, "It is too difficult for God's people to walk all the way up the mountain to Jerusalem three times a year to keep the Feasts. For their ease and convenience, I will build two calves at Dan and Bethel. The pilgrims won't have to walk so far."

Furthermore, this haughty, arrogant king violated the plain teachings of the Law of Moses concerning the Feasts of the Lord (see Lev. 23; Deut. 16) by inventing a false Feast of Tabernacles in the eighth month, and then fearlessly hiring his own priests to administrate it. This affords us a not-so-nice picture of traditional Scofieldian dispensationalism, whose ranks are filled with well-meaning prognosticators who, like Jeroboam, feverishly continue to set their own "dates."

So likewise, whosoever he be of you that forsaketh not all that he hath, he cannot be My disciple (Luke 14:33).

But none of these things move me, neither count I my life dear unto myself, so that I might finish my course with joy, and the ministry, which I have received of the Lord Jesus, to testify the gospel of the grace of God (Acts 20:24).

So when we preach about Christ dying to save them, the Jews are offended and the Gentiles say it's all nonsense (1 Corinthians 1:23 TLB).

Excuse me, but have we read these Scriptures lately? Whatever happened to the responsibilities of biblical discipleship and the accountability of real covenantal relationships? Where is the rugged Pauline altar? What about old-fashioned Holy Ghost conviction and resolve? Many have removed the ancient landmarks which the apostolic fathers set for the Church, and our founding fathers laid down for this great nation (see Prov. 22:28). It is little wonder that our flocks have since been seized and devoured (see Job 24:2 NASB).

In those days there was no king in Israel: every man did that which was right in his own eyes (Judges 21:25).

The Book of Judges is a sad book. In those days, there was no real authority in the land. Consequently, everyone "did his own thing." "Live and let live" was the motto of that day.

This race of faith is not about right and wrong. This Christian journey is about life and death! God, not man, sets the time and the terms of the race. His Word alone has the final say. This contest has a Judge, and each of us will give an "account" to Him about *how* we ran (Rom. 14:12). Destiny awaits, and there is no "easy" way to press toward freedom!

What had happened up until the times of the Judges? What had brought about this tragedy?

> *And it came to pass after these things, that Joshua the son of Nun, the servant of the LORD, died, being an hundred and ten years old.*
>
> *And they buried him in the border of his inheritance....*
>
> *And Israel served the LORD all the days of Joshua, and all the days of the elders that overlived Joshua, and which had known all the works of the LORD, that he had done for Israel.*
>
> *And the bones of Joseph, which the children of Israel brought up out of Egypt, buried they in Shechem....*
>
> *And Eleazar the son of Aaron died; and they buried him...* (Joshua 24:29-33).

Joshua, the great soldier, was gone. Joseph, the great statesman, was gone. Eleazer, the great religious leader, was gone. Godly leadership was nowhere to be found. Now as then, our country desperately needs real leaders to stand up and to speak out.

By boldly writing about these problems that plague our nation and the Church, I am not fooling myself. I will pay a price for being courageous, but if I can awaken the sleeping giant lying dormant in some young man or woman who has been called to prophesy to America and the nations, it is well worth it!

Somebody has to say it. Somebody has to name it. Somebody has to have the courage to tell us to stop it. These "isms" are killing us because they are killing the Seed of our foreordained destiny! These dangerous enemies of our faith are bumps and pitfalls in our way. They slow us down and delay the fulfillment of His promises.

I am astonished that you are so quickly deserting the One who called you by the grace of Christ and are turning to a different gospel

which is really no gospel at all. Evidently some people are throwing you into confusion and are trying to pervert the gospel of Christ (Galatians 1:6-7 NIV).

Easy believism is "another gospel" (Gal. 1:6-10).

Easy Believism Aborts the Seed

Soteriology is the biblical Doctrine of Salvation, taken from the Greek word *soteria*, which means, "a complete deliverance." The sin of easy believism has distorted the Gospel and maimed the Church.

As stated above, there are two primary elements that must be evident for real conversion to take place: *repentance* and *faith*.

Therefore let us leave the elementary teachings about Christ and go on to maturity, not laying again the foundation of repentance from acts that lead to death, and of faith in God, (Hebrews 6:1 NIV).

Every house (life, marriage, or ministry) that will stand must have a solid foundation. "Repentance from dead works, and…faith toward (upon) God" (KJV) are part of the first "principles of the doctrine of Christ." Without them in place, the King will not authorize His building "permit" (Heb. 6:3).

Without repentance and faith, there can be no conversion. In this initial salvation experience, we turn from sin *and* turn to Jesus Christ. The negative element, turning from sin, we call *repentance*. The positive element, turning to Jesus Christ, we call *faith*.

Easy believism is an enemy to the Gospel and an obstacle in our path because it frustrates (sets aside, disregards, violates) the grace of God (see Gal. 2:21). It bypasses the need for real repentance, so there can be no real conversion.

If there is no conversion, there can be no divine Seed planted in the heart.

If there is no divine Seed planted in the heart, there can be no destiny; for, as we learned in Chapter One, the destiny is in the Seed!

The Hebrew word for *repentance* means, "to sigh, breathe strongly; to be sorry; to pity, console." It carries the idea of groaning and lamenting. The New Testament word for "repentance" is *metanoia* and it means, "compunction (for guilt, including reformation); reversal (of another's decision); a change of mind (heart)." It is taken from *meta* (change) and *nous* (mind). Repentance is a change of mind.

There are three aspects of true repentance, impacting the entire soul of man—the intellect, emotions, and will:

Intellectual – I know that I am a sinner.

Emotional – I feel that I am a sinner.

Volitional – I willfully change my mind and turn from sin.

When they heard these things, they held their peace, and glorified God, saying, Then hath God also to the Gentiles granted repentance unto life (Acts 11:18).

The God of our fathers raised up Jesus, whom ye slew and hanged on a tree.

Him hath God exalted with His right hand to be a Prince and a Saviour, for to give repentance to Israel, and forgiveness of sins (Acts 5:30-31).

In meekness instructing those that oppose themselves; if God peradventure will give them repentance to the acknowledging of the truth; (2 Timothy 2:25).

The Bible clearly explains that real repentance is a *gift* from God, ministered to us by the Holy Spirit.

It is God who takes the initiative in repentance. It does not originate with mankind. No one can or will repent of himself (see John 1:12-13). One cannot be born again whenever he or she chooses—there is "a time to be born" (Eccl. 3:2). The Holy Spirit is the One who draws us to God, convicting or convincing us concerning our sin and our consequent need for the Savior (see John 16:8).

Above all, there must be the "fruits" of repentance (Matt. 3:8) or the "works" of repentance (Acts 26:20), the fruit of a changed life that proves that we have repented.[5]

Before we examine real faith, a final example of easy believism must be given with regard to the necessity of real repentance.

There is a growing idea among some preachers and people that all men have been automatically saved. The doctrine of "inclusion," as it is being presently set forth is not true. More than that, it is unclean and dangerous. The word of wisdom, the answer to this thorny issue is that all men have been reconciled, but not all men have been saved.

And all things are of God, who hath reconciled us to Himself by [through] Jesus Christ, and hath given to us the ministry of reconciliation.

To wit, that God was in Christ, reconciling the world unto Himself, not imputing their trespasses unto them; and hath committed unto us the word of reconciliation (2 Corinthians 5:18-19).

"Reconciliation" is the Greek word *katallage*, and it means, "exchange, adjustment; restoration to (the divine) favor; a change on the part of one party, induced by an action on the part of another."

Through the finished work of Jesus Christ in His death (His shed blood), His burial, and His resurrection, the Father has made full *provision* to save. Jesus came to reverse the curse (see Gal. 3:13-14), and to restore mankind to divine favor, the fellowship and dominion we lost in the Garden of Eden because of Adam's sin (see Gen. 3 with Rom. 5:12-21).

God is attracted to *sacrifice*—His own! Just as the "smoking furnace" (a picture of the Father, as in Ex. 19:18) and the "burning lamp" (a picture of the Son, as in John 8:12) sloshed through the blood as They walked down between the pieces of the sacrifice in the days of Abram (Gen. 15:17), so our Savior died between two thieves, two sacrifices, at the Cross, where He and the Father cut the "everlasting covenant" in His own blood (Heb. 13:20)!

Then Moses called for all the elders of Israel, and said unto them, Draw out and take you a lamb according to your families, and kill the passover.

And ye shall take a bunch of hyssop, and dip it in the blood that is in the bason, and strike the lintel and the two side posts with the blood that is in the bason; and none of you shall go out at the door of his house until the morning.

For the Lord will pass through to smite the Egyptians; and when He seeth the blood upon the lintel, and on the two side posts, the Lord will pass over the door, and will not suffer the destroyer to come in unto your houses to smite you (Exodus 12:21-23).

Hyssop is a biblical symbol for the *application* of the blood. While it is true that reconciliation for all men has been provided by our Passover Lamb (John 1:29; 1 Cor. 5:7; 1 Pet. 1:18-20), yet His precious blood must be applied for salvation to take place. The "destroyer" (Exod. 12:23) will only "pass over" the lives of the blood-washed redeemed.

Have you *applied* the blood of the Passover Lamb to the door of your heart? We must repent and turn from sin before we can believe.

What About Faith?

"Faith" was defined in Chapter One. There we learned that this race of faith has to do with *His* faith, not ours. That important information is repeated here.

The Hebrew word for *faith* means, "established, trusty, trustworthiness." Its root *aw-man'* (confirmed, established, sure, reliable, certain) is transliterated to the English, "amen." The Greek word is *pistis*, and it means, "persuasion, credence; moral conviction." *Pistis* is also translated in the King James Version as, "assurance, belief, believe, faith, fidelity."

> *Now faith is the substance of things hoped for, the evidence of things not seen* (Hebrews 11:1).

> *Now faith is being sure of what we hope for and certain of what we do not see* (Hebrews 11:1 NIV).

> *What is faith? It is the confident assurance that something we want is going to happen. It is the certainty that what we hope for is waiting for us, even though we cannot see it up ahead* (Hebrews 11:1 TLB).

> *Now faith is the assurance (the confirmation, the title-deed) of the things [we] hope for, being the proof of things [we] do not see and conviction of their reality—faith perceiving as real fact what is not revealed to the senses* (Hebrews 11:1 AMP).

Hebrews 11:1 is the biblical definition of faith. Furthermore, on page 25 of my book, *The Tongue of the Learned*, we learn that "faith" is:

- A spiritual force; God is a Spirit moved by faith (Heb. 11:6).

- The absence of doubt, the opposite of fear (2 Tim. 1:7).

- In the present tense, for "now" faith is (Heb. 11:1).

- A gift, an impartation from the Lord (Rom. 12:3).

- A fruit that grows (Rom. 1:17; Gal. 5:22-23).

- That which comes by hearing the Word of God (Rom. 10:17).

- That which speaks; faith has a voice (Rom. 10:6-10).

- That by which we live (Acts 17:28; Gal. 2:20).

As with repentance, there are three aspects of true faith that operate in our conversion, impacting the entire soul of mankind—the intellect, emotions, and will:

Intellectual – I know that I am saved.

Emotional – I feel the joy of the assurance that I am saved.

Volitional – I willfully receive the assurance that I am saved.

For I say, through the grace given unto me, to every man that is among you, not to think of himself more highly than he ought to think; but to think soberly, according as God hath dealt to every man the measure of faith (Romans 12:3).

For by grace are ye saved through faith; and that not of yourselves: it is the gift of God:

Not of works, lest any man should boast (Ephesians 2:8-9).

Simon Peter, a servant and an apostle of Jesus Christ, to them that have obtained like precious faith with us through the righteousness of God and our Saviour Jesus Christ: (2 Peter 1:1).

As with repentance, real faith is a *gift* from God, ministered to us by the Holy Spirit.

This faith must be rooted in the heart before it can be declared by the mouth with validity and certainty (see Rom. 10:6-10). The late Charles Price, a great healing evangelist, wrote a classic titled, *The Real Faith*. Rightfully so, he confirmed faith to be a gift. Real faith is not just imputed; it is imparted!

To sum up, it is evident that this brief biblical overview of repentance and faith is far removed from the watered-down compromise of easy believism! We must repent *and* believe the Gospel (see Mark 1:15)!

I challenge every pastor next Sunday morning not to count the saints, but to *weigh* them! The Hebrew word for *glory* means, "heavy, weighty." How much of the substance of Christ, the inward Seed, is resident in the hearts of your congregation?

This race was never meant to be "easy." When introducing other Christian leaders to principles of "present truth" (2 Pet. 1:12), I always begin my saying, "Knowing these things, and getting close to those of us who preach these things, will cost you everything."

And, behold, there was a man in Jerusalem, whose name was Simeon; and the same man was just and devout, waiting for the consolation of Israel [the Messiah]: *and the Holy Ghost was upon him.*

And it was revealed unto him by the Holy Ghost, that he should not see death, before he had seen the Lord's Christ (Luke 2:25-26).

Those who run and win this race must "run all" (1 Cor. 9:24)— a complete death to self. One cannot die the right kind of death until he or she, like Simeon, sees (or has a vision of) the Lord's Christ—Christ fully formed in a people (see Gal. 4:19)! Until we understand God's corporate purposes, the bigger picture, and the greater goal of unity (see the Preface), we will come to the Cross kicking and squealing ("I don't want to die!"). But the Pattern Son came like a Lamb "dumb" (without a sound or voice) before His Shearer, the Father, whose predetermined pleasure (purpose) was to bruise Him (Isa. 53:10).

Focused on the Goal, serious runners have no time or place for easy believism. Too much is at stake to play childish games along the way.

My Personal Race of Faith

As I shared earlier, I backslid my freshman year at Potomac State College. But I will never forget that eventful night in the spring of 1969 on the south end of Keyser when I found myself in Pastor James Williamson's United Pentecostal Church. My Aunt Pearl and my grandmother (my dad's mother), Flatie Carr, attended there. My family had known the Williamsons for years, and I had sung in his services (as I had done in most of the churches in the Keyser area, especially at weddings).

At this significant *kairos* moment of my life, the man of God preached about the backslidden judge Samson, and God smote my wayward heart. I knelt down and cried all over that old-fashioned altar, and the Lord graciously restored to me "the joy" of my salvation (Isa. 51:12).

Earlier that same year, I had received a full scholarship to attend Alderson-Broaddus College in Philippi, West Virginia, to be part of their music department—"Just come and sing," they had said.

But once I had given my heart back to the Lord, He began to deal with me about turning down the scholarship and going to Bible School (at that time I had no understanding of the local church). To the shock, consternation, and dismay of family and friends, I did so. I don't even want to think about what would have happened to my destiny had I not obeyed God at the tender age of 19.

That summer I became very close to one of my friends, George McDowell, Jr. (known to me as "Mac"). Mac was and still is an incredible musician. In his senior year of high school, he toured Europe with the U.S.A. Band, playing the tuba. The Lord taught Mac how to play the piano by ear, and for a season, he was the accompanist for our gospel quartet. He and I were also classmates at Potomac State College, where we both majored in music education.

Mac's parents, George Sr., and Reba, had come out of a certain classical Pentecostal denomination to start an independent ministry. It was at their facility at the old Shaw Mansion where I had received the Baptism of the Holy Ghost in the fall of 1968. I will be forever grateful to the McDowells for their kindnesses. This wonderful, seasoned Pentecostal family "adopted" me and helped me in the spiritual beginnings of my race. It was through their ministry that I was introduced to the real moving of the Holy Ghost through His gifts and graces. They would sit for hours and tell me stories about the supernatural workings and manifestations of the Spirit.

My pace in the race was picking up steam. These spiritual "growth spurts" helped me grow quickly. I was flying around the track.

To make a long story short, Mac was asked to teach at a small Pentecostal Bible School near Pittsburgh, and I sensed that I was to go along, but as a student. The late David J. Beam was the President of Free Gospel Bible Institute (F.G.B.I) in Export, Pennsylvania. It was there in the fall of 1969 where I became acquainted with a beautiful young lady by the name of Joann Dorothy Armentrout.

Joann graduated from "Fig-bee" (as we called it) after three years. Most folks are surprised to learn that I am not a Bible school graduate. I only attended for one year, but the Lord performed a real work in me, chiseling off great chunks of flesh. I would later learn the Bible by sitting at the feet of real apostles and prophets, some of whom never finished high school.

It was at F.G.B.I. during my freshman class of Personal Evangelism when I was introduced to all the aforementioned traditional methods of easy believism. It is cold in the Pittsburgh area all winter, but I still remember handing out tracks on Saturday afternoons outside the mall in nearby Monroeville, as well as visiting folks in their homes (both without much visible results). Again, there is nothing wrong with track evangelism or visitation, but I was just doing what I was told.

Over the years, through the study of the Word, I have come to understand the necessity of real repentance and faith as the elements of conversion. I have witnessed the compromise of easy believism at every level. When I got filled with the Holy Ghost, I saw some of my closest evangelical friends walk away. As I have gradually received the revelation of the present reality of the Kingdom of God (and school is not out yet), I have seen and still see preachers keep me at arm's length. I am somewhat curious to see some of their responses or reactions upon reading this treatise.

What is the answer to this Americanized "pop" Gospel of easy believism?

Where the Bible says "much," let us say "much." Where the Bible says "little," let us say "little." In other words, let us obey the wisest words Paul ever penned to the rest of us preachers.

Preach the word; be instant in season, out of season; reprove, rebuke, exhort with all longsuffering and doctrine (2 Timothy 4:2).

Herald and preach the Word! Keep your sense of urgency [stand by, be at hand and ready], whether the opportunity seems to be favorable or unfavorable. {Whether it is convenient or inconvenient, whether it be welcome or unwelcome, you as a preacher of the Word are to show people in what way their lives are wrong] and convince them, rebuking and correcting, warning and urging and encouraging them, being unflagging and inexhaustible in patience and teaching (2 Timothy 4:2 AMP).

Brothers and sisters, preach the Word!

Endnotes

1. Isaiah received a "burden" for Babylon (13:1), for Moab (15:1), for Damascus (17:1), for Egypt (19:1), for the desert of the sea (21:1), for Dumah (21:11), for the valley of vision (22:1), for Tyre (23:1), and for the beasts of the south (30:6).

2. The "Roman road" in personal evangelism is as follows: (1) Man is a sinner—Rom. 3:10,23; (2) The wages of sin is death—Rom. 6:23; (3) While we were yet sinners, Christ died for us—Rom. 5:8; and (4) We must confess with our mouth the Lord Jesus and believe in our heart that God raised Him from the dead—Rom. 10:9-10.

3. The phrase "born of God" is particular to John's first epistle and is mentioned seven times (1 John 3:9 [twice]; 4:7 [twice]; 5:1,4,18).

4. "Nickels, noses, and names" is a term that I have coined to describe the current trends of many churches and ministries in the United States: (1) Nickels—the love of money; (2) Noses—the numbers game of seeing how many people attend; and (3) Names—the importance of ministerial titles and the desire to be known and seen by others.

5. The "fruits" or "works" of genuine repentance are: a godly sorrow (Ps. 38:18; Matt. 27:75; 2 Cor. 7:10); a confession of sin (see Ps. 32:5; 51:1-4; Prov. 28:13; Matt. 5:23-24; Luke 18:9-14; 15:11; James 5:16; and 1 John 1:9); a turning toward God through Jesus Christ (Acts 26:18; 1 Thess. 1:9; Heb. 6:1-2); a forsaking of sin (see Ps. 119:58-60; Isa. 53:6; 55:6-7; Ezek. 18:20-32; Matt. 3:8-10; and Gal. 5:19-21); a turning from dead religious works (Eph. 2:1-5;Col. 1:21; 1 Tim. 5:6; Heb. 6:1; 9:14); a hatred of sin (Ezek. 6:9-19; 20:43-44; 36:31-33); a desire for forgiveness (Ps. 25:11; 51:1; Luke 18:13); and a restitution where possible (Lev. 6:1-7; Num. 5:5-8; Luke 3:1-14; 18:13; 19:8).

CHAPTER FIVE

Legalism

At this juncture in our race, we are about a third of the way around the course leading to our destiny.

Early on, we must understand that there are three parts to this event, three key sections of the track.

*Have not I written to thee **excellent** things in counsels and knowledge,*

That I might make thee know the certainty of the words of truth; that thou mightest answer the words of truth... (Proverbs 22:20-21, emphasis added).

God's purposes and the biblical understanding of the King and His Kingdom are revealed in three dimensions. The word for "excellent" in this passage means, "three-fold." God's three greatest spokesmen—Moses, Jesus, and Paul—all declared that by the mouth of two or *three* witnesses that all things would be established (see Deut. 17:6; Matt. 18:16; 2 Cor. 13:1).

The grandfather clause of all biblical revelation is the divine "pattern" revealed in the Mosaic Tabernacle (Exod. 25:8,40) with its three dimensions—the Outer Court, the Holy Place, and the Most Holy Place. This pattern holds true through both Testaments and into the Book of Revelation.

> **Three** *times in a year shall all thy males appear before the Lord thy God in the place which He shall choose; in the feast of unleavened bread* [Passover], *and in the feast of weeks* [Pentecost], *and in the feast of tabernacles: and they shall not appear before the Lord empty:* (Deuteronomy 16:16, emphasis added).

Paralleling the Mosaic "pattern" are the three major Feasts of Jehovah—Passover, Pentecost, and Tabernacles. In my book, *Prevail: A Handbook for the Overcomer*, there are 40 examples of three-fold things on pages 84-85.

Simply stated, in the Outer Court, Jesus is our Savior. In the Holy Place, He baptized us with the Holy Ghost. In the Most Holy Place, Jesus is King and Lord, the Pattern Son, the Overcomer, and the Head of the Church.

Thus there are three dimensions of growth in the life of every Christian: in Passover we are born again (John 3:7); in Pentecost we are Spirit-filled (Acts 2:4); and in Tabernacles we are mature, fully grown (Eph. 4:13)—little children, young men, and fathers (1 John 2:12-14).

In the First Day, the emphasis and focus is totally man-centered (all man). In the Second Day, the vision is on two things (double-mindedness)—an outrageous mixture of God *and* man. In the Third Day, our hearts and minds are marked by singleness and simplici-ty as we remain totally focused on one goal—Him! The centrality and supremacy of King Jesus and His finished work constitute our sole emphasis and vision (all God)!

Chapters Two through Four of this writing describe the sins of the Outer Court—the evangelical Church world. These obstacles in our race of faith have compromised the Seed of the Kingdom, and have damaged our destiny in the formative years of our spiritual childhood:

Cessasionism – The belief that the *charismata* (the Gifts of the Spirit), signs, wonders, miracles, apostles, and prophets ceased with the early Church and the Book of Acts. This view insists that once the Canon of Scripture was completed, these things are not for us today.

Stoicism – The belief that one should not show any emotion or passion in the House of the Lord.

Easy believism – The belief that one can be converted without experiencing both basic elements of conversion: repentance and faith, which are gifts from God.

Now we turn our attention to the second dimension—the Feast of Pentecost—the Spirit-filled realm. This includes the classical Pentecostal and Charismatic churches, as well as the Faith Movement. This chapter and the six that follow will expose the dangers that block the road of our spiritual adolescence.

The first of these is *legalism*.

What Is Legalism?

Webster's defines *legalism* as "a strict adherence to law; in theology, the doctrine of salvation by good works."

Legalism binds people to various laws and regulations with the man-made notion unto holiness (see Col. 2:21-23). The legalistic spirit is a doctrine of salvation or sanctification by good works, rather than by grace and faith alone.

For I bear them record that they have a zeal of God, but not accord-ing to knowledge (Romans 10:2).

I know what enthusiasm they have for the honor of God, but it is misdirected zeal (Romans 10:2 TLB).

Legalism is marked by religious, misdirected "zeal" without knowledge. The Message Bible adds that legalists "...are impres-sively energetic regarding God—but they are doing everything exactly backward."

The Book of Genesis is the Book of Beginnings, and is the seed-plot of the Bible. There we are introduced to the essence of legalism.

And out of the ground made the Lord God to grow every tree that is pleasant to the sight, and good for food; the tree of life also in the midst of the garden, and the tree of knowledge of good and evil (Genesis 2:9).

The tree of the knowledge of "good and evil" is rooted in Adam. The "tree of life" is rooted in Christ. Jesus *is* the Tree of Life—He is the true or genuine Vine, the Resurrection and the Life (John 15:1-5; 11:25).

As the sons and daughters of God, we are not called to be a moral people; we have been called to be a Christ-like people. Know this: This Christian journey is not about right and wrong, good and evil; this pursuit of destiny is about life and death!

The real question to ask with regard to any thought or action is, "Is it 'good' or is it God"?

*And certain men which came down from Judaea taught the brethren, and said, **except** [unless] ye be circumcised [peritem-no] after the **manner of Moses** [usage, habit; prescribed by* law; custom, institute] (the **old order**), *ye cannot be* [*duna-mai*] *saved* [*sozo*] (Acts 15:1, emphasis added).

The burning issue that plagued the early Church in the Book of Acts was the demon of legalism which was later dealt with by the Jerusalem Council.

The Protestant Reformation was sparked by Martin Luther. As he studied and meditated on Paul's letters to the Romans and Galatians, this unsaved Catholic monk saw by revelation that "the just shall live by faith" (Rom. 1:17; Gal. 3:11).

Consider what the apostle had to say about "the law" in the following verses taken from those same epistles:

Therefore by the deeds of the law there shall no flesh be justified in His sight: for by the law is the knowledge of sin (Romans 3:20).

Wherefore, my brethren, ye also are become dead to the law by the body of Christ; that ye should be married to another, even to Him who is raised from the dead, that we should bring forth fruit unto God (Romans 7:4).

For the law of the Spirit of life in Christ Jesus hath made me free from the law of sin and death.

For what the law could not do, in that it was weak through the flesh, God sending His own Son in the likeness of sinful flesh, and for sin, condemned sin in the flesh: (Romans 8:2-3).

For Christ is the end of the law for righteousness to every one that believeth (Romans 10:4).

Knowing that a man is not justified by the works of the law, but by the faith of Jesus Christ, even we have believed in Jesus Christ, that we might be justified by the faith of Christ, and not by the works of the law: for by the works of the law shall no flesh be justified (Galatians 2:16).

For as many as are of the works of the law are under the curse: for it is written, Cursed is every one that continueth not in all things which are written in the book of the law to do them.

But that no man is justified by the law in the sight of God, it is evident: for, The just shall live by faith.

And the law is not of faith: but, The man that doeth them shall live in them.

Christ hath redeemed us from the curse of the law, being made a curse for us: for it is written, Cursed is every one that hangeth on a tree (Galatians 3:10-13).

The Word speaks for itself, plainly and powerfully. Moreover, Paul declared that "the sting of death is sin; and the strength (ability) of sin is the law" (1 Cor. 15:56).

Again, the emphasis here is not about right and wrong. It is about life and death. The *law* spells out to one word: *death!*

Legalism will kill you.

Legalism Is at Work

As we run, we meet all kinds of people and situations. Legalism comes in many shapes, sizes, and colors.

First and foremost, legalism is a set of man-made rules and regulations. Webster defines a *rule* as "an established guide for action, conduct, method, or arrangement; a fixed principle that determines a habit or custom; a criterion or standard."

Every church or denomination comes with its own set of rules. We can play in their game if we keep their rules. Break their rules, and we get to sit on their bench (I've been there and done that). This is particularly so with regard to their set of doctrinal beliefs.

Therefore no one is to act as your judge in regard to food or drink or in respect to a festival or a new moon or a Sabbath day— (Colossians 2:16 NASB).

Unfortunately, legalism is rampant in the Outer Court as well as in the Holy Place. Many hardcore Fundamentalists, along with classical Pentecostals have prided themselves in their "holiness" standards. Some have even refused to read any other version or translation of the Bible other than the "good old" King James.

It is hard to believe that some of these examples of legalism given throughout this chapter still exist in the 21st century.

For example, certain standards vary from one geographical region to another—those who live near the ocean may indulge in mixed bathing; those who do not, may not!

Preachers have used the phrase, "dressing the baby before it is born," to describe certain rules for clothing—the dreaded "dress code." We have been especially tough on the ladies.

Certain fringe groups forbid their women to wear anything colorful, and certainly never anything but a full-length dress to go with the head covering on their full-length hair (which, of course, is a sin to cut according to their interpretation of First Corinthians 11:15).

"Men in black" is not just the name of a movie. Black suits and shoes with white, hard-to-press, long-sleeve shirts and white socks; along with these accessories—no shorts, no bright ties, no long hair, or mustaches, or side burns, or beards, and certainly no jewelry—are the things that please God, legalists strictly admonish the brothers.

This man-made list of "do's and don'ts" could go on and on, ad nauseam.

Remember, legalism purports that the keeping of all these rules will please God. We certainly don't want to upset the Lord and get Him "mad" at us! Legalists think that they must "raise the standard."

Then Jehu went to Jezreel. When Jezebel heard about it, she painted her eyes, arranged her hair and looked out of a window (2 Kings 9:30 NIV).

And God forbid that any self-respecting woman would ever wear slacks or shorts, or paint her face like Jezebel of old. This verse has been the text for more than one hard-nosed preacher.

Legalism kills destiny because legalism kills life. It destroys passion and vision, especially among our youth. When they hear about the rules of a man-made race, they don't want to run. Who could blame them? We have told them, "You cannot do this and you cannot go there." In some circles, television and movies (of any kind) are sin. It is not surprising that the kids who grow up in a legalistic household are often overweight—one of the few things that they have been allowed to do is eat!

Another blatant example of legalism among God's people is the adamant refusal of many evangelical and Pentecostal leaders to acknowledge or allow the public ministry of women. "We don't believe in women preachers or pastors," is their unyielding cry. Citing two particular Pauline passages (1 Cor. 14:34-35; 1 Tim. 2:11-15) to substantiate their traditional position, an old order male-dominated priesthood has ignorantly (and too often arrogantly) stifled and snuffed out the anointing upon many of God's handmaidens.

This whole issue of gender prejudice is covered in-depth in my book, *The Three Prejudices*.

Again, the fruit of all this religious stupidity is *death*—death in the spirit, death in the soul (intellect, emotions, and will), and death in the body. We must watch for this deep, black hole in the road, and jump over it.

These useless attempts of our flesh to keep the rules only bring condemnation, frustration, and aggravation, covered with plenty of guilt and shame. Too many young people have taken their talents and gifts to the world because they could never find acceptance and unconditional love in "church."

Legalism works in the home as well as the church. In every domestic dispute between husband and wife, one or both will *insist* on having the last word. Like a spoiled child, some adults demand to have everything done his or her way—"*my* opinion."

Legalism operates wherever one party suppresses another with certain demands. A pastor with a heavy hand on his congregation while in his pulpit preaching or his counseling chambers, or a denominational official handing down the latest ruling from "headquarters," are common examples that the law is at work.

And wherever the law operates, there is death. The sting of death is sin, and the strength of sin is the law (1 Cor. 15:56). Legalism has killed the Seed and aborted destiny.

I am [have been] crucified with Christ: nevertheless I live; yet not I, but Christ liveth in me: and the life which I now live in the flesh I live by the faith of the Son of God, who loved me, and gave Himself for me.

I do not frustrate the grace of God: for if righteousness come by the law, then Christ is dead in vain (Galatians 2:20-21).

The effect of legalism's workings is to "frustrate" the grace of God.[1]

Legalism Aborts the Seed

And He [Jesus] also told this parable to certain ones who trusted in themselves that they were righteous, and viewed others with contempt:

"Two men went up into the temple to pray, one a Pharisee, and the other a tax-gatherer.

The Pharisee stood and was praying thus to himself, 'God, I thank Thee that I am not like other people: swindlers, unjust, adulterers, or even like this tax-gatherer.

'I fast twice a week; I pay tithes of all that I get.'

But the tax-gatherer, standing some distance away, was even unwilling to lift up his eyes to heaven, but was beating his breast, saying, 'God, be merciful to me, the sinner!'

"I tell you, this man went down to his house justified rather than the other; for everyone who exalts himself shall be humbled, but he who humbles himself shall be exalted" (Luke 18:9-14 NASB).

Legalism aborts the Seed of destiny. Pharisees love to condemn and put down other people. The law by nature is very demanding. Driven by that principle, hard-nosed legalists lack love and wisdom. Their "ministry" is to accuse, condemn, judge, and sentence to condemnation's prison house everyone and everything around them.

Judgmentalism always makes comparisons. Legalism drives us to performance. Our unreal expectations of others then create an ungodly rating system. We must stop grading each other, for it is not wise (see 2 Cor. 10:12). By the law is the knowledge of sin (see Rom. 3:20). Sin-conscious Pharisees and self-appointed lawyers are focused on the wrong thing.

But there is another side to the legalism coin. These twelve deadly impediments by no means cover the subject. A case in point: *Legalism* will kill you. But *license* will kill you quicker! License (no rules; anything goes) is the human overreaction to legalism.

The New Testament Saul, who became Paul, was a staunch legalist in his youth. At the proper age (probably about 13), Saul went to Jerusalem to pursue his studies in the learning of the Jews. Here he became a "Hebrew of the Hebrews" (Phil. 3:5), brought up in Jerusalem "at the feet of Gamaliel," the most illustrious rabbi of his day (Acts 5:34; 22:3). Saul's "zeal" without knowledge (Rom. 10:2) for Jewish Law later found a ready outlet in his assault on the infant church of Jerusalem.

Following his conversion (see Acts 9) and his calling as the apostle to the uncircumcised, Paul left Antioch of Syria with Barnabas on the First Missionary Journey (see Acts 13-14). Later, when writing back to these Galatian churches, the apostle dealt with both legalism and license in his powerful letter, the theme of which is the maturation of the Seed (see Gal. 3:1-4:7).

Interestingly, the Galatian saints were the only group of people that this literary apostle addressed for whom he did not give thanks! It was also here in the Galatian letter that Paul relates his correction of even Peter's legalistic prejudices (see Gal. 2:11-16).

You foolish Galatians! Who has bewitched you? Before your very eyes Jesus Christ was clearly portrayed as crucified.

I would like to learn just one thing from you: Did you receive the Spirit by observing the law, or by believing what you heard?

Are you so foolish? After beginning with the Spirit, are you now trying to attain your goal by human effort?

Have you suffered so much for nothing— if it really was for nothing?

Does God give you His Spirit and work miracles among you because you observe the law, or because you believe what you heard? (Galatians 3:1-5 NIV).

Oh, foolish Galatians! What magician has hypnotized you and cast an evil spell upon you?... (Galatians 3:1 TLB).

You crazy Galatians! Did someone put a hex on you? Have you taken leave of your senses? Something crazy has happened, for it's obvious that you no longer have the crucified Jesus in clear focus in your lives. His sacrifice on the cross was certainly set before you clearly enough (Galatians 3:1 TM).

The Galatian churches had been "bewitched" (fascinated, charmed) by a group of legalists known as the Judaizers. These were early converts to Christianity who tried to force believers from non-Jewish backgrounds to adopt Jewish customs as a condition of salvation. Evidence of this movement within the early church first emerged about A.D. 49, when "certain men came down from Judea and taught the brethren, 'Unless you are circumcised according to the custom of Moses, you cannot be saved'" (Acts 15:1). These Judaizers may have been Paul's "thorn in the flesh" (2 Cor. 12:7), his constant enemy, for they followed the apostle everywhere with but one motive—to tear apart and destroy everything that he built!

Again, legalism will kill you, but license will kill you quicker! License is the human overreaction to legalism.

For, brethren, ye have been called unto liberty; only use not liberty for an occasion to the flesh, but by love serve one another (Galatians 5:13).

Now the works of the flesh are manifest, which are these; Adultery, fornication, uncleanness, lasciviousness,

idolatry, witchcraft, hatred, variance, emulations, wrath, strife, seditions, heresies,

envyings, murders, drunkenness, revellings, and such like: of the which I tell you before, as I have also told you in time past, that they which do such things shall not inherit the kingdom of God (Galatians 5:19-21).

The acts of the sinful nature are obvious: sexual immorality, impurity and debauchery;

idolatry and witchcraft; hatred, discord, jealousy, fits of rage, selfish ambition, dissensions, factions

and envy; drunkenness, orgies, and the like. I warn you, as I did before, that those who live like this will not inherit the kingdom of God (Galatians 5:19-21 NIV).

Paul wrote the above passage to a group steeped in license. He said in essence, "Any dummy knows that this stuff is sin and obviously wrong!" These were the Antinomians, whose theology interpreted Paul's teachings on law and grace to mean that the Christian is so wholly in grace that he is in no sense under the law.

"Antinomianism" comes from two Greek words: *anti* (instead of) and *nomos* (law)—it means, "instead of law." We could also call this error "greasy grace" or "sloppy *agape*." In other words, anything goes.

Historically, classical Pentecostals, from 1900 to 1960, were marked by varying degrees of legalism. Then, with the outbreak of the Charismatic Renewal among the denominations in the 1960s and 1970s, the paradigm began to shift.

One could liken the classical Pentecostals to the northern kingdom Israel and the Charismatics to the southern kingdom Judah in the days of Ezekiel. The prophet told the story of the older sister and the younger sister, Aholah and Aholibah (see Ezek. 23). Israel had been carried away because of idolatry, false gods. Judah, her younger sister, never learned from her predecessor's mistake.

Likewise, once we began to climb out of the ditch of historical legalism, we got up a full head of steam, ran across the road, and fell headlong into a deeper ditch called license!

In legalism, there are rules and more rules. In license, there are no rules. Wear what you want, eat and drink what you want, watch what you want, go where you want, and do what you want. As with the Antinomians, there is no restraint, no law, no government, no local church, and no pastor—there is no law, no accountability.

The Galatian epistle has much to say about the Seed. Two things will abort our destiny—legalism and license—law and lust.

This warning is worth repeating: Legalism will kill you. License will kill you quicker.

My Personal Race of Faith

When I began to sing with the Ambassador Quartet, I came to meet many new friends, most of whom were classical Pentecostals. I noticed immediately that most of them were pretty strait-laced and strict, especially the women. Many of them never wore make-up and had their hair styled in a neat little bun. I must have appeared "worldly" to them, and some of them made me feel that way.

The McDowells who "adopted" me after I was filled with the Holy Ghost were from a rigid Pentecostal background. I assumed that what they and other mature Christians believed about "holiness" was right (I had yet to really study the Word). Most of the churches that our Gospel quartet ministered in were classical Pentecostal. I was told later that the particular geographical region where we operated most of our ministry had historically been very legalistic.

I had noticed while a music major at Potomac State that the young people who came from strong legalistic church backgrounds usually went "wild" after they arrived on campus. Out from under the restraint of church and parents, some of my classmates quickly became alcoholics and began to experiment with sex and drugs. While at home, they had kept the rules, but Christ had not ruled their hearts.

Later, when I enrolled at Free Gospel Bible Institute (F.G.B.I.), I, like Saul, became "a Hebrew of the Hebrews." I believed and preached law. All of us had plain uniforms. Make-up and jewelry were taboo.

That was the setting where I met and fell in love with Joann, the love of my life. Now my wife of almost 35 years, she did and does look good wearing anything.

My dilemma: the only time that the boys were allowed to talk to the girls was at mealtime. This was a "faith" Bible school, and we ate what the Lord provided. I gained 40 pounds that year from eating cinnamon toast when talking to Joann at breakfast!

"Social hour" was an exception. Once in a while, for 30 minutes, we could sit and talk to the opposite sex. But—and I'm not kidding—there was a 6" rule (don't touch). To make matters worse, a delightful, never-been-married lady in her 70s was the official overseer of "social hour." She was like those living creatures in the Book of Revelation, with "eyes" all over her!

The funny thing was to watch some of us at Christmas and spring breaks after we left the campus. We weren't a mile down the road before one could hear the screech of tires as we piled out of our cars, found our sweethearts, and cuddled up for the rest of the ride home. So much for rules.

After my year at Free Gospel, I helped the McDowells start their own training center, Zion School of Christian Education, which opened in the fall of 1970. And, yes, we, too, had a dress code and a classical "holiness" standard. I conformed to this because I knew no better. But, as Mac and I studied the Scriptures, the Lord began to show us the balance in these things. We did change the rules somewhat after that (to the dismay of some and the delight of others).

One more story…I have Joann's permission to tell this.

The year at F.G.B.I. and the two years that followed, I courted Joann, a young lady from Moorefield, West Virginia. She had grown up in classical Pentecostalism and had been saved from early childhood. How strange that we grew up only 35 miles apart!

But I am glad that she did not know me before I was saved, especially on the Saturday nights when I stayed late at the downtown dance on the second floor of the Keyser Fire Hall. I was usually dressed in short, tight, white shorts, a bright shirt (unbuttoned, of course), and white tennis shoes without socks. Her mama, Miss Janie, would have told her girl to run from that young man! And rightfully so....

After I met Joann at Bible school, on one of those "courting" weekends, I drove my 1966 light green Ford convertible, with standard shift and baby moon hubcaps, to see my girl. Joann came out of the house wearing a beautiful, fluffy white dress.

Then this wanna-be-preacher, newly-appointed Bible school teacher showed his stupidity to the max (I am almost ashamed to tell you this).

I keenly remember saying, "I am a man of God, and that dress is about one inch too short for my standards!" (Can you believe I said that?) "If you are going on a date with me, you will have change into something else."

What can I say? On the one hand, dumb and dumber. On her part, nothing but grace and mercy, perhaps mingled with pity for a lesser creature. I'm forever thankful that at that awkward moment perhaps love was indeed blind.

She changed the dress....

You do know how I am going to end this chapter, don't you?

Legalism will kill you. License will kill you quicker.

Endnote

1. The effect or fruit of legalism's workings is to "frustrate" the grace of God. This Greek word in Galatians 2:21 is *atheteo*, and it means, to "set aside,

neutralize, violate; do away with, disregard, thwart the efficacy of, nullify, make void; to reject, refuse, or slight." It is translated in the King James Version as, "bring to nothing" (1 Cor. 1:19); "cast off" (1 Tim. 5:12); "despise (-d, -th)" (see Luke 10:16; 1 Thess. 4:8; Heb. 10:28; Jude 1:8); "disannulleth" (Gal. 3:15); and "reject (-ed, -eth)" (see Mark 6:26; 7:9; Luke 7:30; John 12:48).

CHAPTER SIX

Asceticism

For we are His workmanship, created in Christ Jesus for good works, which God prepared beforehand [before the race began] *so that we would walk* [and run] *in them* (Ephesians 2:10 NASB).

The time has come for us to press forward in freedom into all that the Lord has planned for our lives and ministries.

We are sifting through the incredible mixture of negative influences that hinder our ability to run freely after Christ in this race of faith. These sinful trends among God's people have compromised the Word, the Seed of the Kingdom. These evil couriers of carnality have invaded our course to "overtake" the people of God (Amos 9:10).

We have studied the three problems that plague the Outer Court, the evangelical Church world. We are presently looking at seven more "isms" that frustrate the grace the God in the Holy Place among classical Pentecostals, Charismatics, and the Faith Movement.

Chapter Five talks about legalism, the inordinate keeping of rules. Such religious ignorance only breeds death and confusion.

Now we turn attention to one of legalism's unsightly sisters—the religious mind-set of *asceticism*.

What Is Asceticism?

Asceticism according to Webster's, is "the practice or way of life of the ascetic; systematic self-denial for some ideal." Also, an *ascetic* is "one who lives a life of contemplation and rigorous self-denial for religious purposes."

Asceticism as an enemy of our destiny and an obstacle to our faith is a "poverty" mind-set that believes that it is a spiritual thing to be poor in finance and earthly possessions.

This ascetic habit tends toward a more private lifestyle. Spiritual "hermits" stay safely cloistered, tucked away in a monastery, or a cabin in the wilderness, or the comfort of a padded pew in a cavernous sanctuary (inside our "four church walls" on Sunday morning), or as the self-appointed leader of ones own "house church," or as a faithful donor to our favorite television "pastor," or else as one hiding behind the barb-wired protection of our own defense mechanisms. Spiritual "loners" are all afflicted with the same disease—the apostle Paul called this, "not discerning the Lord's Body" (1 Cor. 11:29).

In extreme cases, some religious fanatics have tormented their own flesh (their bodies) in various ways to "purify" themselves. The bottom line: asceticism is another form of salvation or sanctification (or pleasing God) by works.

Asceticism Is at Work

Historically, spiritual asceticism has been widespread among evangelical Fundamentalists and classical Pentecostals. Unfortunately, the latter have all been lumped together, and viewed by others as "the church across the tracks" or "the church on the other side (the poorer section) of town." Store-front meeting places and tents with sawdust for flooring have been and still are a part of that history.

The weakness of asceticism stems primarily from an "other world" point of view. "This world is not my home; I'm just a passin' through" or "I've got a mansion just over the hilltop" are samples of the man-made lyrics to the kind of songs that reflect this view. Many of these folks believe that Heaven is a planet located someplace far away beyond the Milky Way and that God is someplace "over yonder."[1]

Ascetic theology sees this earthly dimension as a sad and desolate wilderness, but this "suffering" will all be worth it, for "one day" in the "sweet by and by," we will be happy after we die and go to Heaven to be with Jesus (the inference being that He is nowhere to be found "down here").

In My Father's house are many mansions: if it were not so, I would have told you. I go to prepare a place for you (John 14:2).

Jesus answered and said unto him, If a man love Me, he will keep My words: and My Father will love him, and We will come unto him, and make Our abode with him (John 14:23).

Evangelical and Pentecostal ascetics in sermon and song long for their "mansion" and their "heavenly home." They reason that since Jesus was a carpenter in Nazareth, He is "up there" now building each of us a mansion.

But the subject of John 14 is not Heaven; however, the Father is mentioned 21 times. Jesus was not on His way to Heaven to "prepare (make ready) a place" for us—He was on His way to the Cross!

Moreover, the Greek word for "mansions" is *mone*, and it means, "a staying, residence (the act or the place); an abiding, a dwelling, an abode; metaphorically, used of God (the Holy Spirit) who indwells believers." The verb is *meno* (to abide, remain); compare the English, "manor, manse." Vine's adds, "There is nothing in the word to indicate separate compartments in heaven."

Mone is only used twice, in the two verses given above—the "mansion" in John 14:2 is the "abode" of John 14:23.

Jesus isn't building a "mansion" *for* us—each of us, as indwelt by the Holy Spirit, the Spirit of the Father and the Son, *is* His mansion! The Pattern Son was the "House" that the Father lived in. When Jesus declared, "In My Father's house are many mansions," He said, essentially, "In Me there is a 'place' for each of you (as members in particular of the Body of Christ, as in First Corinthians 12:12-26).

We are His temple, sanctuary, tabernacle, house, pavilion, dwelling-place, body, and building. In other words, we are His mansion. The mansion "is not for man, for the Lord God" (1 Chron. 29:1).

...and the street of the city was pure gold, as it were transparent glass (Revelation 21:21).

Furthermore, because we are not to have any money or gold "down here," most poverty-stricken folks long to walk on "streets of gold."

The problem with this concept: we are not going to a City; we *are* the City! The first thing that Jesus called the Church was a "city" (Matt. 5:14). The writer to the Hebrews equates "the city of the living God" and "the heavenly Jerusalem" (compare Gal. 4:21-31) with "the church" (Heb. 12:22-23). When father Abraham looked for "a city" whose Builder and Maker is God (Heb. 11:10), he longed to be part of a people, a Church that Jesus said that He would build (see Matt. 16:18).

John the Revelator was shown "the bride, the Lamb's wife" (Rev. 21:9). We know who the Lamb is (see John 1:29).

Have we gone on to read John's next words?

And He...shewed me that great city, the holy Jerusalem, descending out of heaven from God, (Revelation 21:10).

The Church is the Lamb's wife, the "city" of Revelation 21.

One more thought for those who have hampered God-given destiny with a poverty mind-set. There is only one "street," not streets, in Revelation 21:21. I want each of us to try and visualize but one "street" in a city that is 1,500 miles long, 1,500 miles wide, and 1,500 miles high. Go ahead....

No one can do that with his or her natural mind. Perhaps this is because the "city" is a *spiritual* people, not a natural place.

The point is this: as long as we are focused on something "over yonder" in the sweet by and by, we will never acknowledge and appropriate the blessings of the Lord in the evil now and now.

Now I say that Jesus Christ was a minister of the circumcision for the truth of God, to confirm the promises made unto the fathers: (Romans 15:8).

God, who at sundry times and in divers manners spake in time past unto the fathers by the prophets,

hath in these last days spoken unto us by His Son, whom He hath appointed heir of all things... (Hebrews 1:1-2).

As stated in the Preface of this writing, sin is a mistaken identity. We don't know what we have in Christ because we don't know who we are in Christ as the Seed of Abraham and the Seed of David (see Matt. 1:1 with 1 John 4:17).

Giving thanks to the Father, who has qualified you to share in the inheritance of the saints in the kingdom of light (Colossians 1:12 NIV).

And always thankful to the Father who has made us fit to share all the wonderful things that belong to those who live in the Kingdom of light (Colossians 1:12 TLB).

Jesus, the Heir of all things, "confirmed" or "secured" the promises that God made to the "fathers"—Abraham, Isaac, and Jacob (see Acts 3:13).[2] Those who belong to Him are the Seed of Abraham and heirs according to the promise (see Gal. 3:29). Jesus' finished work—His death, His burial, and His resurrection—has qualified us, fitting us for our inheritance as "joint-heirs" with Him (Rom. 8:17). As His Bride, we are "heirs together of the grace of life" (1 Pet. 3:7).

Christ hath redeemed us from the curse of the law, being made a curse for us: for it is written, Cursed is every one that hangeth on a tree:

That the blessing of Abraham might come on the Gentiles through Jesus Christ... (Galatians 3:13-14).

The curse of the law (see Deut. 28) includes sin, sickness, *poverty*, and death. Jesus reversed the curse! The first Adam turned the Garden into a graveyard. Jesus, the Last Adam (who came to bring a lasting end to the first Adam), turned the graveyard back into a garden (see John 19:41; 20:15)!

Jesus, the Author and the Finisher of our faith, came to deliver the creation from natural and spiritual poverty.

Asceticism Aborts the Seed

In a loud voice they sang: "Worthy is the Lamb, who was slain, to receive [take hold of] *power and wealth and wisdom and strength and honor and glory and praise!"* (Revelation 5:12 NIV).

King Jesus is the richest Person in the universe! He is the Heir of all things in Heaven, in earth, and under the earth; all authority has been given unto Him (see Matt. 28:18 with Heb. 1:1-2).

In whom we have redemption through His blood, the forgiveness of sins, according to the riches of His grace; (Ephesians 1:7).

I pray also that the eyes of your heart may be enlightened in order that you may know the hope to which He has called you, the riches of His glorious inheritance in the saints, (Ephesians 1:18 NIV).

But my God shall supply all your need according to His riches in glory by Christ Jesus (Philippians 4:19).

To them God has chosen to make known among the Gentiles the glorious riches of this mystery, which is Christ in you, the hope of glory (Colossians 1:27 NIV).

In and through Christ, we have been made rich, naturally and spiritually. There is nothing spiritual about being poor—broke, busted, and disgusted.

Before we see how that asceticism aborts the seed, a word of balance is needed.

There is an extreme in the Body of Christ, particularly among some in the Faith Camp, regarding the "prosperity" message. "Name it and claim it' or "blab it and grab it" are familiar sayings used to identify these excesses. Every meeting and message has to do with money.

I am not jealous of those who are self-made millionaires. I know what it is to run in the fast lane with the "boy's club." I would rather we read what Jesus said, and stop bragging about what our "faith" can do or has done in the realm of finance.

And He said unto them, Take heed, and beware of covetousness: for a man's life consisteth not in the abundance of the things which he possesseth (Luke 12:15).

And He said to them, "Beware, and be on your guard against every form of greed; for not even when one has an abundance does his life consist of his possessions" (Luke 12:15 NASB).

Beware! Don't always be wishing for what you don't have. For real life and real living are not related to how rich we are (Luke 12:15 TLB).

...Guard yourselves and keep free from all covetousness (the immoderate desire for wealth, and greedy longing to have more)... (Luke 12:15 AMP).

...Life is not defined by what you have, even when you have a lot (Luke 12:15 TM).

God certainly has blessed His people along with faithful Abraham (see Gal. 3:9). But Jesus taught that real Christians would be recognized by their "fruit" (Matt. 12:33; John 15:1-16), not by the size of their house, or the kind of vehicle they drive, or by their clothes, even their "gators" (shoes and pocketbooks).

One simple definition of "prosperity" is that one always has enough. Mature believers use money; money does not use us. We possess things; things do not possess us.

The Lord has indeed come to bring us into a life of "abundance" (John 10:10). He wants to kill the "fatted calf" for each of us (Luke 15:21-32)—this speaks of *excess*. As the Lord causes our lives and ministries to overflow with His blessings, some older brother from the "old order" of working *for* the Father (with the mind-set of a slave) will be jealous and won't like it.

Asceticism, the notion that it is spiritual to be fiscally impoverished, has aborted the Seed of our destiny and slowed us down in the race. Why? We will need *money* to do what God has told us to do! How many of us would be doing so much more for God if we had the means?

Money is not evil in itself. Money is neither moral nor immoral, but amoral, neutral. There is no bad money on the planet, just people who use money badly. Money is not the root of all evil; it is a necessary tool for the journey. The *love* of money is the root of all evil (see 1 Tim. 6:10), and a person does not have to have any to love it.

The Bible, especially the New Testament, has plenty to say about God's money. If preachers are afraid to talk about it, God isn't. The Gospels contain more warnings against the misuse of money than any other subject.

One of every four verses in the synoptic gospels of Matthew, Mark, and Luke deals with money.

One in every six verses in the New Testament as a whole deals with or makes reference to money in some way.

Almost half of the parables of Jesus refer to money, particularly warning against covetousness.

The first apostle to fall was Judas, who sinned because he loved money. He sold Jesus for money that he never lived to spend (see John 12:4-8; Acts 1:25).

The first sin of the early Church concerned the giving of money to the Lord. Note how satan entered the scene when the spirit of giving was on the people (see Acts 5:1-10).

The sin of "simony" concerns money and seeking to buy the gifts of God with it (see Act 8:14-24). Pray for America.

"Stewardship" is the practice of systematic and proportionate giving of time, abilities, and material possessions based on the conviction that these are a trust from God to be used in His service for the benefit of His Kingdom. This long-distance marathon is a divine-human partnership, with God as the senior Partner. The Lord God is the Owner of all things.[3] Men and women are His stewards, responsible and accountable to Him (see Matt. 25:14-30; Luke 19:11-26). We do not own anything; God is the Owner (Ps. 24:1). We can use, abuse, or lose these divine allotments, these possessions:

1. **Life** – what we have received (Gen. 1:27-28; Acts 17:25; James 1:17).

2. **Time** – what we have been allotted (Ps. 90:12; Prov. 24:30-34).

3. **Talents** – what we have given to use (Matt. 25:14-30).

4. **Possessions** – what has been entrusted to us (Matt. 6:19-21; Col. 3:1-2).

5. **Finances** – what we have labored for (1 Cor. 16:1-2).

God's wealth is wealth to be given away, to be redistributed. He blesses us that we might bless others. Currency flows. The law of love is giving (see John 3:16). God is a Giver and His people are all givers. This giving must always be:

1. **Systematic** – Tithes and offerings are given when we get paid.

2. **Sacrificial** – Be ready to give more than usual at times.

3. **Spontaneous** – Always be open to the voice of the Holy Ghost.

4. **Spiritual** – Our principles and motives are Bible-based.

A final reason why asceticism has killed the Seed of purpose in the first two Feasts (among folks who are genuinely born again and Spirit-filled) is their obsession with dispensationalism or futurism, the subject of Chapter Eleven.

The "gloom and doom" preachers are ever harping on the "signs of the times." I have always wondered why they continue to do that, for they also say that everything has been fulfilled (so why look for signs?). Their outlook for the United States of America and the nations is bleak, to say the least. Their sole focus is that we get to leave this planet "any minute" in the "Rapture," that we are "out of here on the first load."

Along the way, I have met classical Pentecostals who never married (and so never had children), never went to college, and never started a business because of the conviction that they might be gone at "any moment;" so why bother?

It is almost unfathomable to begin to consider the lives and what-could-have-been fortunes that have been ruined by such notions.

You are the world's seasoning, to make it tolerable. If you lose your flavor, what will happen to the world? And you yourselves will be thrown out and trampled underfoot as worthless.

You are the world's light—a city on a hill, glowing in the night for all to see.

Don't hide your light!

Let it shine for all; let your good deeds glow for all to see, so that they will praise your heavenly Father (Matthew 5:13-16 TLB).

I want to be a part of a relevant Church!

We must re-define the purpose for our existence, which has been distorted by such traditional eschatology. We must have an adjusted theology and philosophy for ministry and business (the purpose for this writing). The Church is to be salt and light, His witness (see Acts 1:8). These verses from the Sermon on the Mount (Matthew 5:13-16) teach the Kingdom principle of *influence*.

He said therefore, A certain nobleman went into a far country to receive for himself a kingdom, and to return.

And he called his ten servants, and delivered them ten pounds, and said unto them, Occupy till I come (Luke 19:12-13).

...Do business with this until I come back (Luke 19:13 NASB).

...'Put this money to work,' he said, 'until I come back' (Luke 19:13 NIV).

...'Trade with these till I come' (Luke 19:13 RSV).

Before he left he called together ten assistants and gave them each $2,000 to invest while he was gone (Luke 19:13 TLB).

...Buy and sell with these while I go and then return (Luke 19:13 AMP).

...Operate with this until I return (Luke 19:13 TM).

This command and commission of Jesus to the Church—"Occupy till I come"—has to do with business and money.

The word *occupy* here means, "to busy oneself with, to trade; to be occupied in anything; to carry on the business of a banker or a trader." It is derived from the noun *pragma* which means, "a deed; what is done or being accomplished; specifically, business, a commercial transaction." This latter word is translated in the King

James Version as, "business, matter, thing, work." Compare the English, "pragmatic," which speaks of that which is practical.

The King's question to all of us will be, "How much have you gained by trading between My departure and My return (Luke 19:12-26)? We are to engage in profit-making activities. We must make investments, naturally and spiritually. We must live a profitable lifestyle.

Dispensationalism's doctrine of imminence is faulty. We must live and occupy for the long haul! We must "occupy" until He comes! Once and for all, we deliver ourselves from asceticism so that we can make a difference.

When our future makes demands on us that our present cannot provide, then change is inevitable.

There must be the generation that interfaces God, a people who bring the invisible to the visible, who bring Heaven, His Kingdom and His will, to earth! In the Outer Court there is never enough. In the Holy Place, there is just enough. But in the Most Holy Place, there is more than enough.

> *Arise, shine; for thy light is come, and the glory of the LORD is risen upon thee.*
>
> *For, behold, the darkness shall cover the earth, and gross darkness the people: but the LORD shall arise upon thee, and His glory shall be seen upon thee.*
>
> *And the Gentiles shall come to thy light, and kings to the brightness of thy rising.*
>
> *Lift up thine eyes round about, and see: all they gather themselves together, they come to thee: thy sons shall come from far, and thy daughters shall be nursed at thy side.*

Then thou shalt see, and flow together, and thine heart shall fear, and be enlarged; because the abundance of the sea shall be convert-ed unto thee, the forces of the Gentiles [wealth of the nations] *shall come unto thee* (Isaiah 60:1-5).

The end-time Church is going to experience a massive transfer of health and wealth. An in-depth study on this particular aspect of Kingdom economics is one of the major themes of my book, *Moses, the Master, and the Manchild*, based on Exodus 12 (the Passover).

And his master saw that the LORD was with him, and that the LORD made all that he did to prosper in his [Joseph's] *hand* (Genesis 39:3).

Beloved, I wish above all things that thou mayest prosper and be in health, even as thy soul prospereth (3 John 1:2).

The primary Hebrew word for *prosper* means, "to push forward; to advance, to prosper, to make progress, to succeed, to be prof-itable" (see 1 Chron. 22:11; 2 Chron. 20:20; Neh. 1:11; and Ps. 1:3; 37:7). The Greek word *euodoo* means, "to help on the road, succeed in reaching; figuratively, to succeed in business affairs; to grant a prosperous and expeditious journey, to lead by a direct and easy way." It is a compound of *eu* (good, well) and *hodos* (a road or way; a progress; the route, act or distance; figuratively, a mode or means). *Euodoo* is used three times (Rom. 1:10; 1 Cor. 16:2; 3 John 1:2).

For I will pour water upon him that is thirsty, and floods upon the dry ground: I will pour My spirit upon thy seed, and My blessing upon thine offspring: (Isaiah 44:3).

In Noah's day, the Flood could not come until the Ark was built (see Gen. 7). Another flood is coming, not of judgment, but of glory and blessing! After God builds into us all that is needed to handle such stewardship, the flood will come. Let every leader be encouraged, for then every person who is connected to your godly heart and purpose will ride the waves of that blessing!

God wants to prosper His people. Every Christian must learn to make and steward money as he or she runs this race of faith.

My Personal Race of Faith

I grew up poor. My daddy worked hard on the Western Maryland Railroad as a track foreman, bringing home $60 a week. When I was around 10 years old, Dad would give me a quarter every Saturday afternoon so he and Mom could spend some time alone (I never figured out why until later). A dime was enough to get me into the picture show at the old Liberty Theater on Piedmont Street, another dime for popcorn, and a nickel for a Coke.

My dear wife grew up even poorer. For a long time, her family did not have a car. They walked to school, to church, and to work. Like a lot of country folks who lived in the rugged mountains of West Virginia, they ate vegetables from the garden, eggs from the chickens, and drank milk from the cow.

As a teenager, I had a job delivering the *News-Tribune*, Keyser's daily newspaper. I couldn't wait for Friday evening, for that was the night when I would "collect" the 25 cents from each of my 100 customers. I made about $10 a week. I didn't tithe off that because I was still a church-going sinner. But it was enough to pay for my league bowling on Saturday mornings (3 games for $1), and gas for the car (at less than 30 cents per gallon).

I wasted some of my hard-earned money in the shady little upstairs pool room in downtown Keyser by shooting a game of 8-ball for a dime or a game of 9-ball for a nickel. My ever-increasing skills led me to sometimes "gamble" in 9-ball by betting a nickel on the five-ball and a dime on the nine. When I shot "loser pays" with the college boys (I was still in high school at the time) on Saturdays, I could play all day for a quarter. So much for my spendthrift youth.

When I gave up the scholarship (worth about $4,000 a year) in 1969 to go to Bible school, I threw away a "fortune." At F.G.B.I. I gave away the $900 I had saved (from the paper route) to a need in Mexico. Again, Mom thought I was crazy.

Later, after Joann and I were married in 1972, we both worked at Zion School of Christian Education. For that entire tenure of seven years (1970-1977), my salary remained at $10 a week!

Our first home was one room in the upstairs of McDowells' duplex, where I was also the Dean of Men (that was "fun"…). Then a trailer came available next door—an old man and his dog had both died in it. Four ladies from the Bible school took two solid weeks to clean our 8' x 20' long abode. There wasn't enough room in that place to have a good fight, but at least we had some privacy.

After Brother McDowell moved the school to a tract of mountain land in Grantsville, Maryland (Garrett County), Joann and I bought our first home and lived there for five years. The mobile home was 12' by 64' long (a veritable mansion to us) and cost us $98.03 every month at 6 percent interest. It is true that we ate some of our meals at the school (although pot pies were on sale at that time, five for $1). But I was still making the vast sum of $10 per week. You do the math.

To say the least, God taught us to live by faith concerning our finances, a principle that remains at work in our lives after all these years. Back then, I taught more than one Bible study for a $5 offering or a bucket of new potatoes. Joann worked cleaning rooms and bathrooms at the Casselman Restaurant (much to my legalistic chagrin), and I worked part-time in the little craft shop at Penn Alps (and ate there free once a week). During the summer months when school was not in session, I added to our meager income by painting turkey houses.

In the summer of 1977, when the Lord told us to move out from Zion and "to do the work of an evangelist" (2 Tim. 4:5) until He would show us where to pastor (I had received the understanding of the local church principle about 1973), we submitted our ministry to the late Pastors C.S. and Kathryn Fowler from Berkeley Springs, West Virginia. A message preached by Apostle G.C. McCurry over Labor Day weekend of that year in Asheville, North Carolina, on "The Seven Separations of Abraham" saved our lives at that critical *kairos* moment as we stepped out into unknown territory, financially and spiritually.

Brother and Sister Fowler had ministered throughout North Carolina over the years, especially in the Richlands-Jacksonville area (Onslow County). They told us about a little Charismatic prayer group that had just left the denominational church and who were praying for a pastor to start a new work.

Jesse and Linda Futrell and their son Kevin, along with Nathaniel and Carolyn Rand and their five children, were some of the key leaders. I visited these wonderful people (never had I heard such praise and worship) in October 1977 and was asked to return and preach again the following month. It was at that time when the Lord spoke to Joann and me about coming to Richlands full-time.

We went back to Maryland, sold our 12' by 64' long mobile home (at a loss), and went to Apostle McCurry's church in Athens, Georgia, for New Year's Eve.

On December 31, 1977, the man of God prophesied, "I send you to build a Tabernacle for My name. You will build three times, and each time I will fill it with My people and My glory. And then I will give you further instructions." That word is still being fulfilled.

When we arrived in Richlands in January 1978 to start Praise Tabernacle, we drove the 435 miles south from Maryland in a car that was big as a boat—a 1969 green Chrysler without AC that got about six miles to the gallon.

At the beginning, the church gave us $200 a week. We had never had so much money! Our first home in Richlands (from January to May 1978) was another mobile home. We had things, but things didn't have us! We were in the center of God's will.

Everything happened so quickly. In February we incorporated the ministry. In March we went on the radio, and bought a new double-wide home, 24' by 64' long. Wow! We broke ground for the first church building and had our first service in October. That fall we purchased our first new car, a 1978 light blue Buick Electra right out of the show room.

(What you are about to read is important. Please don't misjudge me. I am making myself vulnerable, by giving you private information, to help others see how the Lord will bless a man or a woman who has passed the "money" test.)

That was 29 years ago. The most that the church has ever paid me is $1,000 a week, but I have since given that up to other pastors and ministers sent to help me (Kelley Varner Ministries presently receive $300 a week from Praise Tabernacle).

We have lived by faith all these years. But not without struggling with that stupid spirit of poverty. It took me a long time to get over buying a pair of $200 shoes, or wearing a gold ring that had been given to me. That kind of blessing continues. I wear an

18-carat, handcrafted (the only one like it) gold ring on each pinkie finger; both were gifts from brethren in South Africa.

Please don't let the way that the Lord has blessed me and my family offend you. Things are just not that important to us. We can live with them, or without them. We are but stewards of all that is His. I am trying to tell you in a limited space how good the Lord has been to us over the past 35 years because we know that we are the Seed of Abraham and heirs according to His promise.

A lifetime ago, when I was making $10 a week at Zion, the Lord supernaturally provided me with nice, new suits (I didn't buy one with my own money for years), but the story would take too long to tell. We have seen the supernatural hand of providential blessing rest upon us in numerous ways (that would fill another book).

I presently drive a Denali, but a business person gave me $20,000 to put down on it. The Lincoln that Joann drives was a gift (we had just given our car away to a needy family two days earlier). Our brick and stone house is over 3,700 square feet and paid for. And, yes, in one end of my den is a pool table with an inch of Italian slate with leather pockets (where I have ministered to more than one preacher).

God has graciously provided for us and our four children—April, Jonathan, Joy Beth, and David. We have been blessed. We are being blessed.

When I travel and preach in churches big (over 20,000 members) or small (over 20), I never have or ever will ask for money. I pay my own travel expenses, especially when I fly overseas (business class). I personally believe that those who "contract" for their services are wrong. That would be an abomination to me (but, then, bodyguards are probably expensive).

Joann and me, not Praise Tabernacle, have printed and distributed 16 Destiny Image books since 1982, costing us hundreds of thousands of dollars. We have sown and given away thousands of books over the years, especially throughout South Africa and other nations. I have lost count of the preachers who came to see me, and left with an armload of books (all gifts) under his or her arm. I am grateful that the Lord has positioned us to give and bless like this.

The Lord has brought Joann and me out of poverty and into abundance. Thank you, Jesus. We have been delivered from asceticism. It is not spiritual to constantly be in lack.

At Zion, $10 used to be a lot of money. In 1977, $100 used to be a lot of money. In 1990, $1,000 used to be a lot of money. Now, $10,000 is a lot of money. It doesn't really matter, for all is His, and we are His.

After the Lord delivers you from the "love of money" (1 Tim. 6:10), your faith will stretch out into places that you once thought impossible (He will just keep on adding the zeros to the amount). There is so much to do, and so little time to do it.

You may think me mad, but I need and am asking the Lord for $5 million to do what I sense He wants me to do with the next 50 years of my life. Once a man has been praised to the max and cursed to the max, he learns that neither of these kinds of people or their words can or will move him.

I could share many more experiences. I probably have said too much as it is. I will let King David and apostle Paul (both in their later years) express my closing sentiments on this particular subject.

I have been young, and now am old; yet have I not seen the righteous forsaken, nor his seed begging bread (Psalms 37:25).

I am not saying this because I am in need, for I have learned to be content whatever the circumstances.

I know what it is to be in need, and I know what it is to have plenty. I have learned the secret of being content in any and every situation, whether well fed or hungry, whether living in plenty or in want.

I can do everything through Him who gives me strength (Philippians 4:11-13 NIV).

Endnotes

1. Heaven is the realm of God, and God is omnipresent Spirit. Heaven is real, and is closer that you think! Heaven is not the Goal of our race. Becoming like Jesus is our purpose and end. God is not someone else, somewhere else.

2. The promises that God made to the "fathers" (Acts 3:13)—Abraham, Isaac, and Jacob—are recorded in the Book of Genesis, chapters 12,13,15,17,22,26, and 35.

3. The Lord God is the owner of all things (see Gen. 14:19-22; Ps. 24:1; 50:1-12; 68:19; 89:11; Hag. 2:8).

CHAPTER SEVEN

Dualism

Thou shalt arise, and have mercy upon Zion: for the time to favour her, yea, the set time, is come....

When the LORD shall build up Zion, He shall appear in His glory (Psalms 102:13,16).

Arise, shine; for thy light is come, and the glory of the LORD is risen upon thee.

For, behold, the darkness shall cover the earth, and gross darkness the people: but the LORD shall arise upon thee, and His glory shall be seen upon thee (Isaiah 60:1-2).

These are the greatest days of Church history. The Third Day (from Jesus) and the Seventh Day (from Adam)—the Day of the Lord—is dawning.

As we race toward the fulfillment of destiny, we have come to a *kairos* moment, a strategic season of the Lord. There is before us a "space of grace" as we now stand, individually and corporately, upon the threshold of fulfillment.

The major theme of this writing has been that our destiny is locked up in the Seed, the Word of the Kingdom. The time is at hand for the consummation and manifestation of the workings of that Seed.

We must not allow anyone or anything to deter us in this amphitheater. Every obstacle in the race of faith must be hurdled and overcome. It is good to know that we cannot be defeated, because "greater is He" (1 John 4:4). We cannot be discouraged, for that would mean that our courage had been "dissed." But we can be *distracted* by these besetting sins.

In the Outer Court, evangelical Christians have been distracted by cessasionism, Stoicism, and easy believism.

In the Holy Place, classical Pentecostals and Charismatics have lost their focus and tripped because of legalism (the incessant keeping of rules) and asceticism (a poverty mind-set).

Another enemy is lurking—*dualism*.

What Is Dualism?

Webster's says that *dualism* is "the state of being divided into or made up of two but related parts; duality; in philosophy, the doctrine that recognizes two radically independent elements, as mind and matter, underlying all known phenomenon; in theology, that man has two natures."

Dualism is marked by *two* things. Some synonyms for "dualism" are dichotomy and twofold. Simply stated, duality is *idolatry*!

A double minded man is unstable [unsettled, restless] *in all his ways* (James 1:8).

[For being as he is] a man of two minds (hesitating, dubious, irresolute), [he is] unstable and unreliable and uncertain about everything [he thinks, feels, decides] (James 1:8 AMP).

James called dualism "double-mindedness." In James 1:6 he describes this kind of person as, "he that wavereth" (KJV). The dualist is "hesitating" or "doubting." The old Puritan writers taught that doubt is the wedge of sin.

Moreover, dualism is a *divided heart*, the opposite of *loyalty*.

In the Church and in the world, men and women have experienced disappointment and betrayal. The Hebrew word for *betray* means, "hurl, shoot; throw down; delude, beguile, or mislead" (see Gen. 29:3; Josh. 9:22; 1 Chron. 12:17; and Prov. 26:19). The Greek word is *paradidomi*, and means, "to turn over into the hands of another" (see Matt. 24:10; 26:16-23; John 13:2;11:21). Double-minded folks have a divided heart, and cannot be loyal to one relationship.

Dualism is one of our major obstacles because it compromises the Seed, the Word.

Dualism Is at Work

Having preached the Gospel of the Kingdom for almost 40 years (since 1969), I have learned how to communicate these truths in words "easy to be understood" (1 Cor. 14:9) and words "which the Holy Ghost teacheth" (1 Cor. 2:13). With God's help, profound things can be made simple.

Here in the United States and throughout the nations, I have been encouraged to meet many new, hungry people. These folks remind me of Apollos, who was shown the "way of God" more "perfectly" or "accurately" by Aquila and Priscilla. One rendering of this relationship is that they showed Apollos "the rest of the story." (Acts 18:24-26 TM.) This notable teacher had only experienced the baptism of John. Apollos was only familiar with the dynamics of the previous order.

Let me say to many of you, especially those who handle the Scriptures, "Everything you have learned about God up until now is not wrong; it's just incomplete. Please allow me to show you the rest of the story."

God is moving a people from the Outer Court and the Holy Place into the Most Holy Place. The cloud is moving us on from the Feasts of Passover (in the first month) and Pentecost (in the third month) into the fullness of Tabernacles in the seventh month. We are shifting from childhood and adolescence into the manhood of full sonship.

What does all that mean? Simply, that we who have been born again and Spirit-filled are now hearing the "high (upward) calling" of God to grow up and ascend into full growth, maturity (Phil. 3:12-14 with Eph. 4:13).

For I am jealous over you with godly jealousy: for I have espoused you to one husband, that I may present you as a chaste virgin to Christ.

But I fear, lest by any means, as the serpent beguiled Eve through his subtilty, so your minds should be corrupted from the simplicity that is in Christ (2 Corinthians 11:2-3).

*I am anxious for you with the deep concern of God Himself—
anxious that your love should be for Christ alone, just as a pure
maiden saves her love for one man only, for the one who will be
her husband.*

*But I am frightened, fearing that in some way you will be led away
from your pure and simple devotion to our Lord...* (2 Corinthians
11:2-3 TLB).

The primary difference between the first two legs of this race
and the third is so simple. It is the difference between *two* and *one*.

In the Outer Court and the Holy Place, in Passover and
Pentecost, in spiritual childhood and adolescence, the emphasis is
upon *two*—this is *dualism*.

In the Most Holy Place, the world of worship, the stance of
maturity and fullness in the Third day, the entire focus is upon
one—Paul called this posture the "simplicity" or "singleness" that
is in Christ!

How does this idea of dualism express itself?

Evangelicals and Pentecostals preach as much about the devil as
they do about Jesus, almost to the point of philosophical dualism,
wherein good and evil are equal, "underlying *all* phenomenon."

Moreover, these good folks teach in every one of their Bible
schools and seminaries that there are two natures in the believer—
the "old man" and the "new man"—Adam and Christ.

*Speak ye comfortably to Jerusalem, and cry unto her, that her war-
fare is accomplished, that her iniquity is pardoned...* (Isaiah 40:2).

*"Speak tenderly to Jerusalem and tell her that her sad days are
gone. Her sins are pardoned..."* (Isaiah 40:2 TLB).

When Jesus therefore had received the vinegar, He said, It is finished... (John 19:30).

The exposure of the weakness of this kind of thinking begins with the understanding of its basic flaw—the failure to really know that the *war is over!*

Jesus Christ, the Word made flesh (see John 1:14), wrapped Himself in time and came to earth. The consummate Overcomer and the Pattern Son ran the race of faith and won it wearing a body of flesh (see Heb. 10:5-10). The Author and the Finisher of our faith fought the war and won the war. Jesus crossed the finish line that He might *become* the finish line!

The war is over. It is finished! The devil was finished! The first man Adam was finished!

The underlying reason why dualism can still exist in our minds is our ignorance of the Scriptures, our biblical illiteracy. I believe that a person who does not read cannot think. A person who cannot think has very little to say. Because we don't know from the clear teaching of the Bible that the war is over, we are always fighting against the devil and the old man. Sadly, most of the time we end up fighting against each other!

Somebody rightly asks, "But, Pastor Varner, don't you believe in spiritual warfare?"

Yes, I do. We are to "fight the good fight of faith" as did the apostle (see 1 Tim. 6:12; 2 Tim. 4:7). But Paul was convinced and persuaded that the war was over! He knew that we are not trying to get to a place of victory, but rather that we speak and move out of the procured victory of our risen King and Lord.

Stop asking, "Do you have the victory?" Start rejoicing, "The Victor lives within me!"

Holy Ghost intercession and prayer, "warfare" praise, banners and pageantry, the Gifts of the Spirit, the laying on of hands, and decreeing and declaring are but some of the things that we believe in and practice in our public meetings and private lives.

But thanks be to God, who always leads us in His triumph in Christ, and manifests through us the sweet aroma of the knowledge of Him in every place (2 Corinthians 2:14 NASB).

We fight the good fight of faith from the posture of the *finished work of Jesus* (in His death, burial, and resurrection). We stand in Him and with Him on solid resurrection ground. We live in and live out of the place of His eternal triumph, warding off any other notion or thought that says otherwise. We pull down these "vain imaginations" between our ears by the Word and Spirit of God (2 Cor. 10:3-6).

Simply stated, Jesus defeated the old man and the devil, doing away with dualism at the *Cross*!

There were *three* men crucified. The Man on the middle cross was the God-man, Jesus of Nazareth, God Almighty in the flesh, and humankind's only Savior! Amen? The One who cried out, "I thirst," was God thirsting for man and man thirsting for God in one glorious Person (John 19:28).

And he [the thief on His right] *said unto Jesus, Lord, remember me when Thou comest into Thy Kingdom.*

And Jesus said unto him, Verily I say unto thee, Today shalt thou be with Me in paradise (Luke 23:42-43).

The thief on the right hand of the Savior was *Adam* in the flesh. He pleaded, "Remember me...re-member me—put me back together!" Jesus restored him to the Kingdom, to paradise, to Eden by killing all that was "old" at the Cross (see Col. 2:14).

In justification, it was not Adam who was justified. Adam was put to death at the Cross. It is Christ, the new man, who is declared to be righteous.

So the first thief was Adam. But who was the other thief?

And the devil said unto Him, If Thou be the Son of God, command this stone that it be made bread (Luke 4:3).

And he brought Him to Jerusalem, and set Him on a pinnacle of the temple, and said unto Him, If Thou be the Son of God, cast Thyself down from hence: (Luke 4:9).

And when the devil had ended all the temptation, he departed from Him for a season (Luke 4:13).

And one of the malefactors which were hanged railed on Him, saying, If Thou be Christ, save Thyself and us (Luke 23:39).

The spirit who energized the thief on Jesus' left, the son of perdition, was the same spirit, who, in His Temptation, said, "If Thou be the Son of God...." God the Father had just affirmed His Son from the heavens (Matt. 3:17). The first scheme of satan against Jesus was to get Him to question His sonship.

Learn this: the devil is not God's adversary; he is yours (see 1 Pet. 3:8). Jesus is God, and He has no enemies—not even death. They are all defeated, having been put down under His glorious feet (see Eph. 1:20-23). Our ancient foe has but one weapon: suggestion—"Hath God said?" (Gen. 3:1).

Luke informs us that satan left Jesus after the temptation "for a season." He subsequently returned that awful day in Luke 23:39 to be crucified (just as Haman in the Book of Esther was hanged on his own gallows), dealt with by the cross. The wolf snarled, "If Thou be the Christ, save thyself and *us*." The devil knew that if Jesus completed His predetermined task that the kingdom of darkness would be destroyed. Paul and John attest to this.

And having disarmed the powers and authorities, He made a public spectacle of them, triumphing over them by the cross (Colossians 2:15 NIV).

In this way God took away Satan's power to accuse you of sin, and God openly displayed to the whole world Christ's triumph at the cross where your sins were all taken away (Colossians 2:15 TLB).

He that committeth sin is of the devil; for the devil sinneth from the beginning. For this purpose the Son of God was manifested, that He might destroy the works of the devil (1 John 3:8).

The word for "destroy" in this latter verse is *luo*, and it means, "to loosen, undo, dissolve; to overthrow, to do away with." Jesus dismantled the devil and his works at the Cross! The war is over! So why should we sing songs today about the enemy's camp? What enemy's camp? Jesus destroyed it.

I am He that liveth, and was dead; and, behold, I am alive for evermore, Amen; and have the keys of hell and of death (Revelation 1:18).

A few years ago, some folks got cute and taught that Jesus went to hell to complete His work, and that the Master had to be spiritually born again. What nonsense, whatever its source! To begin with, such notions meddle with His Person and tend to broach His sin-less deity. Jesus didn't go to hell to finish anything—He went there to announce it! He said, "I'll have the keys, please!" Paul sums this whole point up in one verse.

For the preaching of the cross is to them that perish foolishness; but unto us which are saved it is the power of God (1 Corinthians 1:18).

Dualism is at work among God's people. Not only have we been fixated on Jesus *and* the devil, the old man *and* the new man, we see this hurdle of focusing on *two* things expressed in other ways: Some of us still see black and white in our racial prejudice; others still see male and female in our gender prejudice.

Once and for all, let us grow up out of a mind-set of "two" into one "right mind" (see Luke 8:35), out of dualism, and into the sim-plicity that is only to be found in Christ.

For you are all sons of God through faith in Christ Jesus.

For all of you who were baptized into Christ have clothed your-selves with Christ.

There is neither Jew nor Greek, there is neither slave nor free man, there is neither male nor female; for you are all one in Christ Jesus (Galatians 3:26-28 NASB).

Dualism Aborts the Seed

I dare say that this chapter and the section before you constitute one of the most powerful parts of this entire book, addressing one of the greatest needs in the Body of Christ today.

Do you know who you are? Do you know what you have? Do you know how to get it? Do you know what the Lord has already done with who you used to be?

Dualism is double-mindedness. Duality is *idolatry*.[1]

An effective tool to communicate this truth is found in the first chapter of the epistle of James. I call this teaching, "The Man in the Mirror," or "The Genesis Face."

If any of you lack wisdom, let him ask of God, that giveth to all men liberally, and upbraideth not; and it shall be given him.

But let him ask in faith, nothing wavering. For he that wavereth is like a wave of the sea driven with the wind and tossed.

For let not that man think that he shall receive any thing of the Lord.

A double minded man is unstable in all his ways (James 1:5-8).

We commented on James 1:8 in the previous section. But read on.

Do not err, my beloved brethren. Every good gift and every perfect gift is from above, and cometh down from the Father of lights, with whom is no variableness, neither shadow of turning.

Of His own will begat He us with the word of truth, that we should be a kind of firstfruits of His creatures.

Wherefore, my beloved brethren, let every man be swift to hear, slow to speak, slow to wrath:

For the wrath of man worketh not the righteousness of God.

Wherefore lay apart all filthiness and superfluity of naughtiness, and receive with meekness the engrafted word, which is able to save your souls.

But be ye doers of the word, and not hearers only, deceiving your own selves.

For if any be a hearer of the word, and not a doer, he is like unto a man beholding his natural face in a glass:

For he beholdeth himself, and goeth his way, and straightway forgetteth what manner of man he was.

But whoso looketh into the perfect law of liberty, and continueth therein, he being not a forgetful hearer, but a doer of the work, this man shall be blessed in his deed (James 1:16-25).

The key to understanding this passage is found in verse 23—we know that the "glass" or "mirror" is a symbol for the Word of God, which was typified by the laver of the Mosaic Tabernacle. It was made of polished brass and created from the mirrors of the women of Israel (see Exod. 38:8).

The word for "natural" in the same verse is *genesis*, and it means, "nativity, nature; source, origin, a book of one's lineage," (translated in Matthew 1:1 as "generation"). It is literally, "the face of his birth" (that was mentioned in verse 18). This is our Genesis face, which was first mirrored in the Garden in creation, when we were created in His image and likeness and then given dominion (see Gen. 1:26-28).

For God, who said, "Let light shine out of darkness," made His light shine in our hearts to give us the light of the knowledge of the glory of God in the face of Christ (2 Corinthians 4:6 NIV).

The Man in the Mirror is the *New Man*.

The Man in the Mirror is *Jesus!*

The Mirror is the Word of God, revealing the "face" of Jesus.

In the old order, in dualism, men and women take the Mirror, the Word of God, focusing on the face of our old nature, and say to the people, "Behold your sinfulness!"

In this Third Day, in the light of "present truth" (2 Pet. 1:12), we take this same Mirror, contemplating His new nature, and say to the people of God, "Behold Him! Behold His righteousness! And then behold yourself *in Him*!" Our "natural face" in the Mirror is the face of His new nature.

But we all, with open face beholding as in a glass the glory of the Lord, are changed into the same image from glory to glory, even as by the Spirit of the Lord (2 Corinthians 3:18).

The veil of our fleshly understanding must be removed in order to see Christ. As we behold and look unto Him, we worship Him. The blessing of worshiping with this "open (unveiled) face" is that we are ever changed into the "same image." It is only when our hearts turn to the Lord and His Kingdom that the veil and mask, the old mind-set, the "false face," is "taken away," or removed entirely (2 Cor. 3:16).

The light of the body is the eye: if therefore thine eye be single, thy whole body shall be full of light.

But if thine eye be evil, thy whole body shall be full of darkness. If therefore the light that is in thee be darkness, how great is that darkness!

No man can serve two masters: for either he will hate the one, and love the other; or else he will hold to the one, and despise the other. Ye cannot serve God and mammon[2] (Matthew 6:22-24).

The Man in the Mirror is the New Man, and he has but one single eye, not the evil eye of dualism which emphasizes two natures.

We cannot serve or worship "two," with a divided heart; we must be in love with "One" with our "whole heart"[3]—this is the first and greatest commandment, to love the Lord our God with all our heart (see Mark 12:28-30). How sad that we have allowed other lovers to divide our time, our attention, and our affection. As noted previously, dualism is a divided loyalty. But Christians have been espoused (betrothed, joined) to one Husband—Jesus, the Head of the Church (see 2 Cor. 11:2).

> *For if any be a hearer of the word, and not a doer, he is like unto a man beholding his natural* [genesis] *face in a glass* [mirror]:
>
> *For he beholdeth himself, and goeth his way, and straightway forgetteth what manner of man he was* (James 1:23-24).

Herein lies the problem with this obstacle of dualism. Our "Genesis Face" is the face of the new nature—His nature, the "glory of the Lord!" As we contemplate Him by gazing into His Word, we behold ourselves (in Christ), but then "straightway" (immediately, at once) "forget" what "manner" (kind, how great, sort, quality) of *New Man* we were in the Mirror! The word *"forgetteth"* in verse 24 means, "to lose out of mind; neglect, no longer care for." We have misdirected our passion and focus, turning our attention to other paramours.

> *All we like sheep have gone astray; we have turned every one to his own way; and the LORD hath laid on Him the iniquity of us all* (Isaiah 53:6).

We have been called to be worshipers (see John 4:23-24), to ever behold Him, and then become like the One we worship. But instead we have gone our "own way" (go off, aside, or behind) to worship another idea or image.

Remember, Christ is the "image of God" (2 Cor. 4:4), and "antichrist" (instead of Christ) is any other image. These other lovers are other "gods"—duality is *idolatry*.

Remember, we have called each of these "isms" to be sin because sin is a mistaken identity. Sin misses and falls short of the mark, the *charagma*, the character of Christ.

Verily, verily, I say unto you, He that entereth not by the door into the sheepfold, but climbeth up some other way, the same is a thief and a robber (John 10:1).

All that ever came before me are thieves and robbers: but the sheep did not hear them (John 10:8).

The "thief" of John 10:10 is not the devil; stop giving him place (Eph. 4:27). These "thieves" of John 10:8 are "antichrists" (1 John 2:18).

These "thieves" are other ideas and concepts and religious, man-made teachings that try to climb into our minds "some other way." They are the products of the carnal mind, and bring death (see Rom. 8:1-6). These false images are idolatrous. Each is another face instead of the face of Christ. We have maintained "false faces" by continuing to be snared by entertaining "another gospel" (2 Cor. 11:4; Gal. 1:6).

Thou shalt have no other gods before Me (Exodus 20:3).

This first of the Ten Commandments literally reads, "Thou shalt have no other gods *before My face*." Away with graven images!

Every false face is not real, and must pass away—Adam's nickname is "the lie" (Eph. 4:25). The false image that we behold in the circumstances of life is who we say that we are in Adam.

Only the face of Jesus will last (see Heb. 13:8)—the nickname of Christ is "the truth" (Rom. 1:25; 15:8). The true image that we behold in the Mirror of His Word illumined by His Spirit is who God says we are in Christ! Agree with Him (see Amos 3:3).

God is a "jealous" God. Away with these false gods and images, these vain imaginations (see 2 Cor. 10:3-6). Dualism has aborted the Seed and caused us to wander from the path of righteousness. We have been hamstrung by our own ignorance.

My Personal Race of Faith

Having grown up in a traditional, denominational setting, I did not seriously begin to read and study the Bible until I was 21. Hence, the dualistic focus upon Jesus *and* the devil, and upon the new man *and* the old man, was assumed and played out in my thinking until about 1979 (when I was about to turn 30).

I was an only child. Joann has eight brothers and sisters. She and I wanted children, but only after we had moved from Maryland to North Carolina did we discover that our first baby (April Dawn) was on the way.

I will never forget that spring of 1979 when April was born. The Lord visited me and said, "This year I am going to change you!" Soon after, I had an open vision of the Throne Room that John describes in Revelation 4–5. I beheld the enthroned King of glory forever settled in the Mercy-seat of the Most Holy Place. As with the prophet (see Isa. 6), I had an upward vision, an inward vision, and an outward vision. I saw the Lord Jesus, high and lifted up. Only then did I clearly see myself and my world through His finished work.

My book, *The More Excellent Ministry*, flowed out of that relevatory experience.[4] Before that, my limited understanding of biblical sonship had relegated the Most Holy Place (and all that it speaks of) to the future. For the first time, I began to proclaim the third dimension of God to be a *present reality*.

Immediately, my ministry changed as my preaching and teaching declared one, not two (simplicity, not duality). My total focus, emphasis, and vision became fixed upon Jesus and the Christ, the new creation man. As I often tell folks who are hearing me for the first time, "I am a Jesus preacher. I preach a great big Jesus and a wee little devil."

Moreover, Chapter Three of *The More Excellent Ministry*, titled, "A Ministry Without Prejudice," revealed ten kinds of prejudice that continue to plague the Body of Christ. Two of these examples of dualism in particular—the issues of gender prejudice and racial prejudice—were further amplified and clarified in another writing, *The Three Prejudices*.

In the first part of that book, I began with the Book of Genesis and showed God's perspective of womanhood from the beginning. This was followed by two chapters tracing the public ministry of women throughout the Bible and church history. I also provided an exegesis of the two troublesome and widely misunderstood Pauline passages of First Corinthians 14:34-35 and First Timothy 2:11-15 from the Greek text. Hopefully, this once and for all sets the record straight by exposing the primitive teachings of ignorant and arrogant women-bashers.

My personal life and ministry have been blessed by ongoing relationships with outstanding contemporary women ministries and notable prophetesses of the Lord. In *The Three Prejudices*, I list the names of over 20 anointed handmaidens who continue to impact my life.

The second section of *The Three Prejudices* assails the demon prince of racism. I prove that Ham was not cursed (see Gen. 9), and then trace people of color throughout the Bible and church history. I end by setting forth twelve practical ways and means by which we can end racism in the end-times.

As a youth in high school and college, many of my closest friends were Black. In my tenure here in Richlands, I have built and maintained close relationships with men and women of color throughout our region, state, nation, and worldwide.

Adam is prejudiced. Christ is not. Adam is from beneath. Christ is above these man-made walls.

The Lord has delivered me, my family, and my ministry from this dualistic kind of ignorance. Thank God we jumped this hurdle in the race of faith years ago.

Endnotes

1. For a fuller understanding of this statement, read Chapter Seven of my book, *The More Excellent Ministry* titled, "A Ministry Without Idolatry."

2. The Greek word for "mammon" (*mammonas*) is of Aramaic origin and means, "confidence, wealth; avarice; treasure, riches." Vine's adds that *mammonas* is akin to a Hebrew word signifying, "to be firm, steadfast" (whence "Amen"), hence, "that which is to be trusted." Duality is idolatry. We have put our trust in these other "gods" or concepts.

3. The Psalmist mentions the "whole heart" nine times (Ps. 9:1; 111:1; 119:2,10,34,58,69,145; and 138:1).

4. The cover to *The More Excellent Ministry* bears witness to my open vision. In the front material of that book, the "About the Cover" page reads, "The view here is from the eyes of One who is seated between the cherubim on the Ark of the Covenant in the Most Holy Place of the Tabernacle of Moses. The veil has been rent. A ripened harvest of the nations of the earth stands without in the courts of the Lord. This scene was received in a vision of the Lord while attending a prophetic roundtable at Destiny Image in Shippensburg, Pennsylvania. Several attractive cover designs had been

submitted, but all from the perspective of looking into the Holy of Holies. The Lord inspired the cover design to portray the Christ-centered vision of *The More Excellent Ministry*! This is how the Man in the throne with a ministry sees all things." The cover views the creation by looking through the eyes of God out through the rent veil into the nations and peoples of the earth.

CHAPTER EIGHT

Elitism

We have come over half-way around the track. Many obstacles have confronted us in this race of faith.

The Word of God and the joy of the Lord are our strength. From here to the finish line, more will be demanded of us. Some will faint and drop out. Others will be lured away from the way of righteousness, distracted by lesser things. Now is the time for patience and endurance.

The "god of this world" (2 Cor. 4:4) stays busy spinning his web, especially once we enter the Spirit-filled dimension. Legalism, asceticism, and dualism have been placed in our path to impede our forward progress into the high calling.

Another major hurdle is just up ahead—watch out for the besetting sin of *elitism*.

What Is Elitism?

Webster's defines *elite* to mean, "the choice or most carefully selected part of a group, as of a society or profession." Elitism is a mind-set that has pervaded contemporary Christianity.

Elitism contends that one person, or gender, or class of people is superior to another, fostering a spiritual caste system among us.

But this thou [the Church at Ephesus] *hast, that thou hatest the deeds of the Nicolaitans, which I also hate* (Revelation 2:6).

But I have a few things against thee [the Church at Pergamos], *because thou hast there them that hold the doctrine of Balaam, who taught Balac to cast a stumblingblock before the children of Israel, to eat things sacrificed unto idols, and to commit fornication.*

So hast thou also them that hold the doctrine of the Nicolaitans, which thing I hate (Revelation 2:14-15).

A biblical synonym for this impediment is Nicolaitanism. Of note is the attitude of the Lord toward those who hold fast to this teaching and practice: He hates it! This word in Revelation 2:6 means that He "detests" it.

Mentioned only twice in the Bible, the Greek word for "Nicolaitans" is *Nikolaites*, which means "a Nicolaite, adherent of Nicolaus; destruction of the people." It is derived from *Nikolaos* (victorious over the people), which in turn is taken from *nikos* (conquest, triumph; be victor over; to utterly vanquish) and from *laos* (a people, people group, tribe, nation, all those who are of the same stock and language). This could be rendered as, "conquering the laity."

Nicolaitanism is a growing sense of aristocracy that has chosen to rule over the people instead of serving them.

The Nicolaitans were an early Christian heretical sect made up of the followers of Nicolas, who was possibly the deacon of Acts 6:5. In Revelation 2:6,14-15 they are equated with a group holding the doctrine of Balaam, who taught Israel "to eat things sacrificed to idols (thus disobeying Acts 15:29), and to commit fornication (sexual immorality)."

Balaam probably was responsible for the cohabitation of the men of Israel with the women of Moab (see Num. 25:1-2; 31:16). Therefore, the error of this group was moral rather than doctrinal. If the "Jezebel" of Revelation 2:20-23 was a teacher of this sect, as many believe, their sexual laxity was indeed strong. Most likely, they were a group of anti-law practitioners who supported a freedom that became self-indulgent. This historical information is most enlightening, for there has been a spreading moral virus among some leaders who take too much authority upon themselves, and then surround themselves with "yes men" who dare not call them to account.

> *They have gone off the road and become lost like Balaam, the son of Beor, who fell in love with the money he could make by doing wrong;* (2 Peter 2:15 TLB).

> *Woe unto them! for they have gone in the way of Cain, and ran greedily after the error of Balaam for reward...* (Jude 1:11).

> *...For they follow the example of Cain...and like Balaam, they will do anything for money...* (Jude 1:11 TLB).

Beyond this, Nicolaitanism, with its ties to Balaam, is snared with "the love of money." The name of the game in most "successful" (as in numbers) Second Day ministries is money, and more money.

Spiritual elitism has created a Christian caste system of clergy and laity, rather then setting forward the priesthood of all believers.

From Him the whole body, joined and held together by every sup-porting ligament, grows and builds itself up in love, as each part does its work (Ephesians 4:16 NIV).

Under His direction, the whole body is fitted together perfectly, and each part in its own special way helps the other parts, so that the whole body is healthy and growing and full of love (Ephesians 4:16 TLB).

In the nations, we have seen the evil of apartheid and the caste systems of poverty-stricken nations. Elitism believes and practices a respect of persons. But the God who indwells by His Word and Spirit is no respecter of persons, literally, no "accepter of faces" (Acts 10:34).[1]

Elitism Is at Work

The 1970s were marked by an accelerated awareness of theo-cratic government throughout the Body of Christ. The Lord want-ed to bring some semblance of order and government into the early Charismatic outpouring by the revelation of biblical eldership. Divine order, local church structure, along with authority and sub-mission emerged as much-needed truths in the Charismatic com-munity birthed in the 1960s. Sadly, the so-called "discipleship or shepherding controversy" arose because the basic biblical princi-ples of authority and submission were misunderstood and were carried too far with excesses in three fundamental relationships:

- *Domestically*, husbands took too much authority over "their" wives.

- *Ecclesiastically*, local shepherds (elders) took too much authority over "their" sheep (the saints). Nicolaitan shepherds ruled the laity.

- *Translocally*, apostles (bishops) took too much authority over "their" local churches.

Since 1990, there has been an uncontrolled outbreak of elitism in the American Church (which we since have imported to the nations). Many of the brothers sought recognition as apostles and/or bishops. I have often said, "I really don't care what you call yourself. Just do your job."

The whole "bishop" issue could be argued over, historically and biblically. I asked God five years ago to allow me to write a book to "fix" all that. To date, He has not because, (1) My attitude and spirit is not broken enough to handle the subject with love; or (2) He is just letting the thing run its course and then die a slow, gasping death all by itself as men and women see the futility of self-promotion.

The "bishop epidemic" has proven to be weak, limited, and ineffective. We ended up with a bunch of kings on the thrones of independent, fenced-off kingdoms. The fruit of this predicament manifests when one of these leaders dies; the work, based upon his or her personality, usually dies with the founder.

When such a leader leaves the scene, all the young folks who have lusted for power irresponsibly begin to sacrifice motives and morals to take his or her place. These people have always wanted to be "seen," to be a part of the elite, the inner circle. Local church power struggles, church staff pecking orders, and even arguments over the seating order on the Convention platform (rather than a simple love for the people and a desire to bless others) become weakening priorities.

The last 15-20 years has also seen the emergence of elitism in another form. Some have blended the sacred with the sacramental, going back to a "high church" liturgical form and atmosphere. While we are thankful that the Holy Spirit began to invade the Roman Catholic system (beginning in the early 1960s), it is sad to see Spirit-filled men and women retreating to the Romish forms,[2] some even withdrawing to actually live within Vatican City itself.

It is now common to see nominal denominational churches serving up two different kinds of meetings on Sunday—one with contemporary worship for the younger set (with a Charismatic flavor in style and instrumentation), and another with the more familiar, traditional form for the conservatives. Likewise, in Spirit-filled circles, some have gone to having two services—an early, brief Charismatic mass followed by their "regular" Sunday morning service. All this has been done to please the tastes of the people. Give the people what the people want, and the people (and their money) will come.

Whatever liturgical level one chooses, the main point is for us to recognize the high walls (to match the high altar) that elitism has built between a professional clergy and the laity.

It is so much easier and user-friendly[3] for the people to have a professional clergy—someone to pray for us, to read and study the Bible for us, and then to tell us what it all means. This man or woman who stands before us each week is in what we call full-time ministry. Most folks are content to give one or two hours a week. Have we stopped to consider perhaps that our full-time God wants *all of us* to be full-time Christians?

But the grandest truth of the New Covenant is the rent veil.[4] All of us have been given "access" (admission) and permission to come toward the Lord and His throne of grace with boldness and confidence (see Rom. 5:2; Eph. 2:18; 3:12). Jesus' shed blood ripped open every "wall of partition" that separates us from each other (Eph. 2:14). All may now draw near to God with full assurance of faith and enter His Presence through this freshly slain way (see Heb. 10:19-22). How sad that elitism—with the duality (see Chapter Seven) of its clergy-laity paradigm—has, in the name of all kinds of religion, rebuilt the wall that Jesus came to tear down.

> *For there is one God, and one mediator between God and men, the man Christ Jesus;* (1 Timothy 2:5).

Jesus our Savior is the "mediator" of this better New Testament through His blood (see Heb. 8:6; 9:15; 12:24). This is the Greek word *mesites*, which means, "a go-between, an internunciator, or a reconciler (intercessor); one who intervenes between two, either in order to make or restore peace and friendship, or to form a compact, or for ratifying a covenant; an arbitrator." *Mesites* is derived from *mesos* (middle, amongst) and from *eimi* (to go).

> *Neither is there any daysman* [umpire] *betwixt us, that might lay his hand upon us both* (Job 9:33).

Jesus, the God-man, Heaven's answer to Job's prayer, brought reconciliation by arbitration. The chasm of sin had brought an impasse between a holy God and His creation. Jesus alone took hold of God with His right hand and broken humanity with the other, bringing us together at the Cross! He came right into the "middle" (midst) of us to save us, went down into the "middle" of hell to lead us out, and now comes by His Spirit into the "middle" of us to live!

The Lord Jesus, not the Virgin Mary or any of the saints, or some mere priest or preacher, is the sole Mediator between a holy God and broken humanity. No man or woman can be your "door"—that responsibility belongs solely to Jesus (see John 10:1-10), who alone is the "Shepherd and Bishop of your souls" (1 Pet. 2:25).

Many such clergy today pride themselves in being "vanguard" leaders on the cutting edge. But spiritual celebrities are not cutting much. They would rather busy themselves with the building up of their professional portfolio. Men-pleasers are more afraid of people than they are of God, seeking the praises and acceptability of others rather than seeking the face of the One in whose name they minister.

Conferences and camp meetings are filled with preachers "working" the sanctuary before the service and the fellowship hall later on after the meeting. Busy "wannabees" buzz around the room, trading their calling cards, and dropping names along with the latest juicy tidbits about some other preacher. Small people have to make themselves feel bigger by cutting a tall person's legs off. Brothers and Sisters, I implore us to cease from these vain, religious politics. Character is refined by using principles and refusing to use people.

Elitism is even at work in what has come to be known as the Apostolic Reformation or the Third Reformation (Martin Luther in 1517 and the Azusa Street Revival of 1906 being the First and the Second); there still remains the trend for a male-dominated priesthood, the notion that women are inferior to men. This concept is old order (under the law), for it (like the Roman Catholic Mass) is based upon the Levitical system, which was (with some exceptions) biased against women in positions of public ministry and government. Moses led a male-dominated leadership.

Moreover, even among apostles and prophets, some are playing the game of "rent-a-father." It works like this: If you will tithe up to me, I will be your "daddy." Like notches in a gun handle, men boast of their networks and fellowships. Regrettably, some are already busy "mending" (repairing, adjusting) their "nets" (see Matt. 4:21; Mark 1:19).

We have already emphasized that one cannot legislate a relationship. Real relationships must be birthed by the Holy Spirit. The Lord must make our connections and joinings; He alone can build the House, His Church (Ps. 127:1; Matt. 16:18).

Moreover, there is a difference between mentoring and fathering. Your teacher doesn't have to like you. In mentoring, one speaks and the other listens. In fathering, both talk, and both listen. In almost four decades in over 50 nations, I have mentored and do mentor tens of thousands (via books, tapes, CDs, DVDs, and the Internet). Besides my four natural children, I have not really fathered that many spiritual sons and daughters. Real fathers are not elite, separating themselves from their children. My kids can talk to me about anything at any time, and I will listen.

A final observation concerning elitism working among believers: classical Kingdom-sonship theology has been historically marked by pride and arrogance. The culprit here is the false notion that one is made more Christ-like because of spiritual *knowledge*.[5] The fruit of this mentality is that many folks who have received the biblical understanding that there is a Third Dimension (what Bill Britton[6] calls "beyond Pentecost") deem themselves to be more spiritual than their "little sister" (Song 8:8) in the "lesser" realms.

Besides religion, elitism has also reared its ugly head in the marketplace. In the business world, office games and politics constantly vie for the boss's attention. A bigger desk with a better view, a bigger salary with better perks, and a better parking space in a better-lighted part of the lot—workers are ever in competition with each other in the name of promotion.

Not that we [have the audacity to] *venture to class or* [even to] *compare ourselves with some who exalt and furnish testimonials for themselves! However, when they measure themselves with themselves and compare themselves with one another, they are without understanding and behave unwisely* (2 Corinthians 10:12 AMP).

The evil of all this rivalry—friendly or not—is that we, whether in the church or in the world, are constantly grading each other, and that is not wise or healthy.

Elitism, one of the major pitfalls in the race of faith, has killed many a destiny and contaminated the Seed.

Elitism Aborts the Seed

Christ's love controls us now. Since we believe that Christ died for all of us, we should also believe that we have died to the old life we used to live.

He died for all so that all who live—having received eternal life from Him—might live no longer for themselves, to please themselves, but to spend their lives pleasing Christ who died and rose again for them (2 Cor. 5:14-15 TLB).

The Seed within us is without class or distinction. The Seed of destiny is the Seed of love and life; by it, we have become partakers of His own "divine nature" (2 Pet. 1:4). Jesus died for all of us. His great love leveled the field. As stated, God is no respecter of persons. The Lord does not discriminate; His wisdom from above is "without partiality" (James 3:17).

There would have been no "shepherding controversy" had the leaders and the people understood the true nature of biblical authority. It is essential that we all recognize the three basic principles of authority in the Kingdom of God:

1. All authority centers in Jesus.

2. Real authority never has to be enforced, only recognized.

3. Real authority can only work through personal, meaningful relationships, which cannot be legislated.

Then Jesus came to them and said, "All authority in heaven and on earth has been given to Me" (Matthew 28:18 NIV).

First, all authority centers in Jesus Christ. The Greek word for "authority" is *exousia*, and it means, "privilege, force, capacity, competency, freedom, or mastery; delegated influence." It is translated in the King James Version as "authority, jurisdiction, liberty, power, right, and strength."[7]

All authority, whether it is domestic, ecclesiastical, or civil, is delegated authority—*His* authority. The One who divided the five loaves in the Gospel story divided *Himself* into five loaves when He ascended! Jesus is the Apostle (Heb. 3:1), the Prophet (Acts 3:22-23), the Evangelist (Luke 4:18), the Pastor (John 10:11), and the Teacher (John 3:2) of Ephesians 4:11. The Head of the Church has been given all executive authority in Heaven and on earth.

Paul, a servant of God, and an apostle of Jesus Christ, according to the faith [conviction] *of God's elect, and the acknowledging* [recognition, full discernment] *of the truth which is after godliness* (Titus 1:1).

Second, every leader, every parent and pastor, must understand that real authority is never enforced, but only recognized and acknowledged. If a husband, a pastor, or an extra-local ministry has to "bully" people, his authority is not genuine. Psychic manipulation, fear tactics, or intimidation have no place in the life of the believer or the house of the Lord (although the earlier years of most ministries sometimes witness such occasional outbursts of immaturity).

The local church is *autonomous*—it is self-governing, self-propagating, and self-reproducing. Under Jesus Christ, the Head of the Church, there is no higher authority on planet Earth, and there is no court of appeal. There are three sovereign entities, each made in the image of the Sovereign God:

1. The will of the individual.

2. The home; the relationship between the husband and the wife.

3. The local church.

People don't care about how much we know until they know how much we care. One is completely out of order when he pushes his way into another person's heart. If an individual does not want ministry, there is nothing we can do or say that will make a difference. A delegated authority must be invited into a situation. It is wrong to browbeat and "overdrive" (press) the sheep, especially those who are "tender" or weak (Gen. 33:13). The administration of law is always demanding and deadly (see 1 Cor. 15:56; 2 Cor. 3:7).

Flipping the issue, some saints won't (as it were) "blow their noses" or make any kind of decision without their shepherd's consent. The fruit of this ignorant bondage is immature sheep and burned-out shepherds. Foundational ministries—apostles and prophets (see Eph. 2:20)—must be *servant-leaders*, knowing that we are essentially *under*, not over, the people of God. Like the dew, the anointing also comes from the bottom up (see Gen. 2:6 with Ps. 133:3).

Whatever is over us limits and defines us, and we can never be any greater than that. Foundational ministries need to get under the saints and release them up to the only One who is truly over them. We must be sent under authority and be willing to submit to local elders. Some local churches are afraid to breathe without the permission of their "apostle." One with real authority will not make the saints depend on him or her, but will eventually work themselves out of a job. Real authority is recognized when serving the people!

But one of the soldiers with a spear pierced His side, and forthwith came there out blood and water (John 19:34).

Third, real authority only works through personal, meaningful *relationships*, which cannot be legislated. This truth is revealed and demonstrated in the principle of "blood and water." Jesus has shed His blood for you and me; therefore, He has a legal right to wash our feet (see John 13:1-17). He suffered and laid down His life; on that basis, He can speak into our lives. All parents have a right to correct their children. Every pastor has a right to speak into the lives of the people in his or her sphere. Extra-locally, we are reluctant to speak into certain situations until we have "shed blood" for those congregations. After a relationship has been established, after we have served the brethren, our words will be far more effective, fruitful, and life changing. We earn the right to speak to others. Then our words will have real clout.

Much more could be said about biblical authority and submission (which I have addressed in other writings),[8] but we must move on.

Historically, the legalism of classical Pentecostalism (1900-1960) gave way to the rampant license of the Charismatic Renewal (1960-1980), but God is presently bringing both back into balance. In the former, preachers were especially tough on the women. In the latter, some of the women ran to and fro with no regard for divine order, without being accountable to their husbands or to local church eldership.

Biblical theocracy, church government—the sphere in which elitism thrives—is not the end, but the means to the end. When a baby is born, the bones are soft. The structure is there, but it is flexible. The most important thing is that the baby is alive! The life of the risen Christ in the midst of our homes and churches takes precedent over our order or any particular style or brand of government.

True headship or leadership in the home and the local church is horizontal, not vertical. Although He is preeminently the Head over the Church, Jesus is *over* His enemies, but He goes *before* His sheep. This is also true of those called to lead His flock. Genuine leaders demonstrate and focus upon serving *among* men rather than ruling over them. This is the right attitude and understanding that men should have with regard to women, and that leaders should have with regard to the spiritual Woman, the Church.

I weep for the multitudes of men and women in denominational and non-denominationalism systems who have been oppressed by the tyranny of elitism. (As for the arrogant elitist attitude that has historically weakened classical Kingdom-sonship theology, I refer the reader to Chapter Thirteen and the obstacle called Gnosticism.)

The Seed of destiny has been suppressed and replaced by the yoke of being somebody's slave. Content to live the Christian life through a surrogate, some grandiose personality, these people have never discovered the uniqueness of the indwelling Christ calling *them* to come forth. The Old Testament judge Othniel was ever overshadowed by his big brother Caleb. But God had a unique plan for him and each of us—*"the Spirit of the Lord came upon **Him**"* (Judg. 3:10 emphasis added).

My Personal Race of Faith

In my formative years, I never had a problem with elitism. To the contrary, because of my being overweight as a little kid, my awkward and shy personality, and my overall ignorance of what life was all about, I was very insecure, and always fearful of what others might think. Consequently, I didn't consider myself superior to others; I was too busy wondering what others were thinking and saying about me. As a bashful young wimp, I was readily compliant to any and all kinds of authority.

Remember, I didn't really begin to learn the Scriptures until after I was born again (at 17) and filled with the Holy Ghost (at 19). My early experiences in God were with the Ambassador Quartet, the year spent at F.G.B.I., and the seven years working with the McDowell's ministry at Zion (1970-1977).

Through spiritual osmosis, the legalism from those classical Pentecostal atmospheres (that was all I knew in God) created in me a false sense of elitism—after all, I was a "holiness" preacher.

After I began to dig through the Word of God while teaching at the Bible school, my views changed about legalism. What impacted me most were the classes I taught on the Pauline Epistles (in that seven-year stint I taught 44 of the 66 books of the Bible verse-by-verse).

Unfortunately, for years I remained an elitist in my theology and demeanor because of the "sonship" message that I had begun to cut my spiritual teeth on in 1970. I believed that my knowledge of the Scriptures (God had graced my mind with the tool of supernatural retention) made me superior to other ministers. My brash, hard, cocky "bad" self was fed by the residuals of insecurity from my lonely childhood and youth.

It was this immature young man who touched down in Richlands, North Carolina, in January 1978. I get tickled when folks now say, "Wow, Varner sure has changed!" (I hope that *all* of us have changed). After being the daddy to four teenagers and pastoring the same local church in the same town (of about 1,200 people) for almost 30 years, *anyone* would change! Having experienced the good, the bad, and the very interesting, I tell folks that I am now qualified to minister to the "insane."

I have lived through the Shepherding Movement of the 1970s and the Charismatic Masses (blending the sacred and the sacramental) of the 1980s and the 1990s. I have moved in and out of these circles and know many of these men and women personally, having ministered with them and for them.

I have watched many of my friends get caught up in the "bishop" frenzy, including all the Romish regalia, pomp and circumstance. Deep inside I want to tell my brothers and sisters, "No man-made title or religious garb or public ceremony or earthly recognition will give you clout with people." It is the "touch" of God and the anointing of His Spirit alone that equips us to have "power with God and with men" (Gen. 32:25-28 with Zech. 4:6). Real influence begins in the heavens, the realm of Spirit. I often say, "It's not really important how many of us there are, but how big a sound we are making!"

For even the Son of man came not to be ministered unto, but to minister, and to give His life a ransom for many (Mark 10:45).

And there arose also a dispute among them as to which one of them was regarded to be greatest.

And He said to them, "The kings of the Gentiles lord it over them; and those who have authority over them are called 'Benefactors.'

But not so with you, but let him who is the greatest among you become like the youngest, and the leader like the servant" (Luke 22:24-25 NASB).

Where did any of us ministers get the idea that the people were to serve us? Certainly not from the Master. Jesus made it plain that leaders are to serve the people. Every preacher has been commanded to follow His example of servanthood. The King came to earth to "minister," to lay down His life. This is the word *diakoneo*—Jesus is the consummate Deacon!

My present prophetic burden is that I am weeping over the excesses among apostles and prophets, bishops, and pastors who still don't "get it." Like Diotrephes, some have to be the constant center of attention, to always have the "preeminence" (to be fond of being first; ambitious distinction) (see 3 John 1:9-10). The apostle John, from other translations, says that this brother "loves to be first" (NIV) and "loves to push himself forward" (TLB). But the Amplified Bible says it all about this guy (I think that all of us have run into him from time to time, either in ourselves or others).

I have written briefly to the church; but Diotrephes, who likes to take the lead among them and put himself first, does not acknowledge my authority and refuses to accept my suggestions or to listen to me.

So when I arrive, I will call attention to what he is doing, his boiling over and casting malicious reflections upon us with insinuating language. And not satisfied with that, he refuses to receive and welcome the [missionary] brethren himself, and also interferes with and forbids those who would welcome them, and tries to expel (excommunicate) them from the church (3 John 1:9-10 AMP).

I am so grateful for my two sons, Jonathan and David. At the time of this writing, John is 26 and Dave is 19. Both of them have been and are my armorbearers.[9] As my drivers and traveling companions, they have often asked me, "Pop, why does Brother so-and-so act like that?" I am so proud as a Christian father that I can say to anybody on this planet, "If you want to see what a real servant looks like, watch my sons." The main reason for that is the life-long influence of their godly mother, and I also trust that I have been able to somewhat model that behavior before them.

No one of us has any right to feel superior to others. All of us are what we are by the grace and mercy of God (1 Cor. 15:10).

I implore every parent, every preacher and teacher, every leader, every musician and singer, every business person. Read and pray over Ezekiel 34. Then jump over the obstacle of elitism and finish your course. Don't be hampered in this race of faith by such trivia. Paul and Peter, real apostolic fathers who ran this course before us, plainly show us the rest of the way around the track toward freedom from the twelve deadly sins.

Who then is Paul, and who is Apollos, but ministers by whom ye believed, even as the Lord gave to every man?

I have planted, Apollos watered; but God gave the increase (1 Corinthians 3:5-6).

Not for that we have dominion [rule] *over your faith, but are helpers of your joy: for by faith ye stand* (2 Corinthians 1:24).

For we preach not ourselves, but Christ Jesus the Lord; and ourselves your servants for Jesus' sake...

But we have this treasure in earthen vessels, that the excellency of the power may be of God, and not of us (2 Corinthians 4:5,7).

Shepherd the flock of God among you, exercising oversight not under compulsion, but voluntarily, according to the will of God; and not for sordid gain, but with eagerness;

nor yet as lording it over those allotted to your charge, but proving to be examples to the flock (1 Peter 5:2-3 NASB).

Endnotes

1. That God is no respecter of persons is taught throughout the Bible, and is therefore an important Kingdom truth (see Deut. 10:17; 2 Chron. 19:7; Job 34:19; Matt. 22:16; Luke 20:21; Rom. 2:11; Gal. 2:6; 3:28; Eph. 6:9; Col. 3:11,25; James 2:4; and 1 Pet. 1:17).

2. Before you get upset with me for broaching this touchy subject, I would ask one thing of you. Find someone who grew up in the strict order of Roman Catholicism, and who is now genuinely born again and filled with the Holy Ghost, having tasted the liberty of the Spirit. Ask them their opinion on this matter, and then listen carefully to their reply and reaction.

3. This sounds somewhat like the "seeker-sensitive" churches we talked about in Chapter Four.

4. The grandest truth of the New Testament is the rent veil (see Matt. 27:50-51; John 19:30; Heb. 6:19-20; 10:19-22).

5. This thought will be covered thoroughly in Chapter Thirteen when we deal with the obstacle called *Gnosticism*.

6. Bill Britton was a literary prophet who pioneered the biblical message of sonship in the United States through his writing and speaking ministry. There is more discussion about this remarkable man in Chapter Twelve.

7. The Greek word for "authority" is *exousia* (study Matt. 7:29; 9:6-8; 10:1; Luke 4:36; 9:1; 10:19; John 1:12; 5:27; 10:18; Rom. 13:1-3; Col. 2:10; 1 Pet. 3:22; Jude 1:25; and Rev. 2:26; 22:14).

8. I have addressed this issue of biblical authority and submission in my books *The More Excellent Ministry*; *The Three Prejudices;* and especially *The Tabernacle is Jesus, Volume Two*.

9. "Armorbearers" is a term that we have coined from the Old Testament (1 Sam. 14:1; 2 Sam. 1:4-5) to speak of those younger ones who serve more seasoned ministry. In the New Testament John Mark was a "minister"(under-rower, attendant) to Paul and Barnabas on their apostolic journey (see Acts 13:5).

CHAPTER NINE

Tribalism

We are coming into the part of the course that is the toughest. The back stretch of the track is challenging us.

Theologians speak of the "preservation" of the saints, the glorious truth that Jesus, the One who rescued us out of sin, has kept us and will continue to keep us safe to the end. Many of us have learned to cry out with the Psalmist.

Preserve me, O God: for in Thee do I put my trust (Psalms 16:1).

The Hebrew word for *preserve* means, "to hedge about, guard, protect."[1] It reveals that the eyes and ears of the Lord have been attentive to our running as He observes our steps. When the apostle Paul was anticipating his martyrdom in the last chapter of his writings, he placed his unwavering faith on the immoveable Rock of ages.

And the Lord shall deliver me from every evil work, and will preserve [save] me unto His heavenly kingdom: to whom be glory for ever and ever. Amen (2 Timothy 4:18).

As previously stated, this middle part of the course is the most treacherous. The Lord has kept us safe from legalism, asceticism, dualism, and elitism.

But just ahead is another formidable *foe—tribalism*.

What Is Tribalism?

Webster's defines *tribalism* as, "tribal organization, culture, or loyalty." He adds that "tribal" means, "belonging to, or characteristic of a tribe."

The Hebrew word for *tribe* means, "a branch (as extending), shaft; a tribe; also a rod or staff for ruling (a scepter); a company led by a chief with his staff." Its verb means, "to stretch or spread out; to pitch (a tent). This signifies authority or power over a nation.

Tribalism is nationalism. Among Christians in the United States and throughout the nations, there are many spiritual "nations" or denominations. Each of these separate groups has stretched and spread itself. Usually from a centralized "headquarters," their "chief" exercises authority over the tribe with his "staff."

The Greek word for "tribe" is *phule*, and it means, "an offshoot, race or clan; a tribe, a company of people united by kinship or habitation." The primary verb *phuo* means, "to 'puff' or blow, to swell up; to germinate, grow or sprout."

For we are not bold to class or compare ourselves with some of those who commend themselves; but when they measure themselves by themselves, and compare themselves with themselves, they are without understanding (2 Corinthians 10:12 NASB).

The major problem with tribalism is that each particular group tends to deem itself "the" group. The fruit of this ignorance of not discerning the whole Body of Christ (corporate anointing) is that certain groups then tend to criticize, judge, and condemn others. Every tribe tends to puff itself up with pride, especially with regard to ever increasing numbers of people and finances. Tribalism thus becomes another example of the deadly sin of legalism (see Chapter Five).

Tribalism is sectarianism. Men and women are devoted to and prejudiced in favor of some particular group.

Webster's adds that a *sect* is "a troop; a company of one opinion; a group of people having a common leadership, a set of opinions, and philosophical doctrine; a school or a following; any group holding certain views; a religious denomination, particularly a small group that has broken away from an established church."

Tribalism is denominationalism.

Now I beseech you, brethren, mark them which cause divisions and offences contrary to the doctrine which ye have learned; and avoid them (Romans 16:17).

For ye are yet carnal: for whereas there is among you envying, and strife, and divisions, are ye not carnal, and walk as men? (1 Corinthians 3:3).

The word that Paul uses in these two verses for "divisions" is *dichostsis*, and it means, "disunion, dissension": It is a compound of *dis* (twice) and *stasis* (the act of standing; a position) and is thus, "a standing apart." *Dichostsis* is only found elsewhere in Galatians 5:20 listed among the "works of the flesh" and rendered in the King James Version as "seditions" ("dissensions" in the New International Version of the Bible).

For none of us lives to himself alone and none of us dies to himself alone (Romans 14:7 NIV).

Tribalism kills unity and corporate anointing,[2] the key to winning this race. No one has the wisdom and strength to run alone. Tribalism brings division and dissension.

Now I beseech you, brethren, by the name of our Lord Jesus Christ, that ye all speak the same thing, and that there be no divisions among you; but that ye be perfectly joined together in the same mind and in the same judgment (1 Corinthians 1:10).

For first of all, when ye come together in the church, I hear that there be divisions among you... (1 Corinthians 11:18).

Apostle Paul uses a different word for "divisions" in these two verses. This is *schisma*, and it means, "a split or gap ('schism'); a rent; metaphorically, a division, dissension." It is derived from the verb *schizo*, which means, "to split or sever; to cleave asunder; to divide by rending; to split into factions, to be divided."

Used five times in the Gospels (Matt. 9:16; Mark 2:21; John 7:43; 9:16; 10:19), *schisma* is used one other time in Paul's letters.

That there should be no schism in the body; but that the members should have the same care one for another (1 Corinthians 12:25).

Broken lives, broken homes and marriages, and broken churches and ministries are the evil fruit of tribalism. A divided heart, a divided home, and a divided ministry are broken wineskins that spill and waste the joy and life of God. Tribalism's saddest fruit are the broken children (natural and spiritual), the marginalized and abandoned who live in dysfunctional homes and families.

Behold, how good and how pleasant it is for brethren to dwell together in unity! (Psalms 133:1).

Tribalism is the enemy of our unity. As runners in the race, we are to endeavor to keep the "unity of the Spirit" until we all come into the "unity of the faith" (Eph. 4:3,13).

This anointed unity is exampled throughout the Pauline epistles with several key words:

- Fellowlabourer (1 Thess. 3:2; Philem. 1:1).

- Fellowlabourers (Phil. 4:3; Philem. 1:24).

- Fellowworkers (Col. 4:11).

- Fellowprisoners (Rom. 16:7).

- Fellowhelpers (3 John 1:8).

- Workfellow (Rom. 16:21).

- Yokefellow (Phil. 4:3).

All these words are compounds of the primary preposition *sun* with some other word. *Sun* denotes, "union; with or together by association, companionship, process, resemblance, or possession."

This race of faith is not a sprint to the finish line during which each runner must stay within the confines of a particular lane (or group). This is a marathon, a long-distance run where all the participants bunch up and run *together*.

Tribalism is a sin because sin separates. Jesus adds and multiplies. The devil subtracts and divides. Tribalism—sectarianism and denominationalism—tears us apart and keeps us apart.

Tribalism Is at Work

Denominationalism is evil. I don't know the current count of all the different "Christian" denominations in America, but I am sure it is staggering. Add to the nominal churches all the "non-denominational" denominational churches (so-called "independent" works) that are often more sectarian than the larger, major denominations.

That tells us something that we must know as we run this race with patience and endurance. Tribalism is a *spirit!*

Babylon, which means, "religious confusion," is not a particular group of people; Babylon is a *spirit*. A person can be a part of a church that is not part of a sprawling organization under the thumb of some central "headquarters" and still be in confusion. I dare say that any spirit other than the Holy Spirit is an unholy spirit.

Thus saith the LORD, The heaven is My throne, and the earth is My footstool: where is the house that ye build unto Me? and where is the place of My rest?

For all those things hath Mine hand made, and all those things have been, saith the LORD: but to this man will I look, even to him that is poor and of a contrite spirit, and trembleth at My word (Isaiah 66:1-2).

My book, *Unshakeable Peace*, is a study of the life and ministry of the prophet Haggai. Its theme is the bigger picture: the Father's dream and vision for the House of the Lord, the Body of Christ, a people in whom He can tabernacle, rest, and abide—a corporate "Man."

The historical backdrop for the Book of Haggai are the first six chapters of the Book of Ezra. Following the 70 years of Babylonian captivity, the people of God, led by the governor Zerubbabel and the priest Jeshua, returned to Jerusalem with 50,000 hardy pioneers.

Now in the first year of Cyrus king of Persia, that the word of the LORD by the mouth of Jeremiah might be fulfilled, the LORD stirred up the spirit of Cyrus king of Persia, that he made a proclamation throughout all his kingdom, and put it also in writing, saying,

Thus saith Cyrus king of Persia, The LORD God of heaven hath given me all the kingdoms of the earth; and He hath charged me to build Him an house at Jerusalem, which is in Judah (Ezra 1:1-2).

The task of these hardy pioneers was simple and singular. The decree of King Cyrus of Persia in 536 B.C. released them and everything they needed to go back and rebuild the Temple, the House of the Lord.

The Goal of the race that we all are running is the same. At its finish line will stand a people for His name, conformed to the image and likeness of Jesus, our Forerunner (see Heb. 6:19-20).

The Hebrew word for "son" is *ben*. Its verb *baw-naw'* which means, "to build." Therein lies the reason for our running. God's desire is *to build a son*, a corporate Son, the House of the Lord!

In Haggai's day, the greatest obstacle and enemy to the king's mandate was tribalism. The prophet sent a strong rebuke.

Then the word of the LORD came through the prophet Haggai:

"Is it a time for you yourselves to be living in your paneled houses, while this house remains a ruin?"

Now this is what the LORD Almighty says: "Give careful thought to your ways.

You have planted much, but have harvested little. You eat, but never have enough. You drink, but never have your fill. You put on clothes, but are not warm. You earn wages, only to put them in a purse with holes in it."

This is what the LORD Almighty says: "Give careful thought to your ways.

Go up into the mountains and bring down timber and build the house, so that I may take pleasure in it and be honored," says the LORD.

"You expected much, but see, it turned out to be little. What you brought home, I blew away. Why?" declares the LORD Almighty. "Because of My house, which remains a ruin, while each of you is busy with his own house (Haggai 1:3-9 NIV).

As we reach the back stretch of this course, we need to "consider our ways" (KJV). The bigger picture—the House of the Lord—remains unbuilt while each of us busies ourselves with our "own house"—our own life, our own family, our own church or ministry, our own group or denomination, our own "people" (race), or our own finance—our own agenda has replaced the original vision of the Lord, taking precedent over the king's decree.

Sadder still is that the people had taken the financial provision of King Cyrus for the building fund and built their own houses with God's money! Throughout denominations, men and women refuse to tithe and give to God the first 10 percent. Like Achan in the Book of Joshua, they take for themselves what belongs to God. When Achan lost his family along with his finance, he learned the hard way that when we take what belongs to God, it becomes a curse to us. Church parking lots are filled every Sunday morning with stolen vehicles. Stingy church-goers have taken God's tithe and offering (see Mal. 3:10) and bought a car or truck with His money.

We have done the same with our time and talent as well as our treasure. The reason is obvious. We have created a God to serve our own purposes, conforming Him to our image. Each tribe has its own set of rules and opinions. That's why we have a Roman Catholic Jesus, a Methodist Jesus, a Baptist Jesus, a Pentecostal Jesus, a Charismatic Jesus, a Faith Jesus, and a Kingdom Jesus (you can put the name of *your* group in that list). Whatever happened to the real Jesus, the Jesus of the Bible?

This statement is a hard saying, but everybody cannot be right.

Tribalism preaches tribal doctrine, not Jesus.

Tribalism emphasizes tribal rules, not Jesus.

Tribalism creates tribal programs for the people, rather than showing them the ways of the Spirit.

Tribalism has its own style of preaching, its own music and songs and songbook, its own logo, its own schools and seminaries, its own missions program, and its own flavor. Rather then run this race of faith, we have run "every man unto his own house" (Hag. 1:9).

This time in Church history is critical. It is time to press!

Nevertheless I have somewhat against thee, because thou hast left [sent away] *thy first love* (Revelation 2:4).

Runners in this race are shooting off in every direction, following ideas and opinions that are tribal and sectarian. This obstacle has separated us from the Lord and from each other. We have left the path of our first love.

Who or what is more important to you? Jesus or your "church"? Jesus or your "ministry"? Jesus or your "message"? His House or yours?

Again we need prophets who are bold enough to adjust our vision and get us back on the right track. We need a Word from the Lord that will challenge us to "consider [our] ways" (Hag. 1:5,7).

Tribalism Aborts the Seed

The divisions and schisms brought about by tribalism remind us of the obstacle of dualism that we talked about in Chapter Seven. One is encouraged to review all the ways that dualism aborts the divine seed.

Tribalism is similar, for tribalism is "di-vision" or two visions. It stands apart from the Lord in the spirit of "antichrist" (instead of Christ).

...let God be true, but every man a liar... (Romans 3:4).

...God keeps His word even when the whole world is lying through its teeth... (Romans 3:4 TM).

When a Papal Bull or a denominational letter from headquarters carries more extra-biblical weight (whatever the issue) than the plain teaching of the Word of God, it is time to leave. If you can't flow, go.

There comes a time when a person has to draw a line. This race is by God's rules, not man's.

There is only one race and only one course. Jesus Himself is the "Way" (John 14:6). "Way" is the word *hodos*, which means, "a road, path; a progress (the route, act or distance); figuratively, a mode or means; a course of conduct (a way of life)." He is our Course from Beginning to End (see Rev. 21:6; 22:13).

Tribalism aborts the seed because it separates us from God and from each other. We have restricted one another from the Table of the Lord. We have closed our pulpits and churches to ministers who are not of our tribe, or do not have a tribal license. We are snared by preaching or singing a certain tribal style only to our "own people." Parents object or even refuse their children to marry outside of the tribe. Local pastors bow down to the rules and doctrines that flow out of tribal headquarters. In our going out (our public life, including the pulpit) and our coming in (our private life), we are careful to maintain a certain tribal look (in dress and demeanor). All these practices are unclean, and kill the Seed of destiny.

> *I lifted up mine eyes again, and looked, and behold a man with a measuring line in his hand.*
>
> *Then said I, Whither goest thou? And he said unto me, To measure Jerusalem, to see what is the breadth thereof, and what is the length thereof* (Zechariah 2:1-2).
>
> *I asked, "Where are you going?" He answered me, "To measure Jerusalem, to find out how wide and how long it is"* (Zechariah 2:2 NIV).
>
> *"Where are you going?" I asked. "To measure Jerusalem," he said. "I want to see whether it is big enough for all the people!"* (Zechariah 2:2 TLB).

God needs to come to the heavenly Jerusalem (see Heb. 12:22-23), the Church, and to every tribe. He needs to stretch out the measuring line of His Word to inspect our *width*, which is the expanse of our outstretched arms of tolerance and mercy.

How wide are we? Who will we include in our embrace? Who will we love? Who do we love? And receive? And run with?

Tribalism carefully chooses the objects of its affections. Tribalism will only embrace its own people, its own race, its own doctrines and rules, its own agenda.

Are we only preaching and singing "white" to Whites? Are we only preaching and singing "black" to Blacks?[3] Not to mention the browns, reds, and yellows.

Three times in a year shall all thy males appear before the LORD thy God in the place which He shall choose; in the feast of unleavened bread [Passover], *and in the feast of weeks* [Pentecost], *and in the feast of tabernacles: and they shall not appear before the LORD empty:* (Deuteronomy 16:16).

Moses' church in the wilderness (see Acts 7:38) was commanded to keep all three Feasts—Passover in the first month, Pentecost in the third month, and Tabernacles in the seventh month.

As we run more and more of this race, we do not abandon our foundations. The greater realm always swallows up and brings along the lesser realm. Pentecost includes Passover—the oil was predicated by the blood. Tabernacles contains Pentecost and Passover.

But ye are a chosen generation, a royal priesthood... (1 Peter 2:9).

And hath made us kings and priests unto God and His Father... (Revelation 1:6).

And hast made us unto our God kings and priests: and we shall reign on the earth (Revelation 5:10).

A king-priest ministry after the order (manner, similitude) of Melchisedec (Heb. 5:1–8:6) is totally flexible. Having tasted of all three Feasts, that person has the grace, the faith, and the wisdom to minister to anyone on any level. We reach out to all in His name.

The farther we run with God in this race, the more like Him we become. This salvation is progressive as well as once and for all (2 Cor. 1:10). As we run farther and farther, we get wider and wider.

Don't mistake me. We do not agree with or embrace the sin. But, like the Master, we embrace the sinner. Like the Son of man who totally identified with all of us in His humanity, we are not ashamed or afraid to be "among" the people.

We touch the leper, those with AIDS.

We eat at the table of publicans and sinners, the unsaved.

We release the prostitute, refusing to condemn.

We reach out to the unlettered and the unloved.

We minister to all people, not just "our people."

Tribalism does none of these things. It is evil and ugly and biased. It is snobby and particular. It is the enemy of God and His Seed. It will either leave us dead on the racetrack or seduce us into another way altogether.

Quickly now! Let's jump over this beast and go on.

My Personal Race of Faith

As a young Christian, I was plagued with tribalism without realizing it. Having grown up in a nominal church, I did as I was told and behaved as expected.

After my personal Feasts of Passover and Pentecost (in the late 1960s and the early 1970s), I began to run with the classical Pentecostal tribe.

These [Berean believers] *were more noble than those in Thessalonica, in that they received the word with all readiness of mind, and searched the scriptures daily, whether those things were so* (Acts 17:11).

I believed what they believed without ever checking it out for myself in the Scriptures. I acted like they acted. I mostly preached in their churches among their people. I attended their Bible schools and taught in their Bible schools.

I even had the tribal "look." I wore a black suit with black shoes and white socks. My white shirts were long-sleeved and buttoned at the neck to hold my clip-on, conservative, dark, solid-colored tie. My hair was cut short and my face was clean-shaven. I wore no jewelry.

I stopped going to the swimming pool, wearing shorts during the hot summer months, and going to the movies. I rarely watched television. I had become a "Hebrew of the Hebrews" (Phil. 3:5), a real "holiness" preacher.

During my tenure at Zion School of Christian Education, through my diligent study of the Word of God, I gradually became less tribal and more open to the ideas of others.

Shifting away from the classical Pentecostal tribe, moving through the Charismatic tribe, and gradually easing into the classical Kingdom-sonship tribe, I fared better but little. I was still very tribal, and especially proud of my grasp of "present truth" (2 Pet. 1:12).

I brought my tribal ways to North Carolina in 1978, and soon reproduced myself in other people and preachers. I hurt of a lot of people in a lot of ways in my early, formative years (as has any preacher "worth his salt"). Now that I have changed, I do believe I have helped more people than I have damaged by having been "infected with tribalism." Like Peter, I have been converted, so that I can now "strengthen" (confirm, stabilize) the brethren (Luke 22:32).

I can surely say that the Lord has brought this old boy a mighty long way. Today, I have had and do have the privilege of ministering to all of God's people, a variety of audiences. People of all skin colors, male and female, denominational and non-denominational—I embrace them all as ministerial colleagues or congregations.

But he [Melchisedec] *whose descent is not counted from them received tithes of Abraham, and blessed him that had the promises* (Hebrews 7:6).

Again, a king-priest ministry after the order of Melchisedec (see Heb. 5:1–8:6) is totally flexible. Having tasted of all three Feasts, that person has the grace, the faith, and the wisdom to minister to anyone on any level—evangelicals in Passover, Spirit-filled folks in Pentecost, and the Kingdom crowd in Tabernacles (see Deut. 16:16). We reach out to all in His name, and are especially effective among those who have tasted the goodness of His promises.

I have preached to Third Day and Kingdom people all over the United States and throughout the world. I minister in statewide

Pentecostal camp meetings, Charismatics conferences, and evangelical churches—all without having compromised[4] or "watereddown" the Word of God and the "present truth" of the Gospel of the Kingdom, the message of full sonship, and the truth of life and immortality.[5]

I have allowed the Lord to come and measure my width, the wideness of His mercy to me and through me. It has taken the Lord almost 40 years of working with me to get me to the place where I now despise sectarianism in any form. I want to live out of the Mercy-seat that I saw in the vision of early 1979. Then, I beheld a mature Church that really loved God and each other, a people without division, distinction, or distraction. Jesus prayed for that kind of unity.

> *Neither pray I for these alone, but for them also which shall believe on Me through their word;*
>
> *That they all may be one;[6] as Thou, Father, art in Me, and I in Thee, that they also may be one in Us: that the world may believe that Thou hast sent Me.*
>
> *And the glory which Thou gavest Me I have given them; that they may be one, even as We are One:*
>
> *I in them, and Thou in Me, that they may be made perfect in one; and that the world may know that Thou hast sent Me, and hast loved them, as Thou hast loved Me (John 17:20-23).*

I can say little more about this obstacle called tribalism. By His grace, I have hurdled it and it is now behind me, lurking to trip up some unsuspecting runner.

The day will come when there will be no more tribalism. The day will come when there will be just one God with one people, one race from among the races, and one holy nation from among the nations! The Bible prophesies of that day, and it speaks for itself.

The words of the wise are as goads, and as nails fastened by the masters of assemblies, which are given from one shepherd (Ecclesiastes 12:11).

And I will set up one shepherd over them, and he shall feed them, even my servant David; he shall feed them, and he shall be their shepherd (Ezekiel 34:23).

And other sheep I have, which are not of this fold: them also I must bring, and they shall hear My voice; and there shall be one fold, and one shepherd (John 10:16).

Endnotes

1. This Hebrew word for "preserve" is used elsewhere in the Book of Psalms (41:2; 86:2; 121:7-8) as well as the Book of Proverbs (2:11; 4:6; 14:3).

2. The reader is encouraged to read and study my book, *Corporate Anointing*.

3. I have shocked more than one "black" congregation by letting them know that I am a Cushite. Although "Cush" means, "black," a careful study of Second Samuel 18:19-33 reveals that a real Cushite is a person, whatever the skin color, who carries a message that moves the heart of the King!

4. For those who may feel that I must have "compromised" the Word to preach to all these different tribes, I welcome you to peruse the over 50 books and booklets that I have written. They are all online at www.kelleyvarner.org.

5. The message of life and immortality, that there will be an end-time people who will put their feet on the enemy of death, is set forth in my book, *Sound the Alarm*, Chapter Three, "One Among a Thousand."

6. Tribalism fosters division, two parties, and bears the fruit of separation. For a further study on a people who shall become "one," note these Scriptures (see Jer. 32:29; Ezek. 37:16-25; Zeph. 3:9; Zech. 14:9; Acts 2:46; 4:32; Rom.

12:5; 1 Cor. 1:10; 12:12; Gal. 3:28; Eph. 4:3-6; Phil. 1:27; 2:1-5; Col. 3:11-14; and 1 Pet. 3:8-9).

CHAPTER TEN

Traditionalism

Chapters Five through Nine of this writing set forth the sins of the Holy Place—the Spirit-filled Church world. These obstacles in our race of faith have compromised the Seed of the Kingdom, and have delayed our destiny during the developing years of our spiritual adolescence:

Legalism – The belief that the incessant keeping of man-made rules forms the basis of our salvation or sanctification.

Asceticism – The belief that it is spiritual to be poor and lacking in finances and natural possessions.

Dualism – The belief that there are two, not one, underlying principles that govern all things. Focusing on both Jesus and the devil, the new man and the old man, as well as prejudice with regard to race or gender, all exemplify this philosophy.

Elitism – The belief that one person, or gender, or class of people is superior to another.

Tribalism – The belief that emphasizes sectarianism or denominationalism, separating and compartmentalizing us.

Before we round the last turn of the course and head down the home stretch, we conclude the middle section of our race with this chapter and the next.

These last two intermittent problems that hinder the people of God and compromise the Word of God are *traditionalism* and *futurism*. They are mentioned together because Paul mentions them in the same breath (his "one thing") in one of the key Scriptures used for this writing.

> *Brethren, I count not myself to have apprehended: but this one thing I do, forgetting those things which are behind, and reaching forth unto those things which are before,* (Philippians 3:13).

Traditionalism has to do with "those things which are behind."

Futurism (the next chapter) has to do with "those things which are before (in front of)."

What Is Traditionalism?

Traditionalism, according to Webster's, is "adherence to or excessive respect for tradition." He further defines "tradition" to be "the act of delivering into the hands of another; the delivery of opinions, doctrines, practices, rites, and customs from generation to generation by oral communication; a long-established custom or practice that has the effect of an unwritten law." A traditionalist is one who strictly adheres to the authority of a particular tradition.

> *Making the word of God of none effect through your tradition, which ye have delivered...* (Mark 7:13). ·

Beware lest any man spoil you through philosophy and vain deceit, after the tradition of men, after the rudiments of the world, and not after Christ (Colossians 2:8).

Forasmuch as ye know that ye were not redeemed with corruptible things, as silver and gold, from your vain conversation received [handed own] *by tradition from your fathers;*

But with the precious blood of Christ, as of a lamb without blemish and without spot (1 Peter 1:18-19).

The Greek word for "tradition(s)" is *paradosis*, and it means, "transmission, a handing down or on; a giving up or giving over which is done by word of mouth or in writing, that is, tradition by instruction, narrative, or precept." It is taken from *paradidomi* (to surrender, yield up, entrust, transmit; to give into the hands, power, or use of another; to deliver to one something to keep, to take care of, to manage; commit, commend, hand over). Used 13 times in the New Testament (see Matt. 15:2-3; Mark 7:3-13; Gal. 1:14; 2 Thess. 2:15; 3:6), *paradosis* is also rendered as, "ordinances" (2 Cor. 2:11).

Traditions are handed down from a past generation to the following generation.

Traditionalism worships the past.

Therefore leaving the principles of the doctrine of Christ, let us go on unto perfection; not laying again the foundation of repentance from dead works... (Hebrews 6:1).

Traditions vary from person to person, and from group to group. But any and all of our traditions could be summed in what the writer here calls, "dead works." The New International Version of the Bible calls these traditions "acts that lead to death." The Amplified Bible adds that they are but "dead formalism." Men and women waste their present by dreaming about and wanting to live in their past, to return to the "good old days."

Traditionalism Is at Work

Traditionalism, worshipping the past, is hazardous.

Our knowing the Bible and its Author is the key to leaping over this obstruction as we finish this marathon.

But in vain they do worship Me, teaching for doctrines the commandments of men (Matthew 15:9).

"Making the word of God of no effect through your tradition which you have handed down. And many such things you do" (Mark 7:13 NKJV).

The New International Version of the Bible says, *"You nullify the word of God...."*

Jesus made it clear that there is only one thing that is more powerful than the Word of God—the religious traditions of men!

The tradition that trips up more people than perhaps any other is not so obvious.

Command the children of Israel, that they put out of the camp every leper, and every one that hath an issue, and whosoever is defiled by the dead (Numbers 5:2).

He that toucheth the dead body of any man shall be unclean seven days (Numbers 19:11).

Anyone in Moses "church in the wilderness" (Acts 7:38) who "touched" (to reach out and lay the hand upon) a dead person was considered to be "defiled" (made foul, impure, unclean). This first word carries not only the idea of touching a corpse, but also of actively seeking out the dead.

And when [backslidden King] *Saul inquired of the LORD, the LORD answered him not, neither by dreams, nor by Urim, nor by prophets.*

Then said Saul unto his servants, Seek me a woman that hath a familiar spirit, that I may go to her, and inquire of her. And his servants said to him, Behold, there is a woman that hath a familiar spirit at Endor (1 Samuel 28:6-7).

No sensible, born-again (and especially Spirit-filled) believer would ever think of consulting a warlock or witch. We who love and serve Jesus Christ would never seek out a medium that purports to channel the spirits of those who have died. Necromancy or spiritism is part of the occult and New Age thinking, and is a satanic counterfeit.

We learned in Chapter Seven that one example of *dualism* is the belief that two natures still indwell the Christian—Adam *and* Christ, the old man *and* the new man.

But there (in the section about three men being crucified) we beheld Adam's death at the Cross. To affirm him is to revive him, to call him up. Those who believe that Adam is still alive actively preach and practice spiritual *necromancy!*

There shall not be found among you any one that maketh his son or his daughter to pass through the fire, or that useth divination, or an observer of times, or an enchanter, or a witch,

Or a charmer, or a consulter with familiar spirits, or a wizard, or a necromancer.

For all that do these things are an abomination unto the LORD: and because of these abominations the LORD thy God doth drive them out from before thee (Deuteronomy 18:10-12).

...or a spiritist, or one who calls up the dead (Deuteronomy 18:11 NASB).

...or who is a medium or spiritist or who consults the dead (Deuteronomy 18:11 NIV).

The Hebrew word for *necromancer* means, "to tread or frequent; resort, enquire, consult; to follow for pursuit or search; by implication, to seek or ask; specifically, to worship."

Our old life in Adam is gone. We must stop focusing on the past by focusing on our former, sinful lives.

He has removed our sins as far away from us as the east is from the west (Psalms 103:12 TLB).

I, even I, am He that blotteth out thy transgressions for Mine own sake, and will not remember thy sins (Isaiah 43:25).

...I will forgive their iniquity, and I will remember their sin no more (Jeremiah 31:34).

Unlike humankind, when God forgives, He forgets! The blood of Jesus Christ in the New Testament is "better" that that of bulls and goats (see Heb. 12:24), for the blood of these animals can not "take away sins" (Heb. 10:4,11).

The Old Testament Day of Atonement (the tenth day of the seventh month) was marked by the annual "remembrance" of sin. Then, sin was "covered" or "atoned" for (Ps. 32:1). But Jesus has *removed* our sin forever!

The next day John [the Baptist] *seeth Jesus coming unto him, and saith, Behold the Lamb of God, which taketh away the sin of the world* (John 1:29).

And you know that He [Jesus] *appeared in order to take away sins; and in Him there is no sin* (1 John 3:5 NASB).

Our sinless Savior "washed us from our sins in His own blood" (Rev. 1:5). I weep for those who refuse to forgive themselves and do not understand that we have been "accepted in the beloved" (Eph. 1:6). Are we smarter than God? Then why bring up the past by remembering who we were in Adam and what we did as sinners? May God help us to understand what He has already done in Christ with whom we used to be!

No more necromancy! As with the men of Beth-shemesh, when one lifts the "lid" (the Mercy-seat) on what the blood has covered, he releases death (1 Sam. 6:19).

Traditionalism is operating at every level among God's people. Each of the twelve obstacles in this race of faith has become a religious hand-me-down, depending on one's tribe. We cherish these man-made ideas and refuse to change.

And they took them wives of the women of Moab; the name of the one was Orpah, and the name of the other Ruth: and they dwelled there about ten years.

And Mahlon and Chilion died also both of them; and the woman was left of her two sons and her husband.

Then she arose with her daughters in law, that she might return from the country of Moab: for she had heard in the country of Moab how that the LORD had visited His people in giving them bread (Ruth 1:4-6).

Moab has been at rest from youth, like wine left on its dregs, not poured from one jar to another— she has not gone into exile. So she tastes as she did, and her aroma is unchanged (Jeremiah 48:11 NIV).

"Moab" is the place we go when we don't want to change! But spiritual growth denotes change after change after change—"from strength to strength" (Ps. 84:7), "from faith to faith," which was explained in Chapter One (see also Rom. 1:17), and "from glory to glory" (2 Cor. 3:18).

In the Book of Ruth, when the rains poured down from Heaven and broke the famine, Naomi planned to return to Bethlehem-Judah out of the land of Moab. At first, both Orpah and Ruth agreed to leave their heathen land with its heathen gods. Later, under pressure, Orpah decided to stay in the familiar, comfortable place of "ease" and security (Amos 6:1). She needed to heed the advice of the Psalmist.

Hearken, O daughter, and consider, and incline thine ear; forget also thine own people, and thy father's house; (Psalms 45:10).

Many in the 1960s and 1970s were newly filled with the Holy Spirit and began to walk with God. My heart breaks for the thousands of spiritual "Orpahs" who have since then become spiritual orphans. They refused to leave behind their old family and the old church—their excuse: Momma was buried out back of the sanctuary. Their old gods and their previous teachings have disqualified them from the race.

And he [Abram] *went on his journeys from the south even to Bethel, unto the place where his tent had been at the beginning, between Bethel and Hai* (Genesis 13:3).

Far too many of God's people have pitched their tents—their lives, their ministries, and their children—between Bethel and Hai.

Bethel means, "the house of God." *Hai (or Ai)* means, "a heap of (overturned) ruins." The father of all who live and run by faith was westbound "with the hammer down." His future was bright. His past was but a place of desolation.

A fire devoureth before them; and behind them a flame burneth: the land is as the garden of Eden before them, and behind them a desolate wilderness… (Joel 2:3).

Moreover, the army of the Lord is headed back to the Garden, the place of dominion. Keep marching forward, children. All that lies behind us now is a waste-howling wilderness, "a desert waste" (NIV).

Traditionalism has done major damage to the Seed of destiny.

Traditionalism Aborts the Seed

Looking back to our past has destroyed our momentum and sapped our strength. We are about to head down the home stretch. The goal of being like Him is in view and we need every bit of determination and resolve to finish strong. We must keep on running and praying. This is no time to "faint" (Luke 18:1).

Traditionalism has killed godly vision and purpose through the operation of the spirit of fear. The following picture is worth a thousand words.

In Chapter One I talked about three men crucified. Truth is layered like an onion—just keep peeling. Before you now is another picture of Calvary. It illustrates both traditionalism and futurism (the subject of the next chapter).

Jesus Christ was crucified between two thieves—the *past* and the *future*! Chapter Six of my book, *The Priesthood is Changing*, explains this.

Then were there two thieves crucified with Him, one on the right hand, and another on the left (Matthew 27:38).

One of the criminals who hung there hurled insults at Him: "Aren't you the Christ? Save Yourself and us!"

But the other criminal rebuked Him. "Don't you fear God," he said, "since you are under the same sentence?

We are punished justly, for we are getting what our deeds deserve. But this Man has done nothing wrong."

Then he said, "Jesus, remember me when You come into Your kingdom."

Jesus answered him, "I tell you the truth, today you will be with Me in paradise" (Luke 23:39-43 NIV).

The first thief represents the *past*. He was so hopelessly bound and condemned by his former life that he had no hope.

The second thief denotes the *future*, for he had only a futuristic concept of the Kingdom of God (this will be discussed in the next chapter).

For God did not give us a spirit of timidity, but a spirit of power, of love and of self-discipline (2 Timothy 1:7 NIV).

We must not give way to the spirit of fear in any part of our race. That spirit can only work through the *past* and the future. Fear comes up from the past to accuse us of our previous mistakes. We are haunted by the ghosts of past failures and shortcomings.

The Old Testament word for *thief* means, "a stealer." The Greek word is *klepto* which means, "to filch." Webster's notes that as an archaic noun, a "filch" was "the act of stealing; a staff with a hook in one end used by thieves in snatching small articles."

Take us the foxes, the little foxes, that spoil the vines: for our vines have tender grapes (Song of Solomon 2:15).

See to it that no one takes you captive through hollow and deceptive philosophy, which depends on human tradition and the basic principles of this world rather than on Christ (Colossians 2:8 NIV).

Jesus was crucified between two thieves. Traditionalism is a thief. This rascal has run right up on us, and, from behind, has picked our spiritual pickpockets clean! The past has stolen from us through the spirit of fear, using two filches, two nagging questions:

"Why?"

"How long?"

This is the message that came to the prophet Habakkuk in a vision from God:

O Lord, how long must I call for help before You will listen? I shout to You in vain; there is no answer. "Help! Murder!" I cry, but no one comes to save (Habakkuk 1:1-2 TLB).

The thief called "How long?" aggravated the ancient prophet. Fear working throughout the past has "torment," a fear of punishment (1 John 4:18). Those who dwell on the past are constantly asking of God and themselves, "Why?" This thief will cause you to take your eyes off the Goal and possibly forfeit the prize.

Now faith is… (Hebrews 11:1).

To be totally futuristic in one's outlook is to be deceived and robbed by the spirit of fear. There is no future in the past, and the devil doesn't care what we believe, so long as it is in the future. But there is something about a "now" people and a "now" priesthood operating with a "now" faith that scares the hell out of him.

Traditionalism will not let go of the past, either with regard to our past mistakes or our previous teachings. Yet the apostle Paul admonished us to "forget" (lose out of mind) the things that are behind us (Phil. 3:13). Let them go.

But Lot's wife looked back as she was following along behind him and became a pillar of salt (Genesis 19:26 TLB).

Likewise also as it was in the days of Lot; they did eat, they drank, they bought, they sold, they planted, they builded;

But the same day that Lot went out of Sodom it rained fire and brimstone from heaven, and destroyed them all.

Even thus shall it be in the day when the Son of man is revealed.

In that day, he which shall be upon the housetop, and his stuff in the house, let him not come down to take it away: and he that is in the field, let him likewise not return back.

Remember Lot's wife.

Whosoever shall seek to save his life shall lose it; and whosoever shall lose his life shall preserve it (Luke 17:28-33).

Looking back to the past is an issue of life and death. Remember Lot's wife. She "looked back (with favor and care)" at her past. God's Word had been plain—"Don't look back!" (Gen. 19:17 NIV).

In Luke's narration of that Old Testament story, Jesus shows the real reason why folks hang on to the past—to save or preserve their "life." This is the Greek word *psuche* and means, "soul."

Men and women worship the past because they love *themselves* more than God.

You may as well know this too, Timothy, that in the last days it is going to be very difficult to be a Christian.

For people will love only themselves and their money; they will be proud and boastful, sneering at God, disobedient to their parents, ungrateful to them, and thoroughly bad.

They will be hardheaded and never give in to others; they will be constant liars and troublemakers and will think nothing of immorality. They will be rough and cruel, and sneer at those who try to be good.

They will betray their friends; they will be hotheaded, puffed up with pride, and prefer good times to worshiping God (2 Timothy 3:1-4 TLB).

The King James Version calls these compromisers "lovers of their own selves" and "lovers of pleasures more than lovers of God."

To love oneself is to love one's life, or soul. This is our intellect, our emotions, and our will—what we think, what we feel, and what we want. In other words, we want covenant with God on our own terms. We want His blessings without the procedure. Like self-ish, whining children, we want to have our "own way" (Isa. 53:6).

Don't look back. It could cost you the race.

But Jesus said to him, "No one, after putting his hand to the plow and looking back, is fit for the kingdom of God" (Luke 9:62 NASB).

But Jesus told him, "Anyone who lets himself be distracted from the work I plan for him is not fit for the Kingdom of God" (Luke 9:62 TLB).

Now the just shall live by faith: but if any man draw back, My soul shall have no pleasure in him.

But we are not of them who draw back unto perdition [ruin, loss]; *but of them that believe to the saving of the soul (Hebrews 10:38-39).*

The writer to the Hebrews admonishes us not to "shrink back in fear." We are to believe God all the way to the finish.

My Personal Race of Faith

As you now know, I grew up in a nominal church, was saved in a Baptist church, and was then introduced to classical Pentecostalism. I was filled with the Holy Ghost during the Charismatic Renewal during the late 1960s. Each experience brought with it new ideas, each of which had the potential of becoming a tradition in my life.

Therefore, brethren, stand fast, and hold the traditions which ye have been taught, whether by word, or our epistle (2 Thessalonians 2:15).

*Now we command you, brethren, in the name of our Lord Jesus
Christ, that ye withdraw yourselves from every brother that
walketh disorderly, and not after the tradition which he received of
us* (2 Thessalonians 3:6).

Remember, the pure meaning of "tradition" speaks of that
which has been handed down from the past generation to the next.
A word of balance here: not all traditions are evil. Some traditions
are good. Paul made it clear that there are certain apostolic traditions that must be kept and then committed to others.

Indeed, our vision and purpose must be generational as we provide for our seed and our seed's seed. I often remind our four children (and all children) of the privilege of having been raised in the
"nurture" (education, training) and "admonition" (exhortation) of
the Lord (Eph. 6:4). There is no greater blessing than to be raised in
a Christian home, having been loved and discipled by a godly
mother and father. Likewise, there is no higher calling than to be a
godly parent who has given his or her children the good Word of
God, taught them how to pray, and, most of all, has modeled the
Christ-life before them.

Although I came down hard on tribalism and denominationalism in previous chapters, I have appreciated and retained certain
church traditions over the years. For instance, the Church of the
Brethren taught me the sacredness of the Lord's Supper, the Table of
the Lord (Communion), including foot-washing. The Baptists
showed me the importance of sharing one's faith in soul-winning
and evangelism (see Prov. 11:30). Both groups put in my heart a love
for Gospel music. The old hymns are not dead (just some folks who
sing them). We must be thankful for what others have taught us.

As some say, don't throw out the baby with the bath water. Or,
eat the watermelon, and spit out the seeds. Some traditions are

good, and need to be kept and passed down to our children. Although I have laid aside many religious traditions along my way, I have also retained the good traditions of my beginnings.

But, as mentioned previously, I have also run past many of my previous teachings. Legalism with regard to dress was a big one. Asceticism, the notion that it is a spiritual thing to be poor, was also part of my early stubbornness. Dualism did not leave my life and preaching until the mid-1970s. I carried the needless weight of tribalism much farther into my race.

In my mid-20s, I knew and understood 75 percent of the concepts and principles of the Kingdom that I preach and write about these days. God sovereignly dumped revelatory knowledge into me (see Chapter Fourteen for more on this). The problem was, and still is in my present moments of weakness and impatience, that this awesome revelation was just a "message" and had yet to catch up with my character development.

The Lord helped me with the traditional ways with which I viewed myself. The revelation of the "in Christ" message has delivered me from so many negative feelings. For years I battled with what I thought others were thinking and saying about me. Most of those kind of struggles stemmed from the flak—the criticism and hassle from other Christians, even preachers—I have received over the years for preaching the truth.

My release from this prison called condemnation came gradually when I realized that this race has never been about Kelley Varner. Granted, I have made many mistakes (more than most of you), especially in my early years , and, as I still have "hang-ups" that aren't hung up yet. But I have learned that I am not somebody else's problem. The uncompromising Word of the Kingdom that I have kept in my heart and mouth is what most folks have had a problem with.

Behold, the former things are come to pass, and new things do I declare: before they spring forth I tell you of them (Isaiah 42:9).

I am not interested in the "former" days. What Praise Tabernacle was 30 years ago, 20 years ago, ten years ago, five years ago, or even last year—is gone! There is nothing that any of us can do about the past. Truth be told, the "good old days" were really the "good old daze." What I am about to say may sound strong, but we are at the point in the race now where one cannot mince words.

Many Spirit-filled people want to go "back" to the Book of Acts, back to another "Azusa Street" outpouring. What about that?

Positively speaking, that is good. As I travel these days, I am showing Pentecostal and Charismatic folks the key to effective Christian leadership. I am introducing many of them to the Third Day message of "present truth" and "three-fold things" (Prov. 22:20-21) while, at the same time, operating a Holy Ghost, supernatural ministry (see Mark 16:15-20) as I flow among them. We must have pattern with passion, understanding with unction.

The Old Testament "meal offering" (Lev. 2) mingled "fine flour" (the balanced Word) with the "oil" (the moving of the Spirit). Otherwise, our bread, our message and ministry, like Ephraim, will be "half-baked" (Hos. 7:8 TLB)—crummy on one side and gummy on the other! I want to maintain a balanced ministry. I often say, "All Word and we dry up. All Spirit and we blow up. Word and Spirit, and we grow up."

It is surprising for many newer congregations to learn that the Pentecostal experience of the Holy Ghost Baptism is not the fullness of the Spirit. This infilling is in the in-part realm, and is but the "firstfruits" of the Spirit and the "earnest" of our inheritance (Rom. 8:23; Eph. 1:13-14). It is like the "key of David" that unlocks the heavenlies (Rev. 3:7). If these folks want to go "back" to Pentecost to adjust and to realign the foundation, that is fine. But I am admonishing them that we cannot stay in that Feast. We must press on to know the Lord in the full maturity of the Feast of Tabernacles.

What is your Moab?

Moab can be an old dead, dried-up church.

Moab can be our pet doctrine.

Moab can be our favorite pew or a place between our ears.

Moab is the place we go where we don't have to change.

Moab is a voice from our past.

I am praying for Praise Tabernacle and every ministry that we all will change. May every public gathering now be historic; that is to say, life-changing!

We have heard of the pride of Moab, an excessive pride; even of his arrogance, pride, and fury... (Isaiah 16:6 NASB).

I have met thousands of Moabites throughout my journey. Hundreds of them have come in and out of my church and my life in the last 30 years. At some point in the race, they became afraid and looked back. They refused to wrap their arms and minds around anything greater than themselves.

I have sat under mosquito nets in the jungles of South America with covenant brothers, only years later to watch helplessly as they dropped out of the running. I have observed with very mixed emotions as preachers from all three Feasts have lost their marriage, their children, their church, their ministry, and their witness.

The Day of the Lord has dawned and is trying everyone's work and life (1 Cor. 3:13). The lid is coming off everything. Hidden sins are being exposed. Now is the time for us to make our calling and election sure (see 2 Pet. 1:10). Now is the time to strain forward and press into the fulfillment of the promise.

We have come too far in this race. Too much is at stake. Most of our journey is behind us. Sadly, some have come right up to this threshold of destiny, and have fainted.

There is no place here for human sentiment. Some will not make it. As much as we ache to finish with them, we must go on now and focus on what lies before us. We are past the place of looking back, past the point of no return. The fire of God's goodness has graciously burned every bridge behind us.

We are about to round the final turn and head for the Goal. This last part of the course is treacherous and demands our full concentration, "looking unto Jesus the author and finisher of our faith" (Heb. 12:2).

CHAPTER ELEVEN

Futurism

We have now run most of this course; having come to the final turn, the end of its second section.

In the scheme of Moses' Tabernacle, the Holy Place realm typifies the Feast of Pentecost—the Spirit-filled element of the Body of Christ, in particular the classical Pentecostals, the Charismatics, and the Faith Movement.

This second dimension of God's amazing grace has enabled faithful spiritual athletes to leap over the hurdles of legalism, asceticism, dualism, elitism, tribalism, and traditionalism.

But our final obstacle in this leg of the race of faith is one of the highest and hardest to overcome: *futurism* or *dispensationalism*.

What Is Futurism?

My book, *Whose Right It Is: A Handbook of Covenantal Theology*, provides much of the material found in this chapter. One is encouraged to peruse its pages, especially the chapters that set forth the historical and biblical foundations of this futuristic view. Of special consideration is Chapter Ten, titled "Daniel's Prophecy of Seventy Weeks" (found in Dan. 9:24-27). The latter is discussed in the following paragraphs.

Some readers may not be acquainted at all with the different viewpoints of eschatology that are introduced in this chapter. Forgive my brevity of this discussion. A full discussion of these matters awaits any hungry inquirer in the aforementioned, 300-page treatise, *Whose Right It Is*. This book has infiltrated many circles, Bible schools, and even Pentecostal seminaries. Thankfully, it has greatly impacted the thinking of Christian leaders throughout the great nation of South Africa (where I have faithfully ministered the Gospel of the Kingdom since 1998).[1]

My main point is this: futurism has many applications other than traditional eschatology, but the dispensational view is so popular and generally well-known among evangelicals and the Spirit-filled communities that I emphasize it here to illustrate this critical obstacle to our faith.

Futurism is another name in the Christian world for the view of *dispensationalism*. Webster's says that a *dispensation* is "the system by which anything is ministered; management; in theology, the ordering of events under divine authority."

Dispensationalism is taken from the word "dispense" which means, "to weigh or meter out." This school of thought sees God working in different ways in different periods of time.

> For if I do this thing willingly, I have a reward: but if against my will, a dispensation of the gospel is committed unto me (1 Corinthians 9:17).

That in the dispensation of the fulness of times He might gather together in one all things in Christ, both which are in heaven, and which are on earth; even in Him: (Ephesians 1:10).

If ye have heard of the dispensation of the grace of God which is given me to you-ward: (Ephesians 3:2).

Whereof I am made a minister, according to the dispensation of God which is given to me for you, to fulfil the word of God; (Colossians 1:25).

This biblical term, along with "stewardship" (Luke 16:2-4), is the translation of the Greek word *oikonomia*, which means, "the administration of a household or estate; specifically, a religious 'economy;' the oversight of other's property."

Dispensationalism is the eschatological[2] view that God has dealt differently with mankind during distinct eras of biblical history. Cyrus I. Scofield's classic definition states that a *dispensation* is, "a period of time during which man is tested in respect of obedience to some *specific* revelation of the will of God." Influenced by the writings of J.R. Graves, *The Work of Christ Consummated in Seven Dispensations* (1883), Scofield's scheme of seven dispensations has been widely assumed and rehearsed:

1. **Innocence** (before the Fall of man).

2. **Conscience** (from the Fall of man until Noah).

3. **Human Government** (from Noah until Abraham).

4. **Promise** (from Abraham until Moses).

5. **Law** (from Moses until Christ).

6. **Grace** (the Church age)

7. **Kingdom** (the Millennium).

Scofield's famous Reference Bible (first published in 1909) has popularized and polarized these ideas, especially among evangelicals. Finis J. Dake's notable Reference Bible (1961), along with Scofield's, has done the same throughout Pentecostalism.

Scofield's understanding of a "dispensation" undercuts the biblical doctrine of grace in any age. His dispensational distinction between national Israel and the Church denies grace completely, maintaining as it does that there is more than one way of salvation.

Mild dispensationalism teaches the difference between law and grace, the Old Testament and the New Testament.

Extreme or "hyper-dispensationalism" (as shown in Chapter Two concerning cessasionism) relegates the miraculous gifts of the Holy Spirit to the first century Church, and the prophetic promises of the Old and New Testament to the *future* state of natural Israel as a separate kingdom from the Church—thus the synonym, *futurism*.

The basic weakness and flaw of this classical view of futurism is the interpretation of the New Testament on the basis of the Old Testament, rather then viewing the Old Testament in the light of the New Testament. But in the Gospels, Jesus gave us the marching orders and the rules for the race. In the Book of Acts, they did it. Most importantly, in the Epistles, they *explained* it.

Chapter Seven of *Whose Right It Is*[3], titled "A Fresh Historical Look at Dispensationalism," is must reading for any serious reader and runner. We must know where this "ism" came from.

From 1830 to the present, this traditional view has been handed down to us from men and women who were not Spirit-filled. John Darby, founder of the Plymouth brethren and the so-called "father" of this system, brought futurism to the states around 1960. When

Pentecost fell at the turn of the 20th century, his viewpoint was assumed and never questioned until the Latter Rain Outpouring in 1948, when real apostles and prophets began to teach Bible truth about the end-times. The aforementioned Scofield's Reference Bible cemented futurism in the minds of God's people, and has done so to the present.

Essentially based on a difference between the Church and national Israel, this popular eschatological view constitutes one of the greater obstacles in our race of faith. Traditional dispensationalism or futurism, as handed down to us from John Nelson Darby, Cyrus Scofield, and Clarence Larkin,[4] declares:

"The second coming of Christ is in *two stages*. Before the tribulation period, He comes *for* the saints. Seven years later, He will come back *with* the saints. The day of Christ, the 'Rapture,' is the first stage—Jesus comes secretly like a thief in the night for His Bride, the Church. The second stage is called the 'Revelation' or the Day of the Lord, when He returns in judgment to destroy the antichrist and set up His Kingdom."

The purpose of this chapter is not to dismantle futurism (I did that in *Whose Right It Is*, historically and biblically). But a quick note at this point in our race: Jesus didn't leave here in "two stages;" so what makes anyone think that He will come again "in like manner" (Acts 1:11)?

I have noted the last two obstacles in our race of faith to be *traditionalism* and *futurism*. I have lumped them together because Paul did so in the following key Scripture:

Brethren, I count not myself to have apprehended: but this one thing I do, forgetting those things which are behind, and reaching forth unto those things which are before, (Philippians 3:13).

Traditionalism (see the previous chapter) has to do with "those things which are behind."

Futurism has to do with "those things which are before (in front of)."

Traditionalism worships the past. *Futurism*, more widely known as *dispensationalism*, worships the future.

Futurism Is at Work

Nothing has paralyzed the saints more than futurism. It has been completely pervasive and invasive, infecting the first two Feasts—evangelicals and Pentecostals— with its spiritual virus of a "gloom and doom" message, including a seven-year Tribulation Period with its anticipated global, demonized leader, the antichrist. Accordingly, the so-called "Rapture" of the Church could happen at "any minute" (the doctrine of imminence)[5] and the Tribulation would begin. Thus, Jesus must come and rescue His Bride, the Church, before all hell breaks loose.

In camp meetings and in churches (especially on Sunday nights), excited preachers are quick to exclaim that the trumpet may sound at "any minute," before they finish their sermon, or before the saints wake up in the morning. Evangelists tell of cemeteries bursting open and the dead rising, and living Christians zooming off into space to meet the Lord in the "Rapture."

Prophecy buffs prognosticate the rebuilding of the Jewish temple, and some (like Scofield's original notes), even predict the reinstitution of animal sacrifices. I wonder if those who are raising red heifers have ever read the Book of Hebrews?

Who needeth not daily, as those high priests, to offer up sacrifice, first for His own sins, and then for the people's: for this He did once, when He offered up himself (Hebrews 7:27, emphasis added.)

*Neither by the blood of goats and calves, but by His own blood He entered in **once** into the holy place, having obtained eternal redemption for us* (Hebrews 9:12, emphasis added).

*For then must He often have suffered since the foundation of the world: but now **once** in the end of the world* [the Jewish age] *hath He appeared to put away sin by the sacrifice of Himself* (Hebrews 9:26, emphasis added).

*So Christ was **once** offered to bear the sins of many...* (Hebrews 9:28, emphasis added).

*By the which will we are sanctified through the offering of the body of Jesus Christ **once for all*** (Hebrews 10:10, emphasis added).

The word for "once" in all these verses is *hapax*, and it means, "one (or a single) time (numerically or conclusively); once for all."

Jesus' "finished" work on the Cross (John 19:30) was conclusively "once for all." I believe for one to say that animal sacrifice will be offered again (even in a memorial sense) is blasphemous.

Nationwide, preachers unabashedly recite the appearing of a secular world leader—their infamous antichrist, the "beast" of Revelation 13—and the beginning of the Tribulation Period. Fictional series in book form and even movies have popularized these views. Their sad implication is that the Church is too weak to survive the onslaught of such demonic fury (although the whole armor of Ephesians 6:10-18 mentions none for protecting the back). We have been told that while the saints enjoy the marriage supper of the Lamb up in Heaven and receive the rewards of their earthly labors (at the judgment seat of Christ), their unsaved loved ones and untold millions of heathen will suffer untold agonies on earth.

Dispensationalism generates great fear and a dreaded apprehension of the future. As stated in an earlier chapter, any theology or eschatology that is based upon the "spirit of fear" cannot be of the Lord (2 Tim. 1:7).

What are our motives in declaring these things? There is a lot of money to be made in "dispen-sensational" preaching and teaching. Without checking out the Word of God and completely ignoring the historical roots of futurism, God's people, especially here in the United States, can't seem to get enough of this stuff.

But with futurism, the real issue is not eschatological, but Christological. This hindrance has robbed the Church of her true identity as the Seed of Abraham and the Seed of David (see Matt. 1:1 with 1 John 4:17). That thought takes us back to the Preface, where we learned that sin is a "mistaken identity." That's why futurism is such an obstacle in this race. Having ignored sound biblical exegesis, it has evolved into one of our biggest problems, spreading a plague of unbelief and pessimism.

According to futurism, we Christians are "gentiles," and the natural Jews are God's chosen people. This is one reason why futurism is so dangerous. It leaves the true believer feeling like some kind of spiritual "stepchild," unfit to run any race. It has knocked the wind right out of us.

The natural Jew has no advantage over me, and I have none over him. We *both* must be born again! In Chapter Four of *Whose Right It Is*, titled "Jesus is the Seed of Abraham, I write:

> I love the natural descendants of Abraham enough to tell them the truth—salvation is by Jesus Christ or not at all.

Men who are offended by these truths are offended by His cross (Gal. 5:11).... The Law, not the Church, was parenthetical, added because of the transgression (Gal. 3:19). The Church is not an afterthought in the back of God's mind, but is His eternal purpose and program. *God's chosen people are Christians*, whom the New Testament doctrinal epistles designated to be:

- Jews (Rom. 2:28-29).

- The children of the promise who are counted for the seed (Rom. 9:6-8).

- The chosen people (generation)(1 Pet. 2:1-10).

- The holy nation (Matt. 3:7-10; 21:42-43; 1 Pet. 2:9-10).

- The true circumcision (Phil. 3:3).

- The new (heavenly) Jerusalem (see John 4:19-24; Gal. 4:21-31; Heb. 12:22-24; Rev. 21:1-11).

- The Israel of God (Gal. 6:16).

Thank God for all those who have a genuine burden and call to minister to the nation of Israel and to the Jewish people (just as we pray for those with a burden for the United States or South Africa or any other nation). Yet it remains that the Jewish people, upon their conversion through faith in Jesus' blood, are grafted into the ongoing, Messianic Body of Christ made of men and women from every tribe and nation (see Acts 10:34-35).[6]

Some of us have been tagged with preaching what men call "replacement theology" (that the Church has "replaced" Israel). No, we preach "placement theology," and do what Paul did as He placed *both* Jew and Greek in one Body by the Cross, so making *one* new creation man!

Therefore, remember that at one time you were Gentiles (heathens) in the flesh; called Uncircumcision by those who called themselves Circumcision, [itself a mere mark] in the flesh made by human hands.

Remember that you were at that time separated (living apart) from Christ—excluded from part in Him; utterly estranged and outlawed from the rights of Israel as a nation, and strangers with no share in the sacred compacts of the [Messianic] promise—with no knowledge or rights to God's agreements. And you had no hope—no promise; you were in the world without God.

But now in Christ Jesus, you who once were [so] far away, through (by, in) the blood of Christ have been brought near.

For He is [Himself] our peace—our bond of unity and harmony. He has made us both [Jew and Gentile] one (body), and has broken down (destroyed), abolished the hostile dividing wall between us.

By abolishing in His [own crucified] flesh the enmity [caused by] the Law with its decrees and ordinances—which He annulled, that He from the two might create in Himself one new man—one new quality of humanity out of the two—so making peace (Ephesians 2:11-15 AMP).

In recent years, the popular fictional book series, *Left Behind*, has done more to spread the futuristic view than anything else. But what did Jesus the prophet have to say about being "left behind"?

But as the days of Noah were, so shall also the coming of the Son of man be.

For as in the days that were before the flood they were eating and drinking, marrying and giving in marriage, until the day that Noah entered into the ark,

And knew not until the flood came, and took them all away; so shall also the coming of the Son of man be.

Then shall two be in the field; the one shall be taken, and the other left.

Two women shall be grinding at the mill; the one shall be taken, and the other left (Matthew 24:37-41).

They did eat, they drank, they married wives, they were given in marriage, until the day that Noah entered into the ark, and the flood came, and destroyed them all (Luke 17:27).

We will never know what the Bible *means* until we read what is plainly *says*! Jesus obviously declared in this passage that it was the wicked that were "taken" in judgment and "destroyed." Righteous Noah and his family were "left behind" to inherit the earth! No was else was "left" to dispute Noah's claim.

The so-called "Rapture" passage (1 Thess. 4:13-18) confirms this.

*Then we which are alive and **remain** shall be caught up together with them in the clouds...* (1 Thessalonians 4:17, emphasis added).

The word for "remain" (used only here and in verse 15 of the same passage) is *perileipo*, and it means, "to leave all around, survive; to leave over, to remain over; left over." It is us living believers, not the wicked, who are "left over"! Left over what? The shaking that is presently shaking everything that can be shaken, leaving behind an unshakeable people and Kingdom (Heb. 12:25-29).

The Son of man shall send forth His angels, and they shall gather out of His kingdom all things that offend, and them which do iniquity;

And shall cast them into a furnace of fire: there shall be wailing and gnashing of teeth.

Then shall the righteous shine forth as the sun in the kingdom of their Father... (Matthew 13:41-43).

Each of us is a microcosm of planet Earth. In dealing with us, did God remove righteousness and leave behind wickedness, or did He remove the wickedness and leave behind the righteousness of Himself? The truth is that Adam is "taken" and Christ is "left."

"But, Pastor Varner," ask so many, "I thought that the righteous were going to be removed?" I simply ask these folks to read these verses (compare Psalm 37).

They that trust in the LORD shall be as mount Zion, which cannot be removed, but abideth for ever (Psalms 125:1).

The righteous shall never be removed... (Proverbs 10:30).

Futurism is being proclaimed 24/7 on Christian radio and television, not to mention the Internet. The dragon is defeated, but he still has a mouth. There is a "flood" of this stuff that has really muddied up the track and slowed down many a runner (Rev. 12:15-16).

My heart breaks for all the young men and women from other nations who are hungry for the Word of God. I have traveled enough internationally to know that many of them have the idea that if a teaching comes out of the United States, it is of God. Sadly, American theology and popular eschatology has Westernized and not Christianized the nations.

For the record, I still preach the bodily, physical, corporeal, and literal return of Jesus Christ to this planet. Simply stated, I stand with the history of the Church fathers up until 1830, that the coming of Jesus Christ would be *personal, visible, and glorious.*

Futurism is not limited to eschatology, although that is its principal proponent. For example, until 1979, most Kingdom and sonship preachers taught that the Most Holy Place realm, the third dimension and "third day" (Hos. 6:1-3) of grace (and all that it represents) to be future. Even today, to declare that the Most Holy Place is a present reality will start a feud in those circles.

As I have already said, the devil doesn't really care what we believe, so long as it is in the future.

But men and women are tired of satan's lies, the same old cabbage. While an older generation of dispensationalists are still being thrilled and chilled with fits of "rapture fever," there is a whole new wave of thinkers—young preachers and young people—who are finally recognizing that the real future of this planet belongs to Jesus and His Church, if God's people will remain faithful to His Word.

Corporate defeat and heavenly rescue are being steadily abandoned for the view that Jesus Christ is the Lord of all history, and the glorious head of His progressively triumphant Church!

Futurism Aborts the Seed

Real faith is "now" (Heb. 11:1). It doesn't look to the future and claim anything. Real faith possesses.

For the kingdom of God is not meat and drink; but righteousness, and peace, and joy in the Holy Ghost (Romans 14:17).

The Kingdom of God is a present reality. Are righteousness, peace, and joy—right relationships, security, and expression—present realities? Then, of course, this Kingdom is now, as well as the future. It is Kingdom now, but not yet.

The Most Holy Place is a present reality. The Lord Jesus Christ is our Propitiation, literally, our "mercy-seat" (Rom. 3:25). We are to live in Him and then flow out of Him with a present-day, king-priest word and ministry of reconciliation (see 2 Cor. 5:17-21). The "children" or "mature sons" of God are peacemakers (Matt. 5:9).

The rest of this section shows how insidious this doctrine of futurism has become. John Darby's dispensational views, his two-stage theory of Jesus' coming is based on one very critical portion of Scripture. It is the only place in the Bible where one can discover the necessary "seven years" in order to have a future Tribulation Period.

After this key passage is seen in its true biblical light, it cannot be used to substantiate futurism. If it falls, the whole house of cards falls. This Scripture is discussed in voluminous detail in Chapter Ten of *Whose Right It Is*, titled, "Daniel's Prophecy of Seventy Weeks." I will highlight this critical point in the following brief section.

But understand this first. With regard to eschatology and end-time events, each of us is going to believe what he or she wants. Therefore, if someone still believes that there is a seven-year Tribulation Period coming upon this earth, that's fine. But that person cannot use Daniel's famous Prophecy of Seventy Weeks (see Dan. 9:24-27) to prove that view.[7]

The real subject of all of Daniel 9 is *sin* and what God would ultimately do about the sin question. A better title for Daniel 9:24-27 would be, "The Blood Covenant Which Cannot Fail"!

In the first year of Darius the son of Ahasuerus, of the seed of the Medes, which was made king over the realm of the Chaldeans;

in the first year of his reign I Daniel understood by books the number of the years, whereof the word of the LORD came to Jeremiah the prophet, that he would accomplish seventy years in the desolations of Jerusalem.

And I set my face unto the Lord God, to seek by prayer and supplications, with fasting, and sackcloth, and ashes:

And I prayed unto the LORD my God, and made my confession, and said, O Lord, the great and dreadful God, keeping the covenant and mercy to them that love Him, and to them that keep His commandments;

*We have **sinned**...* (Daniel 9:1-5, emphasis added).

Daniel throughout this chapter was concerned with sin. Verses 5-19 record his fervent intercession and concern over the iniquity and transgression of his people, the Jews, and his city, Jerusalem.

*And whiles I was speaking, and praying, and confessing my **sin** and the **sin** of my people Israel, and presenting my supplication before the LORD my God for the holy mountain of my God;*

Yea, whiles I was speaking in prayer, even the man Gabriel, whom I had seen in the vision at the beginning, being caused to fly swiftly, touched me about the time of the evening oblation.

And he informed me, and talked with me, and said, O Daniel, I am now come forth to give thee skill and understanding.

At the beginning of thy supplications the commandment came forth, and I am come to shew thee; for thou art greatly beloved: therefore understand the matter, and consider the vision (Daniel 9:20-23, emphasis added).

The archangel Gabriel, the same heavenly messenger who came to Zacharias (the father of John the Baptist) and to the Virgin Mary announcing the birth of Jesus Christ (see Luke 1:19,26), now comes to Daniel to prophesy Messiah's death!

To punctuate the sentence, Gabriel shows up at the "time of the evening oblation (offering)," at the ninth hour (3 o'clock in the afternoon), at the very same time when Jesus would one day hang on an old rugged cross and die a criminal's death for all our *sin*!

May we allow the archangel to give to us the same kind of "skill" (prudence, intelligence) and "understanding" (discernment) that he gave to Daniel that afternoon, so we can see what these four verses really say. This famous prophecy is Christological (the Person and Work of Christ) and Soteriological (the Doctrine of Salvation), not eschatological in its scope and nature.

Before beginning this brief exegesis of Daniel 9:24-27, we observe that Daniel had been studying the prophecies of Jeremiah. In Daniel 9:2, he by these books understood "the number of the years" (using "a day for a year," as in Ezekiel 4:6). Jeremiah had prophesied that Judah would be in Babylonian captivity for 70 years (from 606 to 536 B.C. and the time of Cyrus' decree in Ezra 1:1-15).

Thus, Jeremiah's 70 years of *uninterrupted time* is the *pattern* for Daniel's "seventy years" or "seventy sevens" or 490 years of *uninterrupted time*. Why is that important?

Darby, Scofield, and Larkin (following the pattern of the Jesuit priest Francisco Ribera in 1585) and their eschatology invented an infamous 2,000-year "gap" between the 69th and the 70th week.

Futurism boldly asserts that Daniel's 70th week is still in the *future*!

Without becoming too detailed, their 70th week is the soon-coming, infamous seven-year Tribulation Period as recorded in Matthew 24 (compare Mark 13 and Luke 17, 21), Revelation 4-19, and which is also known as the "time of Jacob's trouble" (Jer. 30:7). As you can see, this stuff can quickly become complicated.

Their point is simple: futurism says that all of these things are yet to happen, that Daniel's 70th week is still out there in the future.

Seventy weeks are determined upon thy people and upon thy holy city, to finish the transgression, and to make an end of sins, and to make reconciliation for iniquity, and to bring in everlasting right-eousness, and to seal up the vision and prophecy, and to anoint the most Holy (Daniel 9:24).

"Seventy weeks (sevens)" or 490 years were determined. Again, the biblical way to interpret these numbers is to know that a day represents a year (see Ezek. 4:6). What Daniel is about to describe in six major points took place over a span of five centuries of uninter-rupted time. It is interesting in this chapter that deals with *sin* that 490 is the biblical number that denotes *complete forgiveness* (see Matt. 18:22).

These 490 years have been "determined" (divided off; decreed). Grammatically, it is important to know that the subject "seventy weeks" is *plural* but the Hebrew verb for "determined" is *singular*. All seventy weeks or 490 years are thus declared collectively to denote one complete period of time—with *no gap*.

The key to unlocking this powerful Christological passage is to recognize the sixfold prophetic purpose contained in its complete scope and fulfillment. Within the uninterrupted time frame of 490 years, these historical events would take place in *Jerusalem*, Daniel's "holy city," among the *Jews*, Daniel's "people."

In the Jewish city of Jerusalem, Jesus Christ the Messiah once and for all dealt with sin. Jesus' death on the Cross:

- Finished the transgression (see Isa. 43:25; 53:5; John 19:30; Heb. 9:15).

- Made an end of sin (see Matt. 1:21; John 1:29; Heb. 8:12).

- Made reconciliation for iniquity (see Rom. 5:10; 2 Cor. 5:19; Eph. 2:16; Col. 1:19-20; and Heb. 2:17).

- Brought in everlasting righteousness (see Rom. 10:3,10; 1 Cor. 1:30; 2 Cor. 5:21; Phil. 3:9; and Heb. 7:1-2).

- Sealed up the vision and the prophecy (prophet) (see Hab. 2:3 with Heb. 10:37; and Isa. 29:10-11; Matt. 5:17-20; John 5:39; 6:27; 19:28-37; Acts 3:17-22; and Rev. 10:10).

- Anointed the most Holy (place)(see Ps. 45:7; Isa. 61:1; Luke 1:35; 4:16-21; John 14:6; Acts 2:27; 3:14; 4:27; 10:38; Rom. 1:4; Heb. 10:14,19-20; and 1 John 2:27).

Remember, *futurism* teaches these things have yet to happen! I wonder if the "god of this world," the inventor of every confused, man-made religion, had anything to do with creating this view?

Jesus' death on Calvary in Jerusalem among the Jews rent the veil from the top to the bottom, releasing everything that had been hidden for ages and generations. Isaiah 53 is the most beautiful passage in the Bible telling of Messiah's death, burial, and resurrection; but Daniel's Prophecy of Seventy Weeks is the most powerful, pinpointing the time of His death down to the very month and year!

Know therefore and understand, that from the going forth of the commandment to restore and to build Jerusalem unto the Messiah the Prince shall be seven weeks, and threescore and two weeks: the street shall be built again, and the wall, even in troublous times (Daniel 9:25).

This "commandment" is found in Ezra 7, marking the beginning date of the 70 weeks to be 457 B.C. Jesus is "Messias the Prince" (John 4:25-26,42; Acts 3:15; 5:31; Rev. 1:5).

From the autumn of 457 B.C. until the autumn of A.D. 27 is exactly 483 years, or 69 weeks.[8] Jesus was 30 years of age when He was publicly revealed as the "Messiah" in His water baptism by John at the Jordan River (Matt. 3:15-17; Mark 1:14-15; Luke 3:21-23).

The 69th week ended when Jesus stepped down into those cold, chilly waters, and the 70th week of Daniel's prophecy *immediately* began (uninterrupted time) when He stepped back out to begin His three-and-a-half year public ministry.

The latter portion of Daniel 9:25 points to the days of Nehemiah and the rebuilding of the walls of Jerusalem, which took place as part of the 69-week period.

And after threescore and two weeks shall Messiah be cut off, but not for Himself: and the people of the prince that shall come shall destroy the city and the sanctuary; and the end thereof shall be with a flood, and unto the end of the war desolations are determined (Daniel 9:26).

He was taken from prison and from judgment: and who shall declare his generation? for he was cut off out of the land of the living: for the transgression of my people was he stricken (Isaiah 53:8).

Jesus was "cut off" (cut down) at the Cross. This Hebrew word suggests an abrupt, violent death, or a death by the agency of others (cutting a covenant). The rest of the verse 26 is parenthetical,[9] and describes Titus and his Roman army ransacking Jerusalem and the Temple (A.D. 66-70). Jesus Himself prophesied and "determined" those same "desolations" in Matthew 24 (compare Luke 21:20-36).

And he shall confirm the covenant with many for one week: and in the midst of the week he shall cause the sacrifice and the oblation to cease, and for the overspreading of abominations he shall make it desolate, even until the consummation, and that determined shall be poured upon the desolate (Daniel 9:27).

"He" is "Messiah the Prince" of verse 25. The word for "confirm" speaks of a powerful, mighty covenant so strong that it cannot be broken! This "covenant" is not some future covenant that will be made between the natural nation of Israel and a coming antichrist (then broken). This covenant is the "new covenant" of Jeremiah 31:31-34 (remember that Daniel was reading Jeremiah), the New Testament in Jesus' blood reiterated verbatim in Hebrews 8:8-13.

This is *the blood covenant that cannot fail!* It cannot be broken.

Now, once and for all, see the absolute evil of dispensationalim. If "another gospel" (Gal. 1:6-10) dares to broach the precious blood of Jesus, adding, as did Scofield in his original Bible, that animal sacrifice would again be made, it has to be one of the "seducing (misleading) spirits" and "doctrines (teaching) of devils (demons)," causing some to "depart (revolt, withdraw) from the faith" (1 Tim. 4:1).

That's a strong statement, but someone has to draw a line. Any blood-washed preacher with a backbone must agree. When anyone touches or dilutes the blood of the Lamb, that person has gone too far!

Jesus confirmed the New Covenant with "many" elect Jews for the "one week" of seven years, from A.D. 27-34 (see Rom. 9:21-29; 11:15). Then in the "midst of the week," in the spring of A.D. 31, a very real, flesh and blood Jesus died on an old rugged in the holy city among Daniel's people, causing the "sacrifice and oblation (offering) to cease" by the offering of Himself (Heb. 9-10)!

The historical backdrop of the remaining three-and-one-half years of the 70th week, from the spring of A.D. 31 until the autumn of A.D. 34, are found in the first seven chapters of the Book of Acts, ending with the martyrdom of Stephen at the hands of an angry Sanhedrin, the official voice of the Jewish nation. Daniel's words were fulfilled.

Then the center of action relocated from Daniel's city of Jerusalem to Antioch of Syria, 300 miles to the north. And everything shifted:

- Philip preached to the Samaritans (Acts 8).

- Saul, the apostle to the uncircumcision, was converted (Acts 9).

- The Holy Ghost fell upon Cornelius' household (Acts 10).

- Barnabas fetched Saul (Paul) to Antioch (Acts 11).

- The first missionary journey to the Gentiles began (Acts 13).

This "one week" (of seven years) is not some future Tribulation Period with its unveiling of satan in the flesh, and a broken covenant. Daniel's 70th Week is the historical, chronological, moral, and redemptive fulcrum of all the ages of the human race! It heralds the period when God was manifested in the flesh, wherein Jesus Christ paid the full price for sin and conquered satan, wherein the

Holy Spirit came to empower the Church, and wherein the Gospel of the Kingdom was opened to all men. To our Jewish friends throughout the world, it is irrefutable evidence that their Messiah was crucified in Daniel's city among Daniel's people.

The futuristic, dispensationalistic interpretation of Daniel 9:24-27 has been satan's best shot, the most powerful weapon in his arsenal, and the greatest obstacle to hurdle in our race of faith. The evil one himself is so deluded that he thinks that these things didn't happen (in A.D. 27-34), living in denial of his own demise.

> *For God hath not given us the spirit of fear; but of power, and of love, and of a sound mind* (2 Timothy 1:7).

In the previous chapter on traditionalism, we showed that Jesus was crucified between two thieves, the past and the *future*.

Futurism, especially dispensationalism, has picked our pockets, having again come to us through the "spirit of fear," armed and carrying two more filches:

1. "What if?"

2. "How shall it be?"

Again, there is no future in the past, and the devil doesn't care what any of us believe, so long as it is in the future.

My Personal Race of Faith

Some of the most exciting songs that our gospel quartet, the Ambassadors, ever performed in the late 1960s had lyrics that talked about "flying away." When we got to lines like, "My feet won't stay on the ground," you never heard such shouting or saw such carrying on (by us *and* the congregation)!

My first class at Free Gospel Bible Institute in the fall of 1969 was on Dispensational Truth. One on my first textbooks was written by Clarence Larkin. I assumed that this doctrine was correct, and my analytical mind was fascinated and overwhelmed by the intricacies of his many charts. It was not until much later when I actually began to read and study this subject that I discovered on page 102 of Larkin's textbook that the man who was teaching me Bible prophecy also believed (in his section on spiritism) that those of us who speak with other tongues are empowered by the devil to do so!

Whoa! Time out!

Little wonder that Bill Britton (see Chapter Twelve) and other Latter Rain pioneers saw the same thing in 1948 and began to question the standard Scofieldian eschatology that had been handed down through classical Pentecostalism. They, like me in 1970, wanted to know what real apostles and prophets, to whom have been stewarded the mysteries (see Eph. 3:1-5), were teaching about the coming of the Lord.

My eschatology changed, to say the least. I don't even know if I have one anymore. As I said, my apostolic burden has to do with Christology, not Eschatology. I want people to know and understand who they already are in Christ (based upon His finished work) as the Seed of Abraham and the Seed of David. Jesus inherited the "land" and the "throne," the earth and the right to rule it. And we are "joint-heirs' with Him (Rom. 8:17).

Once I began to teach at Zion in Brother McDowell's Bible school, I also began to meet real apostles and prophets. Pastor C.S. Fowler (who introduced me to many others) was the first to really stir my thinking and challenge my traditional futuristic views. This "badger-skin" preacher (he could be rough on a young man at times) showed me one verse of Scripture that changed my life forever.

And if ye be Christ's, then are ye Abraham's seed, and heirs according to the promise (Galatians 3:29).

And now that we are Christ's we are the true descendants of Abraham, and all of God's promises to Him belong to us (Galatians 3:29 TLB).

When I saw that truth, everything changed. As I continued to search and study the Scriptures, the seven points identifying who we really are in Christ as Abraham's Seed (given in the second section of this chapter) were made clear. Then one day, the Lord said it to me in unmistakable language (please indulge my terminology, but I have to tell the story as it happened to me), "Son, the Jew is you!"

Once I knew my identity in Christ, I immediately began to discover three foundational truths that are the birthright of any believer:

1   **A new fellowship** – Abraham is our brother in Christ!

2. **A new promise** – That which heretofore had been given to another time (the future) and to another people (the natural Jew only) was now ours in Christ!

3. **A new authority** – With the realization of identity, possession, and purpose comes a boldness to say it and to become it!

Upon arriving in Richlands, I couldn't wait to tell others about this newfound revelation. I assumed that everyone was as hungry to know the truth. The little Charismatic prayer group that formed the nucleus of our new church ate it up, but not my new daily radio audience.

Back then I was filled with a lot of zeal and not much knowledge. I was on the radio (a 100,000-watt FM station that blanketed the entire region) for 30 minutes every weekday morning and another 30 minutes on Sunday evening. I hammered the "Rapture" teaching, and systematically dismantled it with the Scriptures.

Immediately, other preachers sent signed petitions to the radio station to get that "heretic' off the air. "He is causing our people to ask us questions that we cannot answer," they said.

After almost 30 years, some in this local area still keep me at arm's length because of my "strange" doctrine. I hurt myself and our ministry in 1978-1979 by not using wisdom. There are so many other wonderful Bible truths to teach. Man-made traditions had angered me. I had spoken the truth, but not with much love (see Eph. 4:15).

I implore all the young zealots who just read the truth about Daniel's Prophecy of Seventy Weeks: Don't run out and tell everybody that you do not believe in the "Rapture." They will actually hear you say that you do not believe in the coming of the Lord. And we do.

I am presently teaching seminars on "Apostolic Eschatology" (with *Whose Right It Is* as my textbook) all over the United States. "How do you get away with that?" I am often asked.

My approach to new, hungry people is simply this: You will believe about this stuff what you want to believe. I am not here to "straighten you out" or to get you to believe my views. I want to empower and equip you with the knowledge of history and the Scriptures so you can make wise choices. Besides, there are probably only two areas of consideration that you and I may possibly differ on: first, the contemporary ministries of apostles and prophets, as well as those of evangelists, pastors, and teachers.

And He gave some, apostles; and some, prophets; and some, evangelists; and some, pastors and teachers; (Ephesians 4:11).

Repent, then, and turn to God, so that your sins may be wiped out, that times of refreshing may come from the Lord,

and that He may send the Christ, who has been appointed for you—even Jesus.

He must remain in heaven until the time comes for God to restore everything, as He promised long ago through His holy prophets (Acts 3:19-21 NIV).

Second, the Lord will literally return to this planet, but there will be an unprecedented outpouring of His Holy Spirit in the global Feast of Tabernacles that will precede His Coming.

This present chapter became the longest in this book. But then, futurism or dispensationalism, in my view, has become, at least in the United States, our greatest deterrent in this race of faith.

We have rounded the far turn to head down the home stretch. Behold the Finisher at the finish line! Before we reach the Goal of His full stature (see Eph. 4:13), we must hurdle two final impediments.

Men and women who make it this far in the race are usually shocked to come upon the sins of its third and final leg. But Third Day folks are no an exception. I have preached sonship (the message of maturity) and Kingdom since 1969. I have met these culprits head-on and still do. *Mysticism* and *Gnosticism* are enemies of the faith.

Endnotes

1. I have made seven lengthy (3-5 weeks at a time) ministry trips to the nation of South Africa since June 1998, and have preached to thousands of leaders. I have personally sown (at no cost to the brethren) thousands of my Destiny Image publications to the Church there.

2. Eschatology is the branch of theology known as the Doctrine of Last Things, emphasizing different views of end-time events and various interpretations of biblical prophecy. It is taken from the Greek word *eschatos* which means, "last, farthest, extreme, or final (of place or time)."

3. Kelley Varner. *Whose Right It Is* (Shippensburg, PA: Destiny Image Publishers, 1995).

4. Some Bible teachers affectionately refer to Scofield, Larkin, and Darby as the "three blind mice." What Darby began and Scofield plagiarized, Larkin sealed in print with his *Dispensational Truth* (1918) and its vast array of intricate charts (which now fill other textbooks and even spread themselves across the front of some local churches!).

5. The dispensationalists' "prophecy clock" has taken a licking, but keeps on ticking. Internationally known Bible teachers have set and reset the date for the "Rapture." For example, 1988 (40 years, a "generation" after Israel became a nation in 1948) has since been moved (1992, 1994, 2000) until 2007 (40 years since the Six Day War over Jerusalem). At the time of this writing, 2007 has arrived, so it will be interesting to hear the next latest prediction. With regard to time, the Bible doesn't emphasize "any moment" but rather "until" (Ps. 110:1; Acts 3:19-21; Eph. 4:13; Heb. 10:12-13; and James 5:7). Most importantly, Jesus Himself warned us about setting dates and seasons about such matters (Matt. 24:36,42,44; 25:13; Acts 1:7).

6. For more on this, you are encouraged to read the section of my book, *The Three Prejudices*, that deals with the Jew-Greek issue of Galatians 3:28. That volume contains a verse-by-verse exegesis of Romans 9-11.

7. Now we have a problem, because there is no other place in the Bible to find the seven years. You will find three-and-one-half years, 42 months, and "a time, and times, and half a time" (Rev. 12:14), but not seven years. Without that foundation, futurism's house of cards crumbles.

8. Jesus was born in 4 B.C. Add one year in moving from B.C. to A.D. The 69 weeks of years, or 483 years, takes us from Artaxerses' decree to Ezra in the autumn of 457 B.C. up to the autumn of A.D. 27, when Jesus was 30 years of age!

9. This critical section is where Darby, Scofield, and Larkin begin to insert their infamous "gap" of 2,000 years. Their "prince" of verse 26 is their self-fabricated future antichrist. A much-need exegesis from the Hebrew text is necessary to thoroughly and clearly show what this verse is really saying—I do that on pages 267-275 of *Whose Right It Is*.

CHAPTER TWELVE

Mysticism

The baton has been passed to a new generation. An anointed, overcoming people who will go down in history as the "anchor leg" of His dream team, now strain forward with everything that is in them, pressing toward the mark for the victor's prize.

This is the *kairos* moment (see Chapter Fourteen), the chosen season of the Lord, when His Kingdom will come and His will be done (see Matt. 6:10).

And saviours shall come up on mount Zion to judge the mount of Esau; and the kingdom shall be the LORD's (Obadiah 1:21).

For deliverers will come to Jerusalem and rule all Edom. And the Lord shall be King! (Obadiah 1:21 TLB).

These overcomers and deliverers foretold by Obadiah will run all the way up Zion's hill. They will hurdle every obstacle in their path. Early on, these saw the folly of cessasionism, Stoicism, and easy believism. During the middle and hardest part of the race, they conquered legalism, asceticism, dualism, elitism, tribalism, traditionalism, and even futurism (the previous chapter).

We have "kept the faith" but we have not yet "finished" or completed our course (2 Tim. 4:7). Two hurdles remain. These final obstacles are the deadly sins of the Most Holy Place and the fullness of the Feast of Tabernacles, the realm of maturity, wherein sitting enthroned with Christ are a Third Day people.

Because this "deep end" of the pool (the last leg of our race) is such unfamiliar territory to most folks, these two chapters will be much briefer that previous ones. Nonetheless, we must finally leap over mysticism and Gnosticism.

The first of these mixed-up and exotic teachings in the third dimension is a subtle mixture of "wild" Kingdom truth and metaphysics—spiritual *mysticism*.

What Is Mysticism?

Webster's says that *mysticism* is "any doctrine that asserts the possibility of attaining knowledge of spiritual truths through intuition acquired by fixed meditation." He adds that a mystic is "one who professes to undergo spiritual experiences by which he intuitively comprehends truths beyond human understanding."

Moreover, *metaphysics* is "that branch of philosophy that deals with fixed principles and seeks to explain the nature of being or reality; speculative philosophy; very subtle, abstract, vague, difficult, or perplexing thinking or reasoning."

In the Christian sense, spiritual mystics are men and women who push themselves forward as being very "deep" in God. Often steeped in metaphysics, these folks thrive on mental gymnastics.

Like the brainy Athenians, these spiritual gurus want to sit around and discuss the "deep things of God" all day and all night. Such ministers thrive on any thought or idea that sounds profound, whether scriptural or not. Their conversations are ever abstract and generalized. After one tries hard to listen to these folks talk and talk, a question arises, "What in the world was that all about? What was that person trying to say?"

Most of the so-called "revelation" set forth by spiritual mystics is extra-biblical, something that they insist was "shown" to them by the Lord. They "sensed" that He was speaking this "new truth" to them. God does speak to people (even in an audible voice), but mysticism often replaces real "revelation" knowledge with human speculation.

Mysticism is jacked-up humanism full of man-made ideas that are deliberately fantastic and far-fetched under the guise of so-called "revelation" knowledge.

Mystics love off-the-wall concepts and Bible studies that appear to be "deep." Doing in-depth studies about the spiritual zodiac (biblical astronomy, not astrology), pyramidology, and extremes of biblical typology and numerology all exemplify the kinds of enticing subject matter that lend themselves to this way of thinking.

Folks who are into spiritual mysticism are often very sweet "weird" people, and there are usually one or two in every group.

Now while Paul waited for them at Athens, his spirit was stirred in him, when he saw the city wholly given to idolatry.

Therefore disputed he in the synagogue with the Jews, and with the devout persons, and in the market daily with them that met with him.

Then certain philosophers of the Epicureans, and of the Stoicks, encountered him. And some said, What will this babbler say? other some, He seemeth to be a setter forth of strange gods: because he preached unto them Jesus, and the resurrection.

And they took him, and brought him unto Areopagus, saying, May we know what this new doctrine, whereof thou speakest, is?

For thou bringest certain strange things to our ears: we would know therefore what these things mean.

(For all the Athenians and strangers which were there spent their time in nothing else, but either to tell, or to hear some new thing.)

Then Paul stood in the midst of Mar's hill, and said, Ye men of Athens, I perceive that in all things ye are too superstitious.

For as I passed by, and beheld your devotions, I found an altar with this inscription, TO THE UNKNOWN GOD. Whom therefore ye ignorantly worship, Him declare I unto you (Acts 17:16-23).

The above passage is a tremendous illustration of spiritual mysticism. It is interesting that in all of Paul's travels and journeys, this ancient metropolis of Athens, the cultural center of the pre-Christian world, was the only city in which he did not (or could not) begin a local church. This college town and center of Greek art, architecture, literature, and politics was filled to the brim with mysticism and metaphysical thought, along with any and all kinds of Greek philosophy and polytheism, as well as other religions. After debating these mystics, Paul wrote to Timothy these words.

O Timothy, guard what has been entrusted to you, avoiding worldly and empty chatter and the opposing arguments of what is falsely called "knowledge" (1 Timothy 6:20 NASB).

Keep out of foolish arguments with those who boast of their "knowledge" and thus prove their lack of it (1 Timothy 6:20 TLB).

The characteristics of a spiritual mystic are fully exemplified by the Athenians in Acts 17:

- They were idolatrous (Acts 17:16).

- They were condescending, calling Paul a "babbler" (Acts 17:18).

- They were enamored with "strange" teachings (Acts 17:18).

- They were always looking for some "new doctrine" (Acts 17:19).

- They had itching (liked to be tickled) "ears" (Acts 17:20; 2 Tim. 4:3).

- They were always harping on the latest "new thing" (Acts 17:21).

- They were "superstitious" ("very religious," NIV)(Acts 17:22).

- They ignorantly worshiped the "unknown God" (Acts 17:23).

This next-to-the-last obstacle in our race of faith is a waste of time. The home stretch is not the place for us to stand around and talk about the Kingdom and the deep things of God. It is the place to "stretch" out and run (not walk) with all our might!

Mysticism Is at Work

But refuse profane and old wives' fables, and exercise thyself rather unto godliness (1 Timothy 4:7).

Don't waste time arguing over foolish ideas and silly myths and legends. Spend your time and energy in the exercise of keeping spiritually fit (1 Timothy 4:7 TLB).

There are spiritual "weirdoes" on every level. There were folks running around in the 16th century in the days of Martin Luther claiming to be Elijah the prophet. Just as in the natural, children can be weird, most adolescents are really strange, and many adults are basket cases. So it is in the three levels of this race of faith. We have looked at the sins that so easily beset our evangelical and Pentecostal friends. Third Day or Kingdom folks—those who believe in and preach another realm beyond Pentecost—are also plagued with their own shortcomings.

This chapter deals with the strange folks who are so caught up in the "deep (profound) things of God" (1 Cor. 2:10), and are so heavenly minded, that they are no earthly good.

But the Gospel of the Kingdom in all three dimensions—proclaiming Jesus to be Savior, Baptizer, and King—must be intensely practical. As I said in an earlier chapter, "If it doesn't work in the dirt, I don't want it." The truths of God's Word must be applicable in everyday life, walked out in shoe leather.

There are all kinds of crazy folks running all over this track. One would think that by this point in the contest all the extreme cases would have dropped out of the race or chased after some strange personality or idea off to the side of the road.

Mysticism and Gnosticism (the next chapter), historically, have been the cancers of the Kingdom-sonship realm. These excesses have kept us in the corner of the room, ineffective and alone. Many of the classical sonship ministries have died. Others have become isolated and irrelevant in their communities ("us four and no more"). Their reasoning: "We are so deep in God and have so much that others cannot understand what we know. After all, we are not just the elect. We are the 'very elect' (Matt. 24:24)."

How sad. Paul knew better.

And when I came to you, brethren, I did not come with superiority of speech or of wisdom, proclaiming to you the testimony of God.

For I determined to know nothing among you except Jesus Christ, and Him crucified.

And I was with you in weakness and in fear and in much trembling.

And my message and my preaching were not in persuasive words of wisdom, but in demonstration of the Spirit and of power,

so that your faith should not rest on the wisdom of men, but on the power of God (1 Corinthians 2:1-5 NASB).

This powerful Kingdom message is useless unless we can break it down so that a child can understand it. It is wearisome to see so many who claim to know so much *about* God, but who in reality do not *know* God. These have accrued stacks of study notes, but are woefully lacking in power.

Mysticism, the subtle mixture of Kingdom truth with metaphysics, is spiritual "exotic" food that has usurped the authority of a healthy, balanced, *real* Bible diet. It is what I call "wild" Kingdom.

Truth is often a tension between two extremes.

Let no man beguile you…vainly puffed up by his fleshly mind,

And not holding the Head… (Colossians 2:18-19).

As did the ancient Gnostics (Chapter Thirteen), this obstacle of mysticism here at the end has stopped "holding the Head"—folks who want to appear to be "deep" in the Word have stopped preaching Jesus. Interestingly, the word for *beguile* used here is about our race because it means, "to defraud of the prize of victory."

Fleshly minded folks like these are proud. They have long ago ceased to "hold fast" to the simplicity that is in Christ. As the Athenians made fun of Paul, cocky preachers talk "down" to the saints and the younger men and women. The air of pride that they exude carries the smell of death (see Matt. 5:13). In this they also exemplify elitism, a false sense of superiority over others (Chapter Eight). This smug attitude says, "We have the Word, the truth, and the anointing (more than any other group). Others will have to come through us and our awesome understanding. We are the vanguard ministry."

Just as some Second Day preachers are always looking for a new and different way to take up a bigger offering, these guys are ever looking for "what's hot and what's not," some "new doctrine." Their conferences and conventions often turn into "preaching contests," with the burning question being, "Can you top this?" It sounds like Mar's hill all over again, and a crowd who slobber all over themselves to hear some "new thing" (Acts 17:21).

Getting involved with metaphysics can be dangerous. Real revelatory and prophetic preaching too quickly gives way to humanistic speculation. Sound Bible exegesis goes out the window in exchange for something that sounds really "heavy." That kind of preaching is cute, but it has no life in it. Those speculative notions came right off the tree of the knowledge of good and evil, not the tree of life (see Gen. 2:9).

Empty and insecure, some mystics retreat into their own little world between their ears. Often quiet and contemplative, many of these folks have become spiritual hermits who avoid the local church and the rest of the Body. Their only real relationships are with their books and tapes. Superstitious and very religious, many mystic Christians don't really "know" the Lord (Acts 17:23).

The saddest thing about mysticism is that these men and women have so much to offer. Rich in their knowledge of the Scriptures, they could be such a blessing to others. But they have chosen rather to stay safely cloistered away in their own meditation or the security of their very small little circles of fellowship.

Mysticism is not just a hurdle to leap over. It has become a hole in the road, a dangerous pit that has swallowed up more than one good man or woman.

Apostle Paul knew about these spiritual pitfalls. Listen to these timeless words given by a wise "father" ministry to Timothy and Titus, his sons in the Gospel. This sound advice will help us finish the race.

Keep reminding them of these things. Warn them before God against quarreling about words; it is of no value, and only ruins those who listen.

Do your best to present yourself to God as one approved, a workman who does not need to be ashamed and who correctly handles the word of truth.

Avoid godless chatter, because those who indulge in it will become more and more ungodly.

Their teaching will spread like gangrene. Among them are Hymenaeus and Philetus,

who have wandered away from the truth. They say that the resurrection has already taken place, and they destroy the faith of some.

Nevertheless, God's solid foundation stands firm, sealed with this inscription: "The Lord knows those who are His," and, "Everyone who confesses the name of the Lord must turn away from wickedness" (2 Timothy 2:14-19 NIV).

This testimony is true. Therefore, rebuke them sharply, so that they will be sound in the faith

and will pay no attention to Jewish myths or to the commands of those who reject the truth (Titus 1:13-14 NIV).

But avoid foolish controversies and genealogies and arguments and quarrels about the law, because these are unprofitable and useless (Titus 3:9 NIV).

Mysticism Aborts the Seed

The tragedy of this besetting sin in the Third Day is that men and women in this realm are familiar with the Word and plan of God—we understand and preach Jesus as King, the Goal of the race.

Our destiny is in the Seed, and the Seed is Christ. Mysticism is a higher form of humanism, worshiping the creation rather than the Creator. This top-heavy theology has become a mere message that eventually takes the place of the living Christ from within. Usurping His authority, it is actually an "antichrist," something other than the anointing. We need to be full of the Holy Ghost, not just words. The Kingdom of God is not in word (*logos*), but in power (*dunamis*), the ability of the Spirit (see 1 Cor. 4:20).

The real hazard in our path that mysticism produces is the proud spirit and attitude of hypocrisy. At this stage of the journey, experienced preachers and teachers have the "message" down pat. We have memorized much of the Bible (even entire chapters). The problem is that we have the right theology and the right semantic or terminology, but not the right spirit. We are speaking the truth, but not in love, in the name and nature of the Lord Jesus (see Eph. 4:15).

It is essential that we always hold fast to the Head (see Col. 2:19). We must preach Jesus as Savior in the first part of the race, then acknowledge Him as Baptizer on the back stretch, and, especially after we come around the far turn and head for home, proclaim Him as King and Lord, the Head of the Church! Are you a "Jesus" preacher?

One of the greatest men I have ever met in this third dimension of the Kingdom was a humble, literary prophet by the name of Bill Britton. "Brother Bill," as he was affectionately known by thousands of people here in the United States and around the world, pioneered the message of biblical sonship in the 1950s and 1960s through his anointed writing ministry, called "The Church in Action."

On every piece of literature that Bill sent out to his mailing list, and on every sheet of letterhead were these unmistakable words: "Jesus is wonderful!" To Bill, Jesus was the "Pattern Son." That says it all about this problem, and that says it all about Brother Bill. Although some took hold of his writings, and, with a wrong spirit, misrepresented the man and his message, this great prophet remained faithful to the Scriptures until his untimely death in 1985.

Bill knew what we all must learn. Mysticism will never be able to abort the Seed of the Kingdom and the word of our destiny as long as we preach Jesus. I often say it this way, "Kelley Varner does not preach a message; he proclaims a Person!"

My Personal Race of Faith

I have been a born-again Christian for 40 years. I have been a Spirit-filled believer for almost that long, and have been around the Church world the better part of my life. My conclusion? People are crazy!

I haven't seen or heard it all, just most of it.

In 1970, I began to read (and memorize) Bill Britton's books and to hear the message of biblical sonship. I often say, "Bill Britton taught me how to write, and G.C. McCurry (another one of my early mentors) showed me how to preach." From 1970 until 1985, a sovereign God let me taste almost every spiritual stream that one could think of, including the exotic waters of some mystical preachers. The keenest minds on this planet are mystical in nature. I have had long conversations with some of the smartest men and women in the world. I wanted to know what they knew about God and the Bible, and over these many years, the Lord has helped me remember most of what they told me.

I have thousands of books in my personal library. There are books all over our house—in my office, in two large bookcases in our bedroom, in the living room, and all over our 40'-long den—not to mention the hundreds of my books that are shelved at the church. There is a special section of my library where I have collected some of the now out-of-print exotic stuff (good and bad). I haven't read some of those writings in years. I am too busy writing practical books like this one.

I can remember sitting with Kingdom and sonship preachers around tables for hours, with an open Bible and an open spirit, ready to learn. Along the way, I have heard some "strange" teachings and met some "strange" and (thank God) wonderful people.

I don't want to bore you with "strange" stories of my own encounters with spiritual mystics. One preacher was convinced that he and I were the "two witnesses" of Revelation 11. Another studied biblical numerology using the numbers out of the Strong's Concordance as being significant. One sincere brother taught that clapping the hands or any other kind of passion shown in praise was "sensual" (he felt that he was "beyond" such childish behavior). Others told me that their operation of ministry was beyond the fivefold ministries of Ephesians 4:11 and the writings of apostle Paul (who wrote half of the New Testament). I've been around some far-out folks who claimed themselves to be totally spirit, and that anything done in the flesh was not important (you can imagine the kind the pit they landed in preaching that stuff)—I didn't stay around for lunch on that one.

That's enough nonsense. I thankfully cannot remember a lot of the weird folks with weird ideas. I walked away from exotic sonship and "wild" Kingdom a long, long time ago.

I do not offer the following thoughts to be cute or to strut my grasp of spiritual things. I simply want you to know that there are excesses in all three Feasts. It would be tragic for any of us to come all the way around the track and trip up just before we finish.

I warn everyone who hears the words of the prophecy of this book:
If anyone adds anything to them, God will add to him the plagues
described in this book.

And if anyone takes words away from this book of prophecy, God will take away from him his share in the tree of life and in the holy city, which are described in this book (Revelation 22:18-19 NIV).

I have heard men sit and proudly declare, "I am Jesus. I am Christ." Most of them have already died, so I know that they were not Jesus. We do understand that the "Christ" of the New Testament is both Head (Jesus) and Body (the Corporate Man). He that overcomes—one new Man—is more than an individual (this is the message of my book, *Corporate Anointing*). But mysticism's weakness is to carry a truth beyond the anointing, or beyond what is "written" in the Scriptures (in someone's silly effort to sound "deep" in front of others). For example, we are partakers of the "Divine Nature" (2 Pet. 1:4), but not "Deity." We are called to be *like* Him, but we will never *be* Him (Col, 1:19; 2:19).

Although I have read, and studied, and taught some of the exotic subjects like the zodiac (biblical astronomy, not astrology) and even pyramidology, I don't "harp" on these things, and have, for the most part, stayed away from this kind of teaching for many years. It's not practical, and becomes a head trip that puffs folks up with information that others have never heard.

Knowledge is power. Preachers use knowledge like some athletes use steroids, which are artificial and temporary performance-enhancing drugs. First the natural and then the spiritual—steroids give instant performance, but will eventually destroy one's reproductive organs.

On a positive note, I don't know if we were part of an "Elohim" family who helped to create the worlds or not. I'm not sure if one day each mature son will go and deliver his own planet and then rule it. Have you ever considered that our insides go as deep within as the expanse of the universe goes in the other direction? I have "picked" the heads of the keenest minds in the world over the last 40 years, and nobody can give me a satisfactory answer as to the origin of satan or demons.

Was there a pre-Adamite world? Is Lucifer a fallen angel, or was Adam the "anointed cherub" (see Ezek. 28:14) that covered the earth? Is Heaven or hell a real place? If so, where is it?

Do you see what I mean?

Are any or all of these topics or questions important? It depends on the person to whom you are speaking at the time.

When I first began to preach sonship and learned about the Manchild Company of Revelation 12:1-5 and the Firstfruits Company of Revelation 14:1-4 (both concepts are covered in Chapter Four of my book, *Moses, the Master, and the Manchild*), I emphasized the classical posture that these men and women were an elite company. My message is the same, but my emphasis has changed. There *is* a high calling and a Joseph ministry who is sent ahead of his brothers to preserve life in the earth, but now I place an even greater emphasis upon the Person and Work of King Jesus, and what it means to be conformed to His image.

Once we get past mysticism, we fast approach the last hurdle. The time has come to finish our course. Jesus, the finish line of our faith, awaits with open arms.

Let us press. It's time for our final "kick" and sprint to the end of our race and the end of our faith.

CHAPTER THIRTEEN

Gnosticism

Our gospel quartet used to sing, "We've come this far by faith, leaning on the Lord."

Where have the years gone? Forty years ago, on May 12, 1966, I began to run this race of faith. Joann and I were married on July 22, 1972. Our "baby" (David, our youngest) will be 20 years of age on his next birthday. We have ministered at Praise Tabernacle in Richlands, North Carolina, for almost 30 years. My Dad is in Heaven, my Mom was 81 on her last birthday, and I will be 60 in two more years.

"Just between us, Lord, this has been quite a journey."

Just between us, my friend, you and I have come a long way since the Preface and the Introduction of this book.

The Lord willing and by His grace, we have leaped over and overcome 11 of the 12 obstacles in our path.

There remains one more test—we must hurdle the sinful pride of *Gnosticism*.

What Is Gnosticism?

It is fitting, then, that Gnosticism is the last trial that stands in our way to the finish line, for Gnosticism is the *worship of knowledge.*

Some folks just have to be in the "know." But Eve reached for knowledge, and the heavens closed.

Webster's says that *Gnosticism* is "a system of mythical religious and philosophical doctrines combining Christianity with Greek and Oriental philosophies, propagated by early Christian sects that were denounced as heretical. A *Gnostic* was a "knowing or wise one."

The Gnostics believed that *knowledge* was the way to salvation.

Gnosticism is transliterated from the Greek word *gnosis*, which means, "knowing (the act), knowledge; a seeking to know, an enquiry, investigation."

The fear of the LORD is the beginning of knowledge… (Proverbs 1:7).

The Hebrew word for "knowledge" is used 44 times in the Book of Proverbs.

O Timothy, keep that which is committed to thy trust, avoiding profane and vain babblings, and oppositions of science falsely so called: (1 Timothy 6:20).

…Turn away from godless chatter and the opposing ideas of what is falsely called knowledge, (1 Timothy 6:20 NIV).

Here Paul warned his son Timothy against the Gnostics, against the "knowledge." Spiritual (not philosophical) Gnosticism is the twelfth and final obstacle in this race of faith.

Gnosticism Is at Work

These are momentous days. More genuine "revelation" knowledge has been poured upon the 21st century Church than any other group of people throughout the generations.

Peter therefore went forth, and that other disciple, and came to the sepulchre.

So they ran both together: and the other disciple did outrun Peter, and came first to the sepulchre.

And he stooping down, and looking in, saw the linen clothes lying; yet went he not in.

Then cometh Simon Peter following him, and went into the sepulchre, and seeth the linen clothes lie,

And the napkin, that was about His head, not lying with the linen clothes, but wrapped together in a place by itself.

Then went in also that other disciple, which came first to the sepulchre, and he saw, and believed (John 20:3-8).

The Kingdom and sonship crowd of the 1970s and 1980s gave way to a new crowd of Second Day folks in the 1990s and into the 21st century who are hearing a new thing in this New Day. In those earlier times, the Third Day people, like John, outran everybody to the empty tomb. We looked in and saw the message of life, but did not mix the Word with faith. We did not enter in. Our other brethren have begun to "catch up" with us in understanding the ways of the Kingdom. May we enter in together!

But thou, O Daniel, shut up the words, and seal the book, even to the time of the end: many shall run to and fro, and knowledge shall be increased (Daniel 12:4).

Knowledge is power. Exponentially, both naturally and spiritually, knowledge has "increased" or "become great, multiplied." Every tribe and group (see Chapter Nine) has its own unique, particular strength.

I pray that the temptation and historic, besetting sin of classical sonship—to worship knowledge—will not hinder all these new brothers and sisters who are just now hearing that there is so much *more*. Arise, and shine (see Isa. 60:1).

I pray that evangelicals will not be proud of their numbers.

I pray that Pentecostals and Charismatics will not be enamored by their spiritual giftings.

I pray that the Faith Movement will not be proud of its faith.

I pray that all of us who have moved within the rent veil into the Third Day and the Feast of Tabernacles will not be proud of what we know, but will forever boast in Whom we know!

We say that we know what others do not know (and that is true in some cases), but what are we *doing* with that knowledge? May God give all of us, every tribe and people, the wisdom that is applicable to the knowledge we have already received.

Wisdom will prove to be the right application of knowledge.

Gnosticism Aborts the Seed

We have learned so many things about the Lord. We now know a lot about His acts, His ways, and His Person (see Ps. 103:7). But as my long-time friend and prophetess Dr. Clarice Fluitt says, "The knowledge of a thing is not the possession of it." Knowledge is not appropriation.

For all that is in the world, the lust of the flesh, and the lust of the eyes, and the pride of life, is not of the Father, but is of the world (1 John 2:16).

Gnosticism is spiritual pride that comes through one's preoccupation with what he or she knows (or thinks he or she knows). The worship of knowledge for knowledge's sake is worldly.

For it is God who works in you to will and to act according to His good purpose (Philippians 2:13 NIV).

For God is at work within you, helping you want to obey Him, and then helping you do what He wants (Philippians 2:13 TLB).

Spiritual Gnosticism, in any era and on any level, kills and aborts the divine Seed of destiny because human pride reveals the absence of God's wisdom and strength. It is God who is at work in us! The paradox and seeming contraction is that the more one matures into full sonship, the more child-like and dependent each must become (like a helpless child).

The Third Day from Jesus (see Hos. 6:1-3) is the Seventh Day from Adam (see Jude 1:14), and is the Day of the Lord, a time of day and night at the *same time* in the earth (see Isa. 60:1-2; Joel 2:1-2; Mal. 4:1-2). We are about to enter into the full experience of His

Sabbath rest (see Heb. 3-4). The hardest thing to do, as we "labor to enter in," will be to do nothing.

In the *Olah*, the Burnt Offering of the Old Testament (see Lev. 1), God got it *all*. We must put Him first in all things (see Matt. 6:33).

This final "weight" (encumbrance) of Gnosticism that so easily besets us (Heb. 12:1) must be laid aside. We must "keep it real" in our lives, our homes, our schools, our businesses, and our local churches. The Goal of our race is just ahead. We individually have been apprehended to become like Jesus; corporately, we have been called into "the unity of the faith" (Eph. 4:13).

The highest form of intercession and worship is *personification*. The Church of Jesus Christ is the *ongoing incarnation* of God in the earth.

Our adversary has placed this last obstacle in our way for one reason—he knows at this point in the race that we *will* finish (we have come too far), but he is shaking in his boots at the thought of any of us finishing *strong*.

...Knowledge makes arrogant... (1 Corinthians 8:1 NASB).

...being a "know-it-all" makes us feel important... (1 Corinthians 8:1 TLB).

...Yet mere knowledge causes people to be puffed up—to bear themselves loftily and be proud... (1 Corinthians 8:1 AMP).

...We never really know enough until we recognize that God alone knows it all (1 Corinthians 8:1 TM).

Gnosticism, an ordinate obsession with knowledge, breeds overconfidence and conceit. This final obstacle in our course must be laid aside if we are to finish strong. We will never be like Jesus if we are arrogant in the face of God. Our unity, our being one as the Father and Jesus are one (John 17:20-23), cannot be realized so long as we condescendingly "talk down" to our brothers and sisters who may not know (yet) what we know.

The fear of the LORD is to hate evil: pride, and arrogancy, and the evil way... (Proverbs 8:13).

Pride goeth before destruction, and an haughty spirit before a fall (Proverbs 16:18).

Gnosticism, the worshiping of knowledge, is presumption and pride. The wisdom of Solomon warns us throughout Proverbs about this final hurdle, the twelfth obstacle in our race of faith.

Don't be proud of what you know. Worship God.

My Personal Race of Faith

We are fools for Christ's sake... (1 Corinthians 4:10).

But we have this treasure in earthen vessels, that the excellency of the power may be of God, and not of us (2 Corinthians 4:7).

Our course is almost finished. You and I have run together for quite a distance. I trust that the bits and pieces of my own personal race of faith has blessed and encouraged you.

I submitted this section in Chapters Two through Thirteen to my wife Joann for approval. There was much more to be said, and much more to leave out. Now you have many reasons to put me on your prayer list.

My motive in having been open and vulnerable, exposing my weaknesses as well as my strengths, is to encourage others. The same God who helped me climb over these obstacles will take you by the hand and do the same. In being honest with you, I remember from many years ago a specific moment in my life that turned many things. One afternoon in my office at the church while studying and meditating the Word, the Lord asked,

"Son, why are you so proud?"

"What do you mean, Lord?" (I was still far too religious.)

"Why do you still push yourself forward to maintain your reputation as a great Bible teacher? Why do you continue to uphold your own image? When are you going to come out from behind those chapters and verses and let folks really see you?"

Jesus smote my heart (again) that day to help me see the residual insecurity and compensating pride that were hindering me from being a real person. In those days, when anyone got too close for comfort (my fear that they wouldn't like me), I blew them out the door with my knowledge of the Scriptures (in a good sense).

I am grateful for what I have learned in God. I have become a decent teacher because I have been a great student. It is wise to be able to learn from anyone about anything on any level.

However, let me make it clear that what you and I and everyone else knows (or think that we know) about God could collectively be pushed over to one side of a very small peanut shell. It will take ages piled on top of ages for us to begin to fathom and explore the splendor and the magnificence of Jesus' wondrous Person!

Nonetheless, as I look back over my journey up till now, I thank God for what I know about His Word. I am grateful for the mind and heart He has given me, the ability to memorize these truths, to retain them, and to effectively communicate them to others.

At Free Gospel Bible Institute, over 30 years ago, I met a remarkable Englishman by the name of Albert C. Wilson. He taught me about the gifts of the Holy Spirit and let me preach my first sermon that freshman year in his church at Akron, Ohio. When he wasn't spending hours a day in prayer, Brother Wilson was telling me and others stories about the move of God during the healing revivals of the 1940s and 1950s. In the providence of God, he later served as an elder here at Praise Tabernacle, and I had the honor of helping to officiate at his spiritual "home-going" service (I was told by some that on his deathbed he was conversing with Moses—I believe it).

Early on (1969), at Free Gospel and then during my seven-year tenure at Zion, the Lord taught me many things. As mentioned previously, I studied and taught 44 of the 66 books of the Bible (much of it verse-by-verse), as well as Theology, Greek, English, and many Bible-related subjects. Using the Tabernacle of Moses as a framework, let me illustrate.

At the Brazen Altar, I learned about justification by faith through His blood, and about divine healing.

At the Brazen Laver, I understood the washing of regeneration, water baptism in the name of the Lord Jesus Christ for the remission of sin and the circumcision of the heart, and the Doctrine of Sanctification—once and for all by the blood, and progressively by the water.

At the Golden Lampstand, He showed me the light of His Word, the Holy Ghost Baptism, the Fruit and the Gifts of the Spirit, and about the Man whose name is the Branch (the "seven spirits of God" (mentioned in Rev. 1:4; 3:1; 4:5; 5:6 and enumerated in Isa. 11:1-2).

At the Table of Shewbread came the revelation of real covenant and fellowship, the Lord's Supper, and the fivefold ministry (Eph. 4:11), the border of the Table being a "handbreadth" (Exod. 37:12).

At the Golden Altar of Incense, I learned about Spirit-filled and Spirit-led prayer, and praise, and the pattern of worship as revealed in the restored Tabernacle of David.

Through the rent veil, I was shown the present-day reality of the Most Holy Place, and the message of life and immortality.

At the Mercy-seat, I was given the understanding of His "more excellent ministry" after the king-priest order of Melchisedec (Heb. 5:1-8:6).

At the Ark of the Covenant, I beheld Jesus as our right-now (not soon-coming) King and Lord, the Pattern Son, the consummate Overcomer, and the Head of the Church.

I omitted a lot in this brief sketch. There are so many wonderful truths to know and to learn about the King and His Kingdom!

My race has crossed the paths of great men and women. In my early days with C.S. Fowler and G.C. McCurry, I was introduced to Jack Harris (a tall Texan and former Marine who stood and quoted chapter after chapter of the Bible), Bill Smith, the late J.L. Dutton (who co-authored with me the book, *The Tongue of the Learned*), Alta Smith, Lillie Matthews, J. Preston Eby, and many other classical son-ship preachers and teachers who influenced my life and ministry.

In the late 1970s and the early 1980s I ran up on Bennie Skinner (who taught me the present reality of the Most Holy Place) and Wayne "Doc" Agan (who imparted to me the message of life and immortality, that an end-time people would put their feet on death).

So many others who have run this race before me have enriched and favored my life. To one and all, thank you.

I want to tell one story in particular that was a key to my growing understanding of spiritual things. It happened in the early 1970s while I was teaching the Bible at Zion.

My brother-in-law, Frank Stanley, a wonderful man of God and Pentecostal pastor, sent me a cassette tape that he had received from Bible Temple in Portland, Oregon. On its front was glorious praise and worship (and sometimes prophetic utterances). On the back side was a rich teaching from the Scriptures.

Curious and hungry, I contacted (then) Pastor Dick Iverson and told him who I was and what I was doing. Soon after, I received in the mail a shoebox full of tapes.

Little did I realize upon receipt of this most gracious gift what treasure I held in my hands—dozens of "used" tapes.

I knew none of these people. Dick Iverson, Kevin Conner, Dick Benjamin, Leonard Fox, Violet Kitely, Reg Lazelle, David Schoch, Emmanuel Cannistraci, and many others—who were these people? These speakers were some the greatest voices that came out of the Latter Rain Revival of 1948 (I would later meet Ione Glasier, Charlotte Baker, George Evans, Fuchsia Pickett, Jim Watt, and others).

I memorized that shoebox full of tapes, and my life was changed for all time. Most importantly, those messages birthed into my spirit the understanding and vital importance of the *local church principle*.

That shoebox full of tapes kept my feet on the ground as I walked up to and jumped over the mystical excesses of sonship (see Chapter Twelve) during the 1970s and early 1980s, and down through the years. Thank you, Pastor Iverson.

Justification was "present truth" to Martin Luther and the Reformers (2 Pet. 1:12). Pentecost was "present truth" to Charles Parham and William Seymour at Azusa Street. Principles dealing with the Apostolic Reformation are "present truth" right now.

What would Luther think of Parham and Seymour? What would they think of us?

What will "present truth" be ten years from now? One hundred years from now? One thousand years from now?

We must remain open, ever teachable. School "ain't out" yet!

The following is the last point of our ministry's "statement of faith" (what we believe, found at www.KelleyVarner.org):

"We believe that there are some things that the Lord has yet to reveal to His Church. We have but crossed the threshold of the Most Holy Place. This is uncharted territory: we have not passed this way heretofore. Apostles and prophets will eventually make these things known to the Church in the seasons of the Lord. We remain open to be taught, corrected or adjusted in our vision (Josh. 3:1-5; Isa. 55:9; 1 Cor. 2:9-16; Eph. 3:1-5,16-21). To that end, we declare it more important in *whom* we believe than in *what* we believe!"

To effectively reach this generation, there must be a marriage between the Word and the Spirit. We must boldly proclaim a Third Day message of "present truth" (2 Pet. 1:12) while we operate our ministries in the passionate, supernatural orthodoxy of genuine Pentecostal prayer, praise, and power (real miracles)!

A final word...

I love the Scriptures. I am thankful for what I know. But that is not my priority. Of all the characters in the Bible, I feel a special kinship to Paul, the literary apostle. I will let him say it for me.

But what things were gain to me, those I counted loss for Christ.

Yea doubtless, and I count all things but loss for the excellency of the knowledge of Christ Jesus my Lord: for whom I have suffered the loss of all things, and do count them but dung, that I may win Christ,

And be found in Him, not having mine own righteousness, which is of the law, but that which is through the faith of Christ, the right-eousness which is of God by faith:

*That I may **know Him**...* (Philippians 3:7-10, emphasis added).

Now what do we do? Having hurdled Gnosticism, nothing stands between us and our Goal, our Finisher!

We look to Him and then, for the sake of all those who ran before us, and for all those in the amphitheater—we finish strong!

It's time to press!

CHAPTER FOURTEEN

It Is Time To Press!

From the tribe of Issachar there were 200 leaders of the tribe with their relatives—all men who understood the temper of the times and knew the best course for Israel to take (1 Chronicles 12:32 TLB).

You will arise and have mercy and loving-kindness for Zion, for it is time to have pity and compassion for her, yes, the set time is come—the moment designated (Psalms 102:13 AMP).

…The night is about over, dawn is about to break. Be up and awake to what God is doing! God is putting the finishing touches on the salvation work He began when we first believed… (Romans 13:11 TM).

The goodness of the Lord brought us to the starting-line at the beginning of our race of faith, when we first believed. From day one, we have had an "expected end," a hope and a future, ever confident that the Forerunner Himself would "perfect" (complete) all that concerns us, and assured us that He who began working in and through us at that point would certainly "perform" (fulfill, execute) His eternal purposes—His desire, will, and plan, and our predetermined destiny (Jer. 29:11 with Ps. 138:8; Phil. 1:6).

Twelve Hurdles

For whatever is born of God overcomes the world; and this is the victory that has overcome the world—our faith (1 John 5:4 NASB).

He who overcomes will inherit all this, and I will be his God and he will be My son (Revelation 21:7 NIV).

The word for "son" in this latter verse is *huios*, the mature son. To "overcome" is to subdue, to prevail, to carry off the victory, or to win the case in a court of law.

God's "army" and "glorious Church" (Eph. 5:27), His Bride with combat boots, has learned how to face and overcome many obstacles along the way. In Jesus' name, we have leaped over these negative influences that are aimed to compromise, contaminate, and pollute the Seed of our destiny. These twelve deadly sins or hurdles are impediments, deterrents, problems, difficulties, and complications in the middle of the road that want to hinder and block our progress.

We have discovered three parts of this course, three levels of our Christian maturity.[1] Each dimension has its own challenges.

Evangelicals, those who are born again and baptized in water, must at the outset of the contest face and conquer its first three obstacles: cessasionism, Stoicism, and easy believism (Chapters Two through Four).

Those in the Spirit-filled dimension—including classical Pentecostals, Charismatics, and the Faith Movement—must tackle the most arduous and critical part of the course that has been strewn with the possible snags of legalism, asceticism, dualism, elitism, tribalism, traditionalism and futurism, also known as dispensationalism (Chapters Five through Eleven).

The Kingdom and sonship camps, those who believe and proclaim the third dimension of maturity, the Third Day of God—the home stretch of the track—must hurdle past mysticism and Gnosticism (Chapters Twelve and Thirteen).

And Joshua said, Hereby ye shall know that the living God is among you, and that He will without fail drive out from before you [dispossess, disinherit] *the Canaanites, and the Hittites, and the Hivites, and the Perizzites, and the Girgashites, and the Amorites, and the Jebusites* (Joshua 3:10).

The word for "without fail drive out" in this verse means, "to occupy by driving out previous tenants, and possessing in their place." Jesus commanded, "…Occupy till I come" (Luke 19:13).

We must never step back or step aside to make a deal with any of these heathen ideas. These twelve "isms," like the "seven nations," the "ites" that confronted Moses and Joshua, are not to be bargained with (see Deut. 7:1; 31:19-22). We must not intermingle ourselves with these "strange gods" (Josh. 24:20). Those who run with God must never give in or give up to compromise or negotiation. Idolatry knows no middle ground. As stated in the Preface, we must disinherit these enemies or they will disinherit us!

You've all been to the stadium and seen the athletes race. Everyone runs; one wins. Run to win… (1 Corinthians 9:24 TM).

I press toward the mark for the prize of the high calling of God in Christ Jesus (Philippians 3:14).

Remember, our destiny is in the Seed (see Chapter One)! Our future, our lot, our providence, and our objective is to win the prize of the "high calling"—to be conformed to the image of Christ! The Finisher of our faith (see Heb. 12:2) is our vocation, our destination, our target, and our objective—He is our Goal and the End of this race.

It's time to press, to really stretch out!

The Distant Goal

Not that I have now attained [this ideal] or am already made perfect, but I press on to lay hold of (grasp) and make my own, that for which Christ Jesus, the Messiah, has laid hold of me and made me His own.

I do not consider, brethren, that I have captured and made it my own [yet]; but one thing I do [it is my one aspiration]: forgetting what lies behind and straining forward to what lies ahead,

I press on toward the goal to win the [supreme and heavenly] prize to which God in Christ Jesus is calling us upward (Philippians 3:12-14 AMP).

Brethren, I count not myself to have apprehended: but this one thing I do, forgetting [to lose out of mind] *those things which are behind, and reaching forth* [to stretch oneself toward or forward upon] *unto those things which are before,*

I press toward the mark for the prize of the high calling of God in Christ Jesus (Philippians 3:13-14).

Paul here in this key text notes "one thing" and then mentions two things: the past, "those things which are behind" (Chapter Ten), and the future, "those things which are before" (Chapter Eleven).

Therefore shall a man leave his father and his mother, and shall cleave unto his wife: and they shall be one flesh (Genesis 2:24).

We will never "cleave" (cling, stick to, stay close) to God's will until we "leave" (leave behind, depart from, relinquish) all that lay behind us. Likewise, a man or a woman will never "press" on until he or she runs away from the past and darts toward his or her destiny.

The Greek word for "press" in Philippians 3:14 is *dioko*, and it means, "pursue, run swiftly after, press on in a race to reach the goal."

The word "mark" is *skopos* and means, "the distant goal." Another Greek word for "mark" is *charagma*, and can be transliterated to the English, "character." Chapter Two emphasizes that the Goal in this race of faith is the very character (nature) of Christ. The common objective of our one (high) "calling" (Eph. 4:4) is to be like Jesus![2]

The "prize" in Paul's day was "an award of arbitration, but specially a prize to the victor in the public games;" this word is used only here and in the following verse:

In a race everyone runs, but only one person gets first prize. So run your race to win (1 Corinthians 9:24 TLB).

Only "one"—the overcomer—receives the first prize. John calls these winners the "firstfruits unto God and to the Lamb" (Rev. 14:4).

It's Time To Press![3]

Do you see what this means—all these pioneers who blazed the way, all these veterans cheering us on? It means we'd better get on with it. Strip down, start running—and never quit! No extra spiritual fat, no parasitic sins.

Keep your eyes on Jesus, who both began and finished this race we're in (Hebrews 12:1-2 TM).

Since we have such a huge crowd of men of faith watching us from the grandstands, let us strip off anything that slows us down or holds us back, and especially those sins that wrap themselves so tightly around our feet and trip us up... (Hebrews 12:1 TLB).

...the sin which so easily entangles us... (Hebrews 12:1 NASB).

...the sin which clings so closely... (Hebrews 12:1 RSV).

The twelve obstacles in the race of faith mentioned and discussed in Chapters Two through Thirteen constitute the "sin which doth so easily beset us" (KJV).

The Greek word for "sin" is *hamartia*, and it means, "to miss the mark; wander from the path; to err; to go wrong." The verb is *hamartano* (to miss the mark, and so not share in the prize). It is taken from *a* (the negative particle), and from *meros* (part, allotment, share, lot, destiny). Sin affects our "destiny," our inheritance.

To "sin" is to miss the mark, to come short of the Goal because one *will not "press"*! It is not enough to "walk" in faith and love (2 Cor. 5:7; 2 John 1:6)—we must "run"! To sin is not to press.

Similarly, the Hebrew word for "sin" is *khaw-taw'*, and it means, "to miss, and thus to *forfeit*." Men and women forfeit the race because they refuse to press!

But I keep under my body, and bring it into subjection: lest that by any means, when I have preached to others, I myself should be a castaway (1 Corinthians 9:27).

Paul's greatest fear was not the devil, nor demons, nor the faces of men and women. The apostle dreaded becoming a "castaway." This word is *adokimos*, and it means, "not standing the test; unapproved (used of metals or coins), rejected, worthless; unacceptable." It is also translated as "disqualified" (NAS, NKJ, RSV). The New International Version renders this as, "disqualified for the prize." The Living Bible adds, "Otherwise I fear that after enlisting others for the race, I myself might be declared unfit and ordered to stand aside."

Those who refuse to press will be *disqualified*. Many are defeated before they begin!

Across the nations, millions of saints are walking with God, but they have begged to be excused from making any real effort to run with God.

The heart that has no desire to run sounds like this:

"Don't bother me...."

"I'm too tired...."

"Not today; I'm busy. Maybe tomorrow...."

Procrastinators despise any kind of inconvenience that may interfere with their personal agenda. Exhaustion from lesser pursuits—"the cares (distractions) of this life" (Luke 21:34)—has weighed them down. The effort, the training, and the discipline required to run and to finish this race are not their major consider-ations or priorities. The added responsibility of securing the team victory by running the "anchor leg," the most decisive time to stretch and strain forward (discussed below), is out of the question.

Nominal, "lukewarm" Christians (Rev. 3:16) are like the Levites in the Old Testament—to them, serving God is but a *job*, a religious duty and obligation. These people clock in and clock out on *chronos* time (actual time) every Sunday morning and *maybe* on Wednesday night.

How unlike Aaron's order of priesthood. He and his four sons—Nadab, Abihu, Elezazar, and Ithamar—operated on *kairos* time, the seasons of the Lord! While everybody else was asleep, someone had to be at the Tabernacle, wide awake and watching for the moving of the glory cloud, which could happen at any time, day or night (see Num. 9:15-23).

The *kairos* moments of God are always inconvenient. He does not operate in the lower realm of *chronos* time, and really doesn't care about our schedules. The King of glory carries no Day-timer or PDA. His seasons—those special, critical moments during the race when the contender must really run—always show up as a "sud-denly"!

> *Behold, I will send My messenger* [Messiah], *and he shall prepare the way before Me: and the Lord, whom ye seek, shall* **suddenly** *come to His temple, even the messenger of the covenant, whom ye delight in: behold, he shall come, saith the LORD of hosts* (Malachi 3:1, emphasis added).

> *And the LORD spake* **suddenly** *unto Moses, and unto Aaron, and unto Miriam…* (Numbers 12:4, emphasis added).

The Hebrew word for *suddenly* means, "instantly, surprisingly, or straightway; in the wink of an eye; in a moment," and is used 25 times in the Old Testament, mostly in the poetic and prophetic books to describe the judgments of God that come "suddenly."[4]

*And when the day of Pentecost was fully come, they were all with one accord in one place. And **suddenly** there came a sound from heaven as of a rushing mighty wind, and it filled all the house where they were sitting* (Acts 2:1-2, emphasis added).

Three different Greek words are translated as "suddenly" in the English Bible:

Exapina means, "unexpectedly (out of the non-apparent)" (Mark 9:8; compare Mark 13:36; Luke 2:13; 9:39; Acts 9:3; 22:6).

Aphno means, "unawares" (Acts 2:2; 16:26; 28:6).

Tacheos means, "briefly, (in time) speedily, or in manner) rapidly; quickly, hastily, shortly" (1 Tim. 5:22). It is derived from *tachus* (fleet; prompt, ready; quick, speedy).

The "suddenly" of God is that key juncture of our race of faith when we must kick in with a "sudden" burst of speed.

It is in that season, individually and corporately, that we must *press!*

Too many have been content to saunter along at his or her own (or the group's) pace. To meander and mosey is to play with the call of God. Even good men and women have wandered from the path of destiny because they have refused to press, to run after God.

Draw me, we will run... (Song of Solomon 1:4).

The danger to this kind of spiritual complacency and lethargy is that others—family and friends—are running with us, beside us, and behind us. The Lord is drawing on us to stretch out our necks (and put our lives and ministries on the line) so that others will be inspired to press onward by our example.

Men and women from all three levels (Feasts) have refused to "press;" they have said "no" to the *pressure* of the high calling! Only overcomers are willing to take the pressure of preaching and fleshing out the Word of the Kingdom!

> *To him that overcometh will I grant to sit with me* **in** *My throne...* (Revelation 3:21, emphasis added).

> *...a great multitude...stood* **before** *the throne...*

> *...and God shall wipe away all tears from their eyes...* (Revelation 7:9,17, emphasis added).

The multitudes who stand "before" the throne will one day weep when they finally realize what they could have had and been "in" the throne!

Tribulation Is Pressure

> *These things I have spoken unto you, that in Me ye might have peace. In the world ye shall have tribulation* [pressure]: *but be of good cheer; I have overcome the world* (John 16:33).

> *Confirming the souls of the disciples, and exhorting them to continue in the faith, and that we must through much tribulation* [pressure] *enter into the kingdom of God* (Acts 14:22).

Who comforteth us in all our tribulation [pressure], *that we may
be able to comfort them which are in any trouble, by the comfort
wherewith we ourselves are comforted of God* (2 Corinthians 1:4).

That no man should be moved by these afflictions [pressures]: *for
yourselves know that we are appointed thereunto* (1 Thessalonians
3:3).

I John, who also am your brother, and companion in tribulation
[pressure]… (Revelation 1:9).

Tribulation is *pressure.*

The Greek word for "tribulation" in the verses above is *thlipsis*
(Strong's #2347), and it means, "pressure." It is derived from *thlibo*
(to crowd), and from *tribo* (to rub, to wear down a path). Used 44
times in the New Testament, *thlipsis* is also translated in the King
James Version as, "anguish, affliction(s), persecution, trouble, burdened."[5]

Those who run toward divine destiny are pregnant with
prophetic purpose. The pressure that we bear is not coming from
without—it is coming from *within!*

The Pressure of Birth Pangs

*Trouble and anguish have taken hold on me: yet Thy command-
ments are my delights* (Psalms 119:143).

*For I have heard a voice as of a woman in travail, and the anguish
as of her that bringeth forth her first child, the voice of the daughter of Zion…* (Jeremiah 4:31).

*...our hands wax feeble: anguish hath taken hold of us, and pain,
as of a woman in travail* (Jeremiah 6:24).

This "anguish" (straits, distress; tightness) of childbirth is particularly set forth in the Gospel of John.

*A woman when she is in travail hath sorrow, because her hour is
come: but as soon as she is delivered of the child, she remembereth
no more the anguish, for joy that a man is born into the world*
(John 16:21).

*It will be the same joy as that of a woman in labor when her child
is born—her anguish gives place to rapturous joy and the pain is
forgotten* (John 16:21 TLB).

Compare the "man" born in John 16:21 with the "man child" (company) of full grown sons described in Revelation 12:1-5.[6]

The pressures of corporate destiny—"Christ in (and among all of) you" (Col. 1:27), the indwelling Seed—are kicking hard to come forth! All of creation is groaning for this release (see Rom. 8:19-23). That Christ would be fully formed in a people was Paul's apostolic anticipation!

*My little children, of whom I travail in birth again until Christ be
formed in you,* (Galatians 4:19).

...longing for the time when you are finally filled with Christ
(Galatians 4:19 TLB).

*...until Christ is completely and permanently formed (molded)
within you!* (Galatians 4:19 AMP).

...until Christ's life becomes visible in your lives? (Galatians 4:19 TM).

Used only here and in Galatians 4:27 and Revelation 12:2, the Greek word for "travail in birth" in Galatians 4:19 is *odino*, and it means, "to experience the pains of parturition or childbirth; pang or throe, especially of childbirth; intolerable anguish, consuming grief." Its root *duno* means, "to sink in; to go down or go under, to be plunged into."

There have been moments in our race when we felt like we were "going under" for the last time. Plunged into all kinds of situations and circumstances, we have paid a great price to jump these hurdles. The wear and tear on us has proven costly. This lifestyle of the Kingdom is not without pain.

...weeping may endure for a night, but joy cometh in the morning (Psalms 30:5).

And I will restore to you the years... (Joel 2:25).

Good morning, saints! It's a new day, the Third Day. The race has been long and hard, but God is about to restore the years! Once His purposes are realized through the birthing of His sons of promise (see Gal. 4:28), we will "forget" the pain that it took to get us here. Any and all mourning will be turned into dancing (see Ps. 30:11).

It is of the LORD's mercies that we are not consumed, because His compassions fail not.

They are new every morning: great is Thy faithfulness (Lamentations 3:22-23).

The people of God are laying aside all twelve of these weights, the sins that so easily have beset us (see Heb. 12:1). God is helping us to overcome, to come over these obstacles in our race of faith.

And this word, Yet once more, signifieth the removing [change of place] *of those things that are shaken* [agitated, by winds or waves], *as of things that are made, that those things which cannot be shaken may remain* (Hebrews 12:27).

By this He means that He will sift out everything without solid foundations so that only unshakable things will be left (Hebrews 12:27 TLB).

The Day of the Lord is a day of reversals. Everything that is loosed shall be bound, and everything that is bound shall be loosed. Indeed, everything that can be "shaken" is being shaken. All twelve of these "isms"—these man-made religious ideas—will be removed. All that will remain is His unshakeable Kingdom of love and harmony—the "unity of the faith" for which Jesus prayed (John 17:20-23; Eph. 4:13).

The corporate Overcomer—"he that overcometh" (Rev. 2-3)—will hurdle every encumbrance in the strength of the Pattern Son.

The Forerunner

As we come to the end of this race and this volume, it is imperative that we hear the conclusion from a Third Day and Most Holy Place perspective, from the posture of Jesus' *finished work.*

This writing is not an admonition for us to run. Repentance and faith are *both* gifts from the Lord (Chapter Four). We could not come to Him in our own strength. How much more is it true that we cannot stay in Him and run after Him in our own effort.

There is real difference between the stench of Adam and the savor of Christ.

This hope we have as an anchor of the soul, a hope both sure and steadfast and one which enters within the veil,

where Jesus has entered as a forerunner for us, having become a high priest forever according to the order of Melchizedek (Hebrews 6:19-20 NASB).

The word "forerunner" (used only here) is *prodromos,* and it means, "a runner ahead, scout, precursor; one who is sent before to take observations or act as a spy; one who comes in advance to a place where the rest are to follow." Compare *protrecho* (to run forward, outstrip, precede; to run before, to outrun), which comes from *pro* (fore, in front of, prior, superior to) and *trecho* (to run or walk hastily).

Jesus Christ, our great and merciful High Priest, entered within the veil into the holiest of all. The Pattern Son outstripped us in rank, and ran before us. He has spied out the land of promise and has made us His joint-heirs (see Rom. 8:17). Jesus is the "firstborn" among many brethren, the "firstfruits" of them who slept, the "firstborn" of every creature, and the "beginning" (the Head) of the new creation Man (Rom. 8:19; 1 Cor. 15:20; Col. 1:15; and Rev. 3:14).

And the Word was made flesh, and dwelt among us, (and we beheld His glory, the glory as of the only begotten of the Father,) full of grace and truth (John 1:14).

Wherefore when He [Messiah] cometh into the world, He saith, Sacrifice and offering thou wouldest not, but a body hast Thou prepared Me (Hebrews 10:5).

Again, we are not running or pressing in this race in our own human strength or effort. The Forerunner came here in a "body" of flesh and ran the race before us.

Jesus was the first One who ran the race, and the first One who won the race in a body of flesh.

The war is over (see Isa. 40:2), and the race is over!

Then said He, Lo, I come to do Thy will, O God. He taketh away the first,[7] that He may establish the second (Hebrews 10:9).

Jesus took away the Old Covenant through the violent death of His Cross, and established the New Covenant by the power of His resurrection.

Jesus' first "body" (of flesh) was "taken away" in resurrection and ascension, so that the second "Body" (of Christ) might be established.

Moses, Paul, and Jesus required a "second witness" for anything to be established in the earth (Deut. 17:6; Matt. 18:16; 2 Cor. 13:1).

It is not that we are or can run the race of faith in our own wisdom and strength.

Jesus through His Holy Spirit is running this race "again" through the second Witness, the Body of Christ, the Body of His flesh as His *ongoing incarnation!*

For it is God which worketh [operates] *in you both to will and to do of His good pleasure* (Philippians 2:13).

For God is at work within you, helping you want to obey Him, and then helping you do what He wants (Philippians 2:13 TLB).

It is only in and through Him by His Spirit that we can truly press!

You've all been to the stadium and seen the athletes race. Everyone runs; one wins. Run to win.

All good athletes train hard. They do it for a gold medal that tarnishes and fades. You're after one that's gold eternally.

I don't know about you, but I'm running hard for the finish line. I'm giving it everything I've got. No sloppy living for me!

I'm staying alert and in top condition. I'm not going to get caught napping, telling everyone else all about it and then missing out myself (1 Corinthians 9:24-27 TM).

Jesus Christ, The Little Bird

What must we do?

The praiser David "leaped" over his enemies and obstacles with "all his might" (Ps. 18:29 with 2 Sam. 6:14).

The twelve religious belief systems that formed the bulk of this book have illustrated the "sin" that so easily besets us (Heb. 12:1).

In the Bible, *leprosy* is a picture of this *sin*.[8] Leprosy was *incurable* with no natural answer or remedy. Mankind's religious efforts are futile. Only Jesus Christ can provide supernatural deliverance for the leper and the sinner![9]

What must we do? The answer is found in the passage below, wherein is the law of the cleansing of the leper.

And the LORD spake unto Moses, saying,

This shall be the law of the leper in the day of his cleansing: He shall be brought unto the priest:

And the priest shall go forth out of the camp; and the priest shall look, and, behold, if the plague of leprosy be healed in the leper;

Then shall the priest command to take for him that is to be cleansed two birds alive and clean, and cedar wood, and scarlet, and hyssop:

And the priest shall command that one of the birds be killed in an earthen vessel over running water:

As for the living bird, he shall take it, and the cedar wood, and the scarlet, and the hyssop, and shall dip them and the living bird in the blood of the bird that was killed over the running water:

And he shall sprinkle upon him that is to be cleansed from the leprosy seven times, and shall pronounce him clean, and shall let the living bird loose into the open field (Leviticus 14:1-7).

This was the Word of the Lord, a divine and not a human solution, God's plan, not man's.

The leper (sinner) had to be brought to the priest (see John 6:44). All this was done "outside the camp." The plague of sin separates us from God. We were outside of the family, outside of Christ.

Two birds (little birds, sparrows) were taken, alive and clean (pure). To this was added the cedar wood (the king of the trees) and the hyssop (the smallest of plants), along with "scarlet."

From the cedar to the hyssop, from the greatest to the least, from the deepest of sin to the smallest white lie, provision has been made.

The Hebrew word for "scarlet" is *tola*, and it means, "a worm or maggot." From this crimson grub that attached itself to a tree and died was taken the scarlet dye. The Messianic Worm (Ps. 22:6) attached Himself to the Cross and poured out His blood for our sin.

The priest commanded or ordained that one of the birds would be taken and killed, slaughtered in sacrifice. This was to be done in an "earthen vessel over running water."

Jesus was killed in an "earthen vessel," a body of flesh. The "running water" pictures the life of the Father within Him, ever empowering Him to do the divine will.

Then, like the living bird, each of us was "dipped"—immersed, or plunged, or baptized—in the blood of the bird that was killed.

We have been sprinkled (Heb. 10:22; 12:24; 1 Pet. 1:2) seven times with His blood—we have been completely forgiven. His blood has "pronounced" or declared us "clean" (pure, bright); we have been "justified," declared to be righteous by His blood (Rom. 5:1).

> *But we all, with open face beholding* [worshiping] *as in a glass the glory of the Lord, are changed into the same image from glory to glory, even as by the Spirit of the Lord* (2 Corinthians 3:18).

Finally, those who have been cleansed by the blood, like the living bird, have been "loosed" into the "open field." The word for "open" here is *paniym*, the Hebrew word for "face." We have been "loosed," freed from the fowler and his snare (Ps. 91:3; 124:7).

We who run this race of faith have been cleansed, and now have been "loosed" into the Face of God! We have been "loosed" to worship our King!

> *For a great door and effectual is opened unto me...* (1 Corinthians 16:9; compare Acts 14:27).

I know thy works: behold, I have set before thee an open door, and no man can shut it... (Revelation 3:8; compare Col. 4:3).

Moreover, we who run this race of faith have been "loosed" into the "open field" of evangelism (the Great Commission of Matthew 28:18-20), the "open door" of a global harvest in the Feast of Tabernacles!

But if we walk in the light, as He is in the light, we have fellowship one with another, and the blood of Jesus Christ His Son cleanseth us from all sin.

...If we confess our sins, He is faithful and just to forgive us our sins, and to cleanse us from all unrighteousness (1 John 1:7,9).

Have you sinned? Be dipped in the blood of Jesus Christ, the little Bird. Has one of these obstacles in the race of faith easily beset you? Let the blood of the little Bird "loose" you!

And Jesus answering said, Were there not ten [lepers] cleansed? but where are the nine?

There are not found that returned to give glory to God, save this stranger.

And He said unto him, Arise, go thy way: thy faith hath made thee whole (Luke 17:17-19).

Do you not know that those who run in a race all run, but only one receives the prize? Run in such a way that you may win (1 Corinthians 9:24 NASB).

This passage in Luke 17:12-19 tells the story of the ten lepers. One out of ten, the tithe, "returned to give glory to God." This one who returns to worship and to serve, falling at the feet of the Master, is the "one" who wins the "prize."

This is the "one" who overcomes every obstacle, the "one" who *presses into destiny!*

Endnotes

1. The primary "pattern" used throughout this volume for these three sections of the race is revealed in the Mosaic Tabernacle (Exod. 25:8,40)—the Outer Court, The Holy, and The Most Holy Place. Paralleling that are the three Feasts of Jehovah (Deut. 16:16)—Passover in the first month, Pentecost in the third month, and Tabernacles in the seventh month. The runners in this race of faith are born again, Spirit-filled, and then mature. Forty examples of these "excellent" or "three-fold" things (Prov. 22:20-21) are listed on pages 84-85 of my book, *Prevail: A Handbook for the Overcomer*. This Kingdom principle also underlies two other writings that complete the trilogy—*The More Excellent Ministry*, and *The Priesthood is Changing*.

2. To be like Jesus is the Goal of the high calling. The "fruit" of the Spirit (Gal. 5:22-24) is His *nature*, and the gifts or "manifestations" of the Spirit (1 Cor. 12:1-10) constitute His *ministry*.

3. "It's Time to Press!" is the title of the message I preached here at Praise Tabernacle in Richlands, North Carolina, on Sunday morning, October 22, 2006. Call our office at 910-324-5026 to order this teaching that sparked the original inspiration for this writing.

4. The Hebrew word for "suddenly" is used 25 times in the Old Testament (see Num. 12:4; 2 Chron. 29:36; Ps. 64:7; Isa. 48:3; Jer. 51:8; and Mal. 3:1).

5. The Greek word for "tribulation" is *thlipsis*, and it means, "pressure." Used 44 times in the New Testament, *thlipsis* is also translated as "anguish, affliction(s), persecution, trouble, and burdened" (including Matt. 13:21; 24:21,29; Rom. 2:9; 5:3; 8:35; 12:12; 2 Cor. 1:4; Eph. 3:13; 2 Thess. 1:4,6; Heb. 10:33; and Rev. 2:9-10,22; 7:14).

6. The Manchild Company of Revelation 12:1-5 is thoroughly discussed in Chapter Four of my book, *Moses, the Master, and the Manchild*.

7. "He Taketh Away the First" is the title of Chapter Three of my book, *The Priesthood is Changing*. The reader is encouraged to study that chapter for a full understanding of Hebrews 10:9.

8. In the Bible, leprosy is a picture of sin; note its characteristics: (1) Leprosy begins as a small, insignificant spot or blemish; (2) The individual does not realize his condition at first; (3) Leprosy is progressive, sure to grow (the rate of growth varies with each individual); (4) Leprosy affects the whole man; the worse kind of leprosy—the forehead (see 2 Chron. 26); (5) Leprosy is contagious and can affect others (see Matt. 12:30-33); (6) Leprosy causes the hair to fall out (no submission; note the Nazarite vow of Numbers 6); Leprosy causes insensibility (the hardened heart that is past feeling) (see Eph. 4:19; 1 Tim. 4:1-2); (7) The leper was separated, shut out from the camp because the camp was holy (see Deut. 23:14 with Eph. 2:11-12); and (8) Only Jesus can heal the leper (sinner)!

9. Only Jesus Christ can provide supernatural deliverance for the leper and the sinner! (See Lev. 13-14; Num. 5:2; 2 Kings 5; 2 Chron. 26:11-13; Matt. 8:2-4; 10:8; 11:5; 26:6; Mark 1:40; 14:3; and Luke 4:27; 5:12-14; 7:22; 17:12-14.)

OTHER RESOURCES BY KELLEY VARNER

All resources (including DVDs) from Dr. Kelley Varner
are available at www.kelleyvarner.org (Order online)

KELLEY VARNER MINISTRIES
P.O. Box 785
Richlands, NC 28574-0785

Phone: 910-324-5026 or 324-5027
FAX: 910-324-1048

Email: jpvarner1@earthlink.net
OR
kvarner2@earthlink.net

E-MAIL NEWSLETTER

Subscribe to Dr. Varner's bi-weekly E-mail newsletter,
"The Praise Report," a resource for leaders, at www.kelleyvarner.org.

CD OF THE MONTH

Two CDs (including sermon notes) by Dr. Varner and other ministries
are available each month on an annual offering basis. Write, call, or
go online to join this growing family of listeners.

CONFERENCES AND SEMINARS

CAROLINA LEADERSHIP INSTITUTE is a monthly weekend seminar
imparting a biblical foundation for understanding and expressing
Kingdom principles (see our schedule online).

Other regional and national gatherings take place during the year at
Praise Tabernacle. Dr. Varner and his apostolic team are also
available for ministry to your church and local area.

Additional copies of this book and other
book titles from DESTINY IMAGE are
available at your local bookstore.

Call toll free: 1-800-722-6774.

Send a request for a catalog to:

Destiny Image® Publishers, Inc.
P.O. Box 310
Shippensburg, PA 17257-0310

"Speaking to the Purposes of God for this
Generation and for the Generations to Come."

For a complete list of our titles,
visit us at www.destinyimage.com